The Entrepreneur's Guide To Getting Your Shit Together Volume Two

By John Carlton

(Author of "Kick-Ass Copywriting Secrets of a Marketing Rebel")

Psst… wanna tear down the obstacles standing between you and real wealth and happiness in business, no matter where you're at right now? Step #1 has got to be feasting on the specific advice from Carlton's 30-year career as a marketing and advertising legend.

These tactics are straight from the real world, where they've been tested, proven and deeply appreciated by the vast mob of entrepreneurs who've already been transformed by this man's shocking… outrageous… and very, *very* successful directives on making business pay off while enjoying life at a level unimaginable to most folks…

Published by Carlton Ink Copyright 2019

Praise From The Big Dogs In Marketing And Advertising

"John Carlton is that cool, street-wise, curmudgeonly, heart-of-gold uncle that you always wished you had... the one who played guitar in a rock-and-roll band, and who just happens to be an incredible wizard of sales copy and marketing. When you read what John writes you will be wildly entertained, and you'll also become a much better entrepreneur."

Jeff Walker
#1 New York Times Bestselling Author of "Launch: An Internet Millionaire's Secret Formula To Sell Almost Anything Online, Build A Business You Love, And Live The Life Of Your Dreams"

"You should all know of John Carlton. He's a long-tenured major leaguer. Now a graybeard. It seems to me all the *real* rebels are aging. Most of today's direct response copy that I see churned out is derivative and formulaic and safe. Not Carlton's. Anyway, he has now written a book ("The Entrepreneur's Guide To Getting Your Shit Together"). It's *good*. It is a poke in the eye, a whack on the head, a blunt dissertation.

One thing we completely agree on is that most do NOT have their shit together. Not even close. And, to the salesmen go the spoils."

Dan Kennedy
Legendary and influential business coach, author of the "No B.S." book series

---

"I first met John Carlton at one of Gary Halbert's classic seminars. I soon hired him to bust my chops and coach me to master copywriting. A lot of folks talk about getting serious corrective advice and correction. But few people truly desire it or act on it -- let alone come back for more punishment.

But once I had a John Carlton "alter-ego" installed in my head, I possessed a guiding voice for writing persuasive, punchy copy. "You're putting me to sleep here. Stop selling from your heels and swing for the customer's passionate sweet spot." "Geez Perry, you need to take your inner salesman out for a walk every once in awhile." I now instantly knew whether what I'd just written was going to make the cut or not.

It suddenly became easier to write winning promotions. John is difficult to hire, because frankly he doesn't need the dinero. So if you want the voice of John Carlton installed in your head, I recommend you pick up this book ("The Entrepreneur's Guide To Getting Your Shit Together"). In case the title didn't alert you, it's edgy.

Everything John does is edgy. There just aren't many people who can alert you to the mind-bending *irrationality* of real human beings - and show you how to work with it, flow with it. If humans confuse you and you need a teacher, John's your man."
Perry Marshall
Best-selling author of "80/20 Sales And Marketing" and "The Ultimate Guide To Google Adwords"

"Occasionally you get to meet gods among men - those who go beyond expertise and have managed to become iconically associated with their craft. They alter the zeitgeist and define what must be for those following in their footsteps. John Carlton is a

living deity of copywriting and word-smithing -- a guy who I'm proud to call both a mentor and a friend. If he is offering anything, you'd be a fool not to take it. You'll find the experience of earning more money and feeling your cerebral cortex evolving at the same time infinitely rewarding."
Jon Benson
Godfather of the Video Sales Letter
Sellerator.com

"If you ever entered my office where I've made millions of dollars for myself and hundreds of millions for my clients, you'd probably be puzzled by the number of picture frames around the office. These frames have little snippets from John Carlton's emails and blog posts. Whenever I find one that hits home, and that's often, I cut them out and frame them. Above my computer is the famed "all clients suck" email. John's writings - whether in emails or blog posts - have helped guide me for over a dozen years.

His writing cuts through all the BS and goes to the core or what it means to have marketing chops. Now, you'll never find Carlton pushing the latest trick of the month -- in fact he shies from this crap like the plague. You'll only find proven techniques and advice from someone who's been there.

Today, due to Facebook and Twitter, we are used to seeing the same material regurgitated *ad nauseum*. The same video clips, the same stories, and the same click bait headlines. If you've become immune to the idea you can learn something new, then John's books will be like oxygen to a man in a vacuum."
Harlan Kilstein
Top Dog, DogingtonPost.com

"John Carlton is a rebel with a cause. His no-BS, hold-nothing-back attitude speaks to the heart of the entrepreneur and teaches them to create messages that compel customers. John is a disruptor, a trail-blazer, and a visionary. Get ready for a wild ride, and then reap the benefits. You are about to enter a relationship you'll never forget."
Dave Lakhani
Inc. 500 business owner, author of "Persuasion: The Art Of Getting What You Want"

"John Carlton's blog posts interweave savvy marketing advice with guidance on how to be a good human. And he does it in a breezy, casual style I wish like mad I could capture as a writer. Practically every article has at least one nugget I write on a post it in my office to remind me how to be more successful in everything."
Lorrie Morgan-Ferreo
Owner, Red Hot Copy

"I picked up one of Carlton's books in my young 30's and sure damn glad I did. It significantly altered the last decade of my life in an extremely profound way. As I approach 40 years old I often look back at my 30's and say "What a fucking ride!" and much of that wouldn't have been possible without what I learned from John along the way. Good choice picking up this book. Hope you get the kind of results I did!"
Jason Moffatt
Marketing Wizard at ProfitMoffatt.com

"John Carlton scares the shit out of me. And I mean that in the absolute best way possible. When I first got started in the direct marketing world as a young and cocky copywriter John beat the daylights out of me (Figuratively. He didn't actually HIT me for real until after I'd earned his respect.). He tore my copy (which I naively thought was AWESOME) to tiny, whimpering shreds, forced me to question every assumption and belief I had about marketing and life, insulted my haircut, destroyed my illusions, mocked me viciously for my high fallutin' vocabulary and cackled with absolute glee when I took everything he could throw at me and came back for more.

In other words, John made me a better copywriter, a better marketer, a better thinker and a better man.

A long time ago I realized that getting to a world-class level as a marketer and copywriter means fundamentally fucking with the way you look at the world. There's simply no way you can be GREAT at this unless you're able to have an unflinching love affair with reality and are willing to toss everything you WANT to be true off a bridge.

And when it comes to thinking critically, seeing the world the way it ACTUALLY IS, having the guts to be GREAT at something and the wisdom not to buy your own BS or fall victim to your own reputation, John is the greatest mentor a young 'up and comer' could ever have.

Thanks, John. I wouldn't be anywhere near where I am now in my life without you. I feel bad, though. Thanks to you I've got it burned into my bones and into my marketing DNA that the only way to take folks with 'potential' to the next level is with aggression, brutality and truth. So the folks who have been through one of *my* scathing copy critiques have *you* to blame =-).

Read every word John lets you. This man cuts through bullshit like a hot knife through . . . um . . . bullshit."

Chris "Mr. Moneyfingers" Haddad
9-Figure (and counting) copywriter, ridiculously-priced marketing consultant, niche-dominating info-marketer, highly-innapropriate public speaker and amateur drummer. (Also bad at doing dishes.)

"When I was 21 years old, I lived and worked with the legendary Gary Halbert for three years. One of the first lessons he taught me was this: Be protective of who you let into your mind. It takes a short time to learn a lesson.

But it could take years to unlearn that lesson if it was bad advice. And so, Gary restricted my quest for knowledge to just two people. The first was Gary. The second was John Carlton. Now what I learned from John is that you don't need to live and work with a legend to have him as your mentor. I say that because while I did not live or work with John, he's been no less a mentor to me for the past 14 years. Next only to Halbert, I learned more about salesmanship from Carlton than anybody else on earth. I attribute much of my success to the concepts, principles, tactics and strategies John teaches in his books and his courses."
Caleb O'Dowd
Founder of Multi Channel Marketing.

"The thing I love about John is that he was a public cheerleader for women in this biz long before it was front page news or popular to do so. He supported me and my female-only community of the Titanides while other men were still asking me, "Why?". John Carlton holds the door open for female entrepreneurs in a still mostly male led business world. Best of all, he doesn't expect a Scooby snack just for acting like a decent human being. That's a

true hero in my book."
Marcella Allison
Female Entrepreneur, Owner, Copy Harvest LLC, and Founder of
the Titanides

"John Carlton has always been a thorn in my side.

Over my entire career, spanning decades, I have read his countless
rants with insatiable curiosity while also soaking up his wisdom
with every encounter (when I've been fortunate to be in the same
zip code with him).
But truth be told, I often tried to dismiss everything he said that
made me feel uncomfortable—you know, stuff I *knew* he had to be
wrong about.

And the more uncomfortable he made me, the more I wrote him
off as that "hippie who can't be that smart."

I'm here to tell you that he IS that smart—that this book is a must
read--and that he is not wrong about much.

A few years ago I attended one of his unique mastermind meetings,
all hot seats, no fluff, all truth and no coddling—and after I talked
about my newest, brilliant idea on my own hot seat, John peered
into my soul and said, *"Rookie mistake, Brian."*

There are very few people who could say that to me and be 100%
correct (i.e. that my idea had so many fatal flaws that I better start
from scratch).

It also mattered little that this "rookie" had already been in the
business for 30 years.

He was just telling me it like it is. That's what he does. Didn't matter who I was.

Thank goodness there are prophets like Carlton around who never shy away from telling the truth no matter how painful it might be to hear. And in this book, he also goes way beyond his main areas of expertise of copywriting and marketing too.

You are so lucky to own it.

He bears all and shares all—all of the time—and since he has he made the mistakes you won't have to, you can avoid a lot of grief in the future by reading it.

In this book he will also give you the secrets to having the most meaningful life as an entrepreneur (which are not so "secret" to hear John tell them). You just need to pay attention.

If you dismiss this book rather than pay close attention and devour every page, *you* will be making a "rookie mistake" too."

Brian Kurtz
Titans Marketing LLC, author of *The Advertising Solution* and *Overdeliver*...and former business builder at Boardroom Inc.

"As far as I am concerned Carlton's blog (**www.john-carlton.com**) is THE #1 resource on the planet for exactly the kind of hard-fought, grizzled wisdom that every copywriter, entrepreneur and business owner needs by the bucketful. I must have read every single post and archive entry a dozen times, maybe more. Whenever a friend or family member asks me for business advice, I tell them to devour everything Carlton's ever written.

If you read this stuff, re-read it, then read it again, in a short space of time you'll find you have more business acumen and more honest-to-goodness moneymaking chops than even the fanciest MBA holder with a six-figure education under his belt. Believe the hype.

Read these books immediately. Then read them again. They are that good."
David Raybould
Freelance copywriter and Conversion Rate Optimization Specialist
DavidRaybould.com

"John's incredible wisdom in the fields of entrepreneurship, copywriting and business is priceless -- he is the ultimate triple crown winner! He has years, actually decades of a successful track-record. Following and implementing John's advice will only result in major improvements for your own business."
MaryEllen Tribby
#1 Best Selling Author, "Reinventing the Entrepreneur: Turning Your Dream Business into a Reality"

"Carlton's a unique one-of-a-kind cat, with a deep grasp on all the important springs and gears that make people tick. More importantly John can actually communicate that insight to pals (like me) so we can get busy dominating markets and crushing evil competitors.

Acting on John's advice has earned me and my partners millions (yes, millions) and transformed my life into something resembling an amusement park. I'd suggest that any serious marketer get on board and listen to this dude. Then, let the thrills begin."

Jimbo Curley
CEO, FightFast.com

"I have to say that John Carlton has been the biggest influence on my marketing mindset and writing drive, and I hope you enjoy his grit (that is snark x 10)... and if you ever get a chance to learn from him directly, grab the opportunity. He's one of the few marketers out there I know that is not completely full of BS."
Lisa Wagner
Owner, RugChick.com

"Listen up guys, I made a gazillion bucks way before even hearing of John Carlton. However, if I *had* listened to his CDs and read his books beforehand I would have saved myself at least 10 years of time, pain, and suffering. And I would have earned infinitely more money. Some people just have "it". I have listened to or read everything John has produced at least once a year. I recommend that you do the same. Better yet, buy it for someone you love or care about."
Michael T. Irvin
CEO of MLTC Consulting, NY, NY

Acknowledgements

I've been blessed to be surrounded by extremely good and savvy people my entire career… especially when it comes to technology and the details of getting things done.

With deep gratitude, I'd like to thank these folks for helping me finally get this second volume published:

Pete Hudson, the tech and design wizard.

Virginia Drew, whose eagle eyes helped catch those last-draft errors that otherwise would have slipped by (and also for helping with the final chapter arrangement).

Rick Allen, for the cover design.

Stan Dahl, my long-time and very patient business partner and good friend.

Michele Attaway, my life partner.

Gary Halbert, the one mentor who helped me realize the potential he saw in me from the beginning.

And finally, **Pop**, dearly missed but never far from my thoughts.

What You're In For:

Introduction

With a few exceptions, this Volume 2 is (like Volume 1) a collection of the best of the "Marketing Rebel Rant" newsletters I wrote monthly over the course of eight years to a very exclusive group of marketers, copywriters, business owners and industry big shots.

As you can see from the rabid testimonials I've included (a mere fraction of the deluge of praise I've earned during my notorious career), the advice, strategies and insight to human behavior as a customer has influenced a large snarling mob of successful folks... many of whom are now household names for any entrepreneur who's been paying attention.

I've enjoyed a great life in the marketing and advertising world. For over 40 years now, I've had a global reputation as "the most respected and ripped-off copywriter alive"...

... as well as being one of the *first* consultants the Big Dogs think of when they need help. I've also hosted the legendary insiders-only Platinum Mastermind for more than a decade, and remain close friends of icons in the biz.

You tend to build up a backlog of good stories and life-changing advice in a career like that.

Which is a good thing, because my goal for the past twenty-odd years has been to give deserving entrepreneurs and copywriters access to the *same* brain-rattling revelations that transformed me from a clueless nobody into one of the most effective and skilled marketers in the game.

My teaching style is very much NOT for everybody. Just spilling out the secrets of success in a "do this, then do that" manner, I've found, doesn't stick in your mind.

The better method of sharing -- proven in the front-line trenches of the remorseless Real World -- is to *couch the lessons within a damn good tale that makes it memorable.*

So it melds into your cerebral cortex and stays there, cooking away as you trundle off to make your own fortune in this crazy modern world.

I started out back in the 1980s as a direct response freelance copywriter – the guy that Los Angeles agencies snuck in the back door to create the killer ads their own in-house writers couldn't pull off.

Then I worked my way into the "A List" of copywriters for the largest publishers of financial and health information (still the biggest market out there). There were (and still are) just a handful of copywriters worldwide capable of writing controls for the most competitive direct response markets like these. It's a high-wire balancing act that demands deep knowledge of human psychology, persuasion tactics worthy of a world-class salesman, and the deft touch of communicative skill that only dedicated copywriters can ever achieve.

However, I soon grew bored with those markets. There were layers of corporate creatures always hovering, trembling with anxiety over the irreverent and sometimes outrageous copy I wrote, forcing diluted versions to go out.

That's when I met the legendary Gary Halbert. I was presented with a stark choice – stick with my current career, earning fat royalties while writing for markets that left me unexcited...

… or chunk it all and go off into the wild entrepreneurial world with Halbert. Where there was no playbook, few restrictions on creativity (other than remaining ethical and within the law), beholden only to the ultimate demand of the market: *Convince prospects to become eager customers.*

I made the decision to go off into the wild with Halbert in a heartbeat. One of the easiest decisions I've ever made, and one of the most profoundly life-changing.

It was fun, because every new job brought us into a new market, with new clients to wrangle with and fresh problems to solve. No one came to us without massive trouble brewing in their business. We were the "fixers" entrepreneurs sought out after everything else had collapsed, and they'd hit a wall.

We thrived on turning around failing campaigns, creating massive profit where none existed before, and causing complete disruption in the competition hierarchy across the capitalistic landscape.

I can't think of a single market segment we didn't eventually go after. We were fearless, because we understood the power of direct response advertising, and had honed the skills required to make it work.

Just before the turn of the century, I coupled up with a client I still call "The Boys" – a small group of enthusiastic entrepreneurs who begged me to come write exclusively for them in the golf and self-defense markets. I was semi-retired at the time, having taken off a few years to write some novels and form a small rock band to play all the biker bars in Northern Nevada. (Yes, it was one of many mid-life crises I've had, and I've enjoyed them all immensely.)

To bring me out of my vacation, The Boys made me a promise I simply couldn't refuse: They would run every ad I wrote, *as I wrote it*, with no editing or interference from them whatsoever.

And they'd handle any heat that came from it.

Basically, they "took the leash off"… all of the restrictions I'd had with my former corporate clients, and all of the reticence I'd experienced with the nervous entrepreneurs Gary and I had engaged with… was now *gone*.

I could field-test *every* idea, theory, and hare-brained creative notion I had… and The Boys would run it.

So I happily spent a decade writing the most outrageous and rule-stretching advertising I could muster… employing all the tactics and strategies I'd learned from my long career, but had never been able to fully employ before (because of the Nervous Nellies who feared offending anyone or being too "out there" and having someone question their mental state as a "normal" marketer).

Of course, The Boys and I were on the right side of history. We upended the staid, boring ads and direct mail clogging up the markets we went after…

… actually succeeding where every other entrepreneur had failed miserably.

We even changed the look of some of the large magazines in golf. Our ads didn't look anything like the other ads – because we went directly after that slice of the market every other competitor ignored.

Which just happened to be the larger slice. While the competition preened and sopped up to the pro golfers, we went after the *older* end of the market – the guys hobbled a bit by arthritis, who couldn't break 100 if their life depended on it, who didn't have "windmill" swings like Tiger Woods…

… but who desperately wanted the accessible secrets of finally hitting long, accurate drives and putting like true masters. So they could at long last beat their buddies who had been humiliating them over the years.

It's easy to find those notorious ads online.

For one thing, many of them are still running… twenty-five years after I first wrote them. They went from direct mail, to magazine ads (often 3 entire pages of just copy, no photos), to websites, and then to video sales letters… with *minimal* editing.

I *still* get royalties every month from dozens of ads I wrote back before the Web was a viable marketing vehicle. A true testament to the power of damn good (and damned *outrageous*) copy that delivers.

Here, in this Volume 2 collection of my Marketing Rebel Rant newsletters, you now can share in the advice and tactical advantages formerly available only to a select few marketers who were on my exclusive list.

It is life-changing stuff. Insight you would otherwise never come close to unless you also spent 40 years on the inside of the roiling marketing world. Strategies that would remain *hidden* to you unless you were able to weasel your way into the back rooms where the Big Decisions are made.

Here is a real taste of the fun, excitement and bottom-line success now within your reach, if you take all of this to heart and *use* it.

I've enjoyed a wild and wonderful ride. I am opening up my experiences here, revealing *everything* that was critical to my success and happiness.

It's here for the taking.

Go feast on it.

Stay frosty,

John

P.S. And if you're still jonesing for more, after reading this…

… just hop over to www.john-carlton.com, where I've maintained one of the first marketing blogs since 2004. The entire archive (crammed with more excellent advice and insight) is **free**. Plus, it's "action central" for everything else I offer (including all my copywriting courses, books, and consulting opportunities).

Like I said, I'm not for everyone. I've always gone for the gusto in life and business, and refuse to suffer fools or tolerate bullshit. My teaching style is story-based, because *that's what works best* for nailing the good stuff down inside your brain.

I also offend dainty ears, and outrage uptight people. Which I consider a badge of honor.

So, if my style clicks with you (as it has with so many of the top marketing minds around), then you've got plenty more to enjoy on the blog.

But first, dive into Volume 2 here…

Forward
By Perry Marshall

I first met John Carlton at one of Gary Halbert's classic seminars. I soon hired him to bust my chops and coach me to master copywriting.

A lot of folks talk about getting serious corrective advice and correction. But few people truly desire it or act on it - let alone come back for more punishment.

But once I had a John Carlton "alter-ego" installed in my head, I possessed a guiding voice for writing persuasive, punchy copy.

Like: "Geez Perry, you need to take your inner salesman out for a walk every once in awhile." "You're putting me to sleep here. Stop selling from your heels and swing for the customer's passionate sweet spot."

I now *instantly* know whether what I'd just written is going to make the cut or not. It suddenly became easier to write winning promotions.

John is difficult to hire, because frankly he doesn't need the work anymore. So if you want the voice of John Carlton installed in your head, I recommend you pick up this book. In case the title didn't alert you, it's edgy.

Everything John does is edgy. There just aren't many people who can alert you to the mind-bending irrationality of real human beings - and show you how to work with it, flow with it. If humans confuse you and you need a teacher, John's your man.

One time I got in a tiff with a client over a project. They weren't happy, they didn't want to pay the other half of the bill, they disagreed with this and that. I used my access to John to ask him how to handle it.

He shakes me by the lapels, via email: "You did all THAT - for only six thousand dollars???"

He continues: "You should have charged them at least fifteen. Listen Perry, if the client's hand isn't *shaking* when he writes you the check, you're not charging enough. As THEE marketer on their team, you're not a mouth in the food chain. You ARE the food chain!"

John's got this funny way of drilling things into your head. Has a lot to do with his talent for turn-of-phrase. Which, by the way, is learnable. Great communicators obsess over the nuances of how to deliver a message. Jerry Seinfeld deliciously chews on the delivery of a single line for months. Then makes it look effortless onstage.

And sure, he does it behind closed doors in his practice room, but he also does it while he's flossing his teeth or driving home after he drops his kid off at school. Copywriters do that too. This skill of wordsmithing isn't born, it's acquired.

When I wrote my first Google book, I sent John all the chapter titles. He flogged me to make it more interesting. So instead of "Your USP - The Most Important Ingredient" which is was the original title, now it's "The Most-Ignored Secret Behind the Most Profitable Marketing Campaigns in the World."

Whether someone reads the first third of your book vs. setting it aside for "later" might be the difference between getting a $100,000 client or not. Chapter titles matter a lot.

I sent him a writing sample for another book project, and once again, he pinpointed the #1 question that I was circling but never quite getting to. Subsequent readers frequently commented on how stimulating that section was.

That's the way it is with John. Get straight to the point, point out the elephant in the room, spay-paint it pink, spear it with knives and serve up elephant meat for your evening guests.

Finally as you read I want you to notice the *density* of John's writing, his headlines. Great communicators pack kilovolts of emotional energy into few words. People always argue about long copy but what always gets ignored in that conversation is, long or short, the demand that you pack as much mojo into every word and phrase as possible.

Study John's headlines and his opening paragraphs - even in his newsletters and book chapters. Notice how his thoughts stick in your brain like cockleburs on wool socks. That's intentional.

That's why YOU need to be more intentional. I recommend to you this politically incorrect, edgy bottle of marketing *habanero* sauce.

Perry Marshall
Marketing Strategist & Author of *The Ultimate Guide to Google AdWords* and *80/20 Sales & Marketing*

Chapter One:

The Savvy Entrepreneur's "Starter" Checklist.

What do you really need to get moving as fast as possible with your entrepreneurial adventure, or on a harrowing new project in your established business, without crashing and burning?

As I was gathering the courage to attempt my first bumbling foray into the entrepreneurial world as a freelance copywriter (having zero experience in the gig and no idea yet how to pull it off)…

… an actual professional copywriter (who freelanced on the side) earnestly informed me that I should not even try.

I was working as a low-level graphic artist for a computer supply catalog at the time, and the copywriters had cubicles in the same art department.

What I had at the time was a totally expendable grunt job. (And yes, I did eventually get fired for insubordination. I'm still proud of that mark on my permanent record.)

She was the first copywriter I'd ever met, and writing snappy little tales about cables, monitors and floppy discs looked like something I could handle (and possibly thrive at, for the first time in my life).

She seemed happy, well-paid, respected and competent. (All of which I wasn't at the time.)

And I thought maybe she could slip a few pointers my way.

You know, a hint.

A clue.

Anything at all.

She scoffed at the very thought.

"It's too hard, John," she said. "You'll never be a professional writer."

That was, of course, the BEST thing she could have ever told me.

I figured out how to become a copywriter anyway, just to show her I could do it…

… and I doubt I would have survived the first harrowing year of my fledgling freelance career without that burning determination to prove her wrong.

It's called "**negative motivation**"…

… and it's actually one of the most powerful forces available for getting stuff done.

I never saw that surly copywriter again, and don't even remember her name…

… so I never experienced the fun of flaunting my eventual success in her face.

I didn't need to.

The motivation was all internal for me – I used her as the "personification" of the obstacles in front of me as I stumbled through the nerve-wracking early days...

... and I even laughed when I later realized I was finally in a position to tell that image of her in my mind "Screw you, I made it anyway."

Yes, my internal ego is an immature twerp sometimes. Chip on the shoulder, snarling underdog attitude, and an almost stupidly-aggressive and irrational refusal to let others tell me what to do.

I am so grateful for it, too.

You do not need to be a belligerent rebel to be a good entrepreneur...

... but it can help sometimes.

Certainly, given the choice of sitting down to dinner with a table full of standard-issue business goons in suits, who are uber-polite, calculating, and careful in their conversations...

... or, instead, sitting with that rowdy crowd of rule-breaking ne'er-do-well whack-job entrepreneurs who may easily get us kicked OUT of the restaurant....

... well, you know which one I'd pick.

I wandered into the entrepreneurial world precisely because I don't "fit" in the normal rule-bound corporate environments.

And I'll bet the appeal of a lifestyle where you set your own damn rules is a big part of why you got into the game, too.

For the last 30-some years, I've had the privilege of advising, writing for, and hanging out with many of the top entrepreneurs alive.

I've also spent massive time counseling struggling entrepreneurs who haven't quite got it all together yet. My proudest moments are when I've helped someone break through the chaos and problems holding them back, and ushered them (sometimes kicking and screaming) into a better life full of moolah, happiness and fun.

This has got me thinking a lot, lately, about what you DO need to be a successful entrepreneur.

So I've put together a quick-start list, based on the most common advice I dole out to struggling folks getting pummeled by the business world.

Let's just get into it.

Here are the main things you'll need in your "toolkit" as an entrepreneur (whether you're starting out or getting ready to move up a level):

Tool #1: **Survival resources.**

This includes:

(a) **Books** (both the ones you read for general knowledge and put on your shelf or into your virtual ebook shelf…

… and the ones that stay on your desk, dog-eared, because they are advice-and-tactic-dense manuals that help in your day-to-day work)…

(b) Plus an ever-expanding network of **experts, mentors, colleagues and go-to-guys** (including tech geeks, vendors, hosting services, spies, friendly competitors, advisors, support staff, and helpmates in your quest for animal-level contentment)…

(c) Plus whatever **courses, seminars, podcasts, blogs, and tutorials** you need to attain a mastery of the details of whatever biz you're in or about to lay siege to. (I have a list for you at the end of this book, if you're interested in what I recommend.)

Books are the fastest way to access the wisdom of experts. Make the effort to discover what the classics are in your chosen niche, and stay current with the newer best-sellers (asking other business owners what they've read is an excellent starting point).

But, simply reading books just stuffs your head with ideas. You've got to take the next step of putting those tactics, strategies and insights to work in the real world.

That's where networking with people already in motion brings it all home. It's one thing to have a great idea – it's quite another to make it manifest in the world.

And you can short-cut the process of strengthening the weak spots in your skill set – whether it's writing copy, building websites, creating products or whatever task is between you and success – **by taking full advantage of the many "here's how you do it" courses and seminars available.**

Knowing what to do…

… and how others have already done it…

… plus the details of how you can start doing it, too…

… are the keys to getting your entrepreneurial game on.

Tool #2: **Goal-setting skills.**

You need to understand, clearly, where you're headed and what you want from both your journey and your final destination.

It's okay, early on, to not be entirely clear on your ultimate goals.

Sometimes you work hard to attain something, and only then realize it wasn't what you wanted after all. That's how life works. The universe has a cruel sense of humor sometimes.

So, as a savvy entrepreneur, you will constantly re-adjust your long-term goals as you go…

… to make sure the end-game is still something you desire.

Short-term, however, you need to get good at breaking down the best (and fastest) path to your target…

… while also learning how to fix problems and deal with unexpected emergencies. (This kind of looking ahead will always be the **best business plan** you ever create.)

First, decide what you want.

Then, make a plan to go get it.

Finally, implement your plan. Go get what you want.

That's the fundamental process.

Most folks forget the third step, or can't decide specifically what they really want in the first place. And disaster awaits them.

Dream, plan, execute. It's a simple technique…

… but following through takes effort, critical thinking, and the honing of required skills.

Nevertheless, it's massively easier to become successful when you're clear on what you want, and what you need to do to attain it…

… and then actively get moving on completing the process.

Movement is what turns dreams into realities.

Tool #3: **Thick skin.**

You need to put your ego aside when entering the entrepreneurial world…

… because you're gonna get stomped, bullied, abused, insulted, back-stabbed, cheated and assaulted.

Often.

In new and fascinating ways that your civilian pals will never believe possible.

Your motto must be "eyes on the prize", at all times. There will be setbacks, disasters and breathtaking failures…

… but you must consider these setbacks as temporary annoyances, an opportunity to learn what not to do next time.

Then you readjust after each failure (filling in the gaps that created the failure – which will likely include new knowledge, better mastery of required skills, higher-level network connections, and probably dialing up your attitude to kick-ass levels).

(Also, your readjustment may possibly include firing or hiring someone, or raising venture capital, or whatever you figure out was missing or corrupting your first effort).

This is your basic Reality Check, where you refuse to wallow in self-pity, and instead focus on honestly examining everything.

Keep your ego out of it. (What's your stubborn, fragile and too-easily-offended ego done for you lately, except get you into trouble?)

Don't be swayed by coulda-woulda-shoulda regrets. (Regrets are for civilians. You're an entrepreneur now, and that means you move forward no matter what. Fix what you've broken, clean up your messes, make amends to those you've wronged, and do what's necessary to handle things better next time. Don't promise to do better – instead, fill in the gaps of your toolkit so you WILL do better.)

And don't allow even a hint of feeling like a "failure" creep into your brain.

For smart entrepreneurs, not getting it right is just another step on the sometimes-long path toward success.

Dust yourself off, get better prepared, and climb back into the ring with the resources, skills and attitude to win the next time.

You know you've "arrived" as a true entrepreneur when all of this becomes just part of the process, and you even enjoy the constant challenges raining down on you.

Tool #4: **Risk tolerance.**

This is what sets most entrepreneurs apart from the civilians who never try their hand at creating a business.

Against the advice of your drinking buddies (who really do not want you to succeed, because that will destroy their own belief that the little guy can't win)...

… and contrary to the fears of your family (who are terrified that going after your wild-ass dreams will humiliate them)...

… and in utter defiance of your own fears (flashing constantly from the scaredy-cat part of your brain)…

… you're going to have to lay your reputation on the line, and climb into a fight with the forces of capitalism armed only with your wit, sometimes meager resources and weak-ass skill sets, and raw determination.

And no one else except other entrepreneurs will even vaguely understand what you're going through.

It's like working without a net.

Or daring the universe to slap you down.

And going into situations, over and over again, where you're a complete rookie, apt to make embarrassing mistakes.

In short, **living with risk**.

And the consequences of risk, which can include icky failure.

Of course, as we established already, a true entrepreneur regards "failure" as just another step on the rocky path to breakthrough success.

It really is a process. Few get it right the first time.

So, you need to assess your capacity to accept and deal with risk.

If the very notion of taking a risk terrifies you into inaction, it's probably a sign from the universe that you need to go find a regular job somewhere safe. There's no shame in that. The world needs folks filling normal jobs.

However, if contemplating risk steels your determination to move forward (despite the butterflies in your stomach and the doubts that cause a few sleepless nights)…

… welcome to the club.

Tool #5: **Your basic bag of tricks.**

You may have to learn the basics from books at first, or by observation…

… but no matter how you learn them, you need to understand:

The fundamentals of a sales funnel (where qualified leads in a market full of your best prospects are captured and closed)...

… the details of **fulfillment and customer management** (where you offer a quality product and follow through on the customer experience)…

… and **how to craft a sales message** that can be easily communicated to prospects.

It's not rocket science, but you're an idiot if you think you can "fake it" as you begin marketing your business for real.

Fortunately, there are a lot of courses out there to shortcut your efforts...

... or, you can dive into the many books out there on these subjects.

In a weekend (even if you're a slow reader) you can begin your self-education by reading one book on product creation, one on marketing, one on sales, and one on writing copy.

Yes, you really can do this. You may have to miss out on bowling with your buddies, and skip all your usual TV shows… but you're setting up the framework for a successful entrepreneurial adventure here, Bucko.

You'll survive a few weekends of hitting the books.

Or, heck, just use the bolded phrases above in a determined Google search. There are blogs, reports, and wiki-sources all over the Web on these very subjects.

Your first choices of books or blogs may be the wrong ones to read (the Web is overflowing with rotten advice and dubious expertise) but that doesn't matter…

… **because you'll have started the process**, and that's the critical part of this step.

Next weekend, read four different books on the same subjects, and go deeper into your online research.

Rinse and repeat until you feel you have a toe-hold in each subject, at least.

The longest journey begins with a single step.

Just try not to fall on your face immediately, all right? Read critically and intelligently, and continually seek out authors you can trust and identify with.

Take notes. Imagine you're building a virtual house in your head, and you want that sucker to look good and stand tall for a very long time…

… which requires a solid foundation and sturdy supports.

Bonus tip: The more you research any given topic, the more you'll start to see certain names, ideas, phrases and techniques pop up.

Write these down – despite the mountains of crap out there, the best stuff does tend to rise to the top…

… and what gets referenced and mentioned the most is almost always something important you need to know.

This is why the best entrepreneurs alive are voracious readers, and never consider their self-education "done". They continue to learn, seek out better options, and stuff their network with experienced, smart connections on the cutting edge of whatever market they're in.

Things can change fast in business.

That's a huge advantage for rookies and entrepreneurs looking to kick their act up a notch…

… and a disadvantage only for anyone who refuses to learn new tricks.

Tool #6: **A budget, or war chest.**

You will need cash for your business adventures. No getting around that.

I'm not a great role model. I started my freelance career with one tank of gas in my rattle-trap car, one month's rent paid, and enough spare change to feed myself for a couple of weeks.

I had no Plan B.

Much better to have a planned budget, and the money to fund that budget for at least a few months (or even years). This is my recommendation to rookies.

If you're already in business, and you want to expand or get into a new project...

... then set aside a "war chest" of cash you're willing to invest in the new adventure.

Don't go in broke or clueless about what resources (money, time, employees) you may need to pull out of your existing biz.

Sit down and plan it out.

Most entrepreneurs hate budgets and planning.

Do it anyway. There are plenty of misadventures awaiting you in biz -- don't stumble on stuff like budgets, which you have control over and can figure out fairly easily.

And stick to your budget. Give yourself a deadline where you'll pull the plug if you haven't conquered this new adventure...

... and never look back on any money or time already spent.

That's the "sunk cost" blunder that can destroy empires. When you've budgeted money and time to put into a venture, with a deadline for calling it quits if you don't succeed...

... then you can walk away without regret. You planned, you went after it, and it didn't happen. That's life, and that's biz.

Move on to the next project, bringing with you any lessons learned.

Tool #7: **The ability to judge what's worth doing, and what's going to hold you back.**

This is a biggie.

You may suck at it right now, but one of your goals must be to quickly get pro-level good at judging client requests, job offers, new projects, partner assessment (in both biz and love), and all the little and big decisions that will cascade upon your head every single day.

One tactic: Apply the 1-10 "pain scale" measurement many doctors use in assessing patients.

Use it on yourself: What level is the value… the risk… the reward… and the danger of any decision you encounter?

Is it a big deal, a medium-sized deal, or a little deal of no lasting consequence?

Be decisive about these measurements. Saying "I don't know" isn't an option.

Dig deep into your heart, your fears, your dreams and your abilities… and figure it out.

Another tactic: I use the "5 Seconds After" technique all the time.

Here's how it works: When you're conflicted about a choice, put yourself into the headspace you'll be in five seconds after making a decision on one option.

Really immerse yourself into that feeling immediately after deciding.

Are you relieved? Panicked? Think it was a mistake that will haunt you? Feeling rueful but ready to charge ahead?

Your body will reveal a lot to you right afterward about what you really want.

Then, apply this same future-based evaluation on the next choice, and so on.

You will often find the correct path forward this way, based on how you'll feel after making the decision.

Get good at these tactics, as fast as possible.

One of the **main failure points** of unsuccessful biz owners is an inability to make prompt, good decisions.

Tool #8: **Stress management.**

You're going to encounter stress as an entrepreneur.

That's a given.

Ignoring this stress is a very, very, very bad idea. It will never leave, it will build up, and in due time it will fry your brain like an egg in a skillet.

You are not a superman. Your body and mind are vulnerable to the ravages of poor diet, lack of exercise, and constant hormone dumps of adrenaline and other bad chemicals.

Massage, meditation, lots of vacations and sex, reading satisfying books (not biz books) to relax, having "safety zones" in your week where you are free from the tentacles of your biz (no phone, no email, no nothing)…

… are the best tactics for battling stress. And they are easy to research and experiment with.

Find out what works for you, and give it PRIORITY status in your life.

For example, I began getting weekly massages early in my career… long before I started buying better clothes, a newer car, or eating out more often. I put money into my body.

Massage "re-set" my physical stress levels, and I'm convinced it has saved me from ulcers and worse. And kept me mega-productive for decades.

Burnt-out, tense entrepreneurs seldom make good decisions.

Relaxed ones do.

I started out with a "business before pleasure" mindset…

… but included in that "business" part was de-stressing and being a good animal (loose, in shape, well-fed, lots of restorative sleep, etc.).

If you're not healthy and having fun while making your business thrive…

… then you're not living large.

And wasn't that part of your motivation to become an entrepreneur in the first place?

Finally (for this short "starter list")…

Tool #9: **Have an exit plan.**

Go after your goals like a terrier chasing a squirrel, with total focus and commitment.

However, realize that sometimes your goals need to be adjusted, radically altered, or even abandoned.

When the facts and circumstances change, your goals change.
(This includes sudden changes in technology like Google slaps…
booming new opportunities that didn't exist earlier… skilled and
better-funded competitors chewing up your market… and – most
importantly – realizing you no longer crave what motivated you so
desperately before.)

I'm not suggesting you have an easy "bail-out" plan that you can
take whenever things get dicey.

Like Cortez burning his ships when starting his conquest of Central
America, a lot of entrepreneurs do better when there is no turning
back. Having your eye on the exit sign will affect your ability to
charge forward with commitment and verve.

No, I'm talking about visualizing your life after success.

Many entrepreneurs, right after "making it", immediately begin to
sabotage the business.

Why? Because the fun is in the building-up of the beast, the
adventures of tackling challenges and working without a net.

Once you've been successful, you either need to pivot to
management of the biz (yawn)…

… or consider the consequences of cashing out, selling your
business, moving into something else, or just becoming an
"intrapreneur" like Steve Jobs did at Apple.

At least consider what your life will be like when you succeed.
And consider options for yourself.

Right now you're engaged in the greatest adventure possible –
becoming or strengthening your position as an entrepreneur.

However, the path you're on will veer wildly in different directions (possibly way sooner than you anticipated)…

… and it's a good thing to be prepared for both failure and success.

Visualize your bad self sitting back one day, after having "made it".

What's your NEXT set of goals?

A cushy retirement of luxury and debauchery?

Writing your autobiography?

Starting another business?

Most civilians believe (incorrectly) that the goal of becoming an entrepreneur is to make a bundle of moolah, and sit back doing nothing for the rest of your life.

That idea just makes most entrepreneurs squirm.

Most of the ones I've met during my many decades in the game would shrivel up and die if forced to sit on a beach somewhere drinking beer the rest of their days, no matter how much money they'd socked away.

What else do you want, after you've made your business successful?

I plan on remaining active in both biz and my lifestyle until I'm cashed out entirely (and off to that big marketing seminar in the sky). I already kick back occasionally on a beach, swilling beer… for brief periods during vacations.

It's fine for an afternoon, but not for longer than that.

No, I've always had a vision of myself in deep old age, and it's all about writing better than ever, and helping people as much as possible.

That's what floats my boat, teaching.

And teachers just get better with age.

I don't see a need to ever call it a day and quit business. Scale it back, sure. Try new things, sure. Travel more for fun (rather than the globe-trotting I do now as a professional speaker and consultant), sure.

But living without grandiose goals that I have every intention of fulfilling?

Never.

I have a healthy suspicion you're the same way.

But figure it out, regardless.

Peer into your future, and see what kind of lifestyle makes you smile.

Okay.

That's the starter list. Not a bad checklist to have on the wall above your desk as you move forward, either.

One last thought on reality: Yes, I have, on occasion, ignored the reality of who I am, and what I bring to the game, as I've plowed through life going after what others have considered unrealistic goals.

And I've done pretty well with that brazen attitude. (Great Gary Halbert quote: "Nothing is impossible for a man who refuses to listen to reason.")

However, there is ONE reality I never ignore.

That would be the reality of results.

I love seeing how ads and tactics work, or don't work, through actual sales numbers (and click-through and open rates, and so on).

However, I look at these results CRITICALLY. I never accept them blindly.

They are tools for moving forward.

Where did, or where could the ad have failed? Can we fix it? What other things can be done to navigate a sales problem? Where IS the main problem, anyway?

My stupidly-aggressive and irrational refusal to face certain realities has served me well over the years.

If I'd listened to the nay-sayers, or even my own fears, my life would have been much less exciting and happy.

And less rich, in every respect.

Still, all vices in moderation. That's my motto.

Find out what works for you. I hope this list is a good starting point.

Chapter Two:

"Operation MoneySuck"

The only reality-based mindset that will relentlessly cram piles of moolah into your bank account.

You hear me nattering about "Operation MoneySuck" all the time. And some folks are confused about what it means.

So let's do a refresher.

Here's the story: Early in my career, I was hired by advertising legend Gary Halbert to help him write ads for clients.

The first day I arrived at his offices on Sunset Blvd (in West Hollywood), we were scheduled to slam out copy and plot "next moves" with some current clients.

However, just as my butt hit the chair across from his desk, two (count 'em, two) secretaries AND his red-headed girlfriend (notorious for getting her way) burst in with bad news.

Lots of bad news, in fact. The printer had just broken down, and important papers needed to get copied NOW. Some guy was ranting and raving on Line 2, threatening legal action over something. The landlord was on the way up in the elevator, because there was a problem with the lease. The bank was on Line 1, and so on.

These women were shaking with panic and consternation, freaked out by the urgent crisis-level emergencies that...

... *HAD*...

... to be dealt with...

...*NOW!*

I sighed, assumed our meeting was not gonna happen, and started to gather my stuff, ready to split until Gary had attended to all of this mayhem.

Instead, he held up his hand...

… shushed everyone...

… gently ushered the secretaries AND his red-headed girlfriend (notorious for getting her way) out the door...

... and *locked* it.

Returning to his desk, he picked up a pen and said "Okay, let's get busy."

I was stunned. *What... what... wait a minute... what about all that...* "Operation MoneySuck," he said, rifling through his Rolodex for the number of a client we needed to call.

"Screw all that irrelevant stuff. We're gonna bring in the bucks." **And we did.** For the next several hours, we finished ads, nailed down deals, and consulted with clients.

All behind a locked door, ignoring the commotion outside, which eventually subsided.

When we finally opened the door again, all was calm in the outer offices. Line 1 and Line 2 were quiet, the landlord was gone, the printer chattering happily and kicking out dot-matrix copies. (It was a while back, folks.)

*All the "emergencies" had been taken care of, **without us**.*

And we had put in a solid session of writing and wrangling with clients.
Which generated income, new business, and a good deal of killer brainstorming.

The lesson of Operation MoneySuck couldn't have been clearer.

It's this: If you are the person in charge of bringing in the money, then *that* is your Number One job -- *to bring in the money.*

It's also your Number Two job, your Number Three job, and so on.

More: ALL problems are "emergencies", in one way or another. They're a show-stopper to some, an ulcer-inducing nightmare for others.

However, if your job is to bring in the moolah...

… and an hour of you doing that can generate, say, a thousand bucks in fees or sales...

... then, when you scurry over to start looking at the printer when it snarls up...

... that means you're paying someone (you) a *thousand bucks an hour* to read the manual and pull out jammed paper with uncoiled paperclips.

While NO ONE is picking up your job of bringing home any bacon.

So you lose *twice.* Net loss of two thousand smackeroo's per hour. (Plus, you'll most likely just fuck up the printer and have to go buy a new one anyway. What are office printers running nowadays? $150? *Phht.* Spare change when you're bringing home thousands.)

The importance of this attitude kept getting nailed home for me as I noticed how many entrepreneurs and biz owners *routinely* took their eye off the ball...

... trying to "save" a few bucks by doing everything themselves.

And, at the same time, I noticed that the really *successful* dudes had personal assistants, secretaries, and grunt labor at their beck-and-call to do all the "small shit" (as Halbert called it).

Which guaranteed that their lives bopped along smoothly (with dishes washed, dry cleaning picked up, bills paid, fridge stuffed, landlords mollified, and so on)...

... and ALL of their main energies went into doing what they did best: **Create wealth.**

So that's Operation MoneySuck.

For me, it's a code-word for my colleagues (and my brain) that means we're gonna focus on the raw greenback core of business right now. *And nothing else.*

You are free to interpret it however you like...

... as long as, when you're done, you've made serious progress toward your goals of feeding the financial monkey in your life.

Yes, the emergencies in your life need to be tended to.

And you need to pay attention to your health, the rent, your Significant Other's needs, family obligations, and all the nagging details of being a fine upstanding member of modern civilization.

But you BEGIN with a solid understanding of what your JOB is in life.

Make sense?

Get clear... and be specific... on *what it is*, exactly, you do that causes cash to be delivered into your bank account.

In this "2.0" modern world, you may need to include some things that are, say, one step removed from the actual act of converting a customer. If you have an online biz, for example, then writing the sales message is critical to make sales happen.

However, generating traffic (if you haven't got any) is a precursor to hauling prospects in front of your wonderful sales pitch.

So all the things you may need to do right now to divert leads into your world becomes Operation MoneySuck, ahead of even writing the sales message.

Including hiring someone to do it for you.

Or hiring someone to find someone to do it for you.

Radical example: This attitude of "get it done", at the highest professional levels, is something awesome to behold.

Let's say you're a copywriter, and you have a deadline tomorrow morning at 8 am for something you need to write tonight.

And you drop your laptop in the toilet at 1 am...

... so it's not just dead, but it's Ugly Dead. All files flushed, gone, not backed up.

What do you do?

Less focused folks would punt. Call the client early, apologize profusely, and try to negotiate more time.

Not the "real" pro.

He would immediately figure out his options.

Borrow a computer, even if it means calling and waking up an old girlfriend (who hates your guts). Steal one. Call up pawn shops, all-night stores, anywhere that might have a working computer.

BUT... he would only spend a *short time* on this side project.

As soon as bribing, begging, theft and shopping were ruled out...

... he would pick up a pen, pencil or crayon, and start *writing* (using notebooks, napkins, paper towels, anything that worked).

And FINISH the writing part of the gig.

Grab a 20-minute nap, proof-read the scribbling... and be waiting at the most logical place to score a way to get it into a Word document the moment that place was open: The city library, Susie's apartment, the nearest computer store, a hotel business center.

So he could *finish* the rest of what was required to meet his deadline.

So he would get *paid*.

That's Operation MoneySuck.

Give that man a round of applause.

That's a pro.

And yes, I've done (more or less) versions of this kind of insane meet-the-deadline-no-matter-what behavior throughout my career.

Because I'm the guy whose job it was to bring home the moolah.

If this kind of dedication, determination and raw discipline is not in your toolkit right now... it *can* be.

You start by committing to a goal.

And you move forward from there.

You really can astonish yourself with your ability to do things that -- yesterday -- you would have routinely regarded as "impossible"...

... but you can't get there by *dreaming* about it.

You may even need guidance, from a mentor or coach to watch your back as you establish your private beach-head in the world of professionalism.

Lemme tell you, though...

... once you get a taste of living life with this kind of verve, awareness and Zen-warrior "get it done" mojo...

... you will feel and *be* more alive than you ever believed possible.

And that's why successful entrepreneurs sometimes seem so cocky.

It's because they've experienced Operation MoneySuck (whether they call it that or not)...

... *and it rocked their world.*

I dunno... are you buying all this?

It's all the dead-solid truth... but I know that most people recoil in horror at the thought of going after a goal like a terrier after a squirrel. (Pure lethal focus.)

I learned the methods of living this way slowly...

... because I had to pull myself out of the Slacker Mire, with little guidance or advice.

So when I realized what Halbert was doing in that long-ago office on Sunset Blvd, I grasped that lesson close to my heart and *kept* it there until it became a part of me.

It's worth it.

<u>Chapter Three:</u>

Goal Setting & The Notorious "January 15th Letter"

Tricking your bad self into attaining every goal on your Master List For Living Well (cuz you'll never attain ANY of it, left to your own methods)…

Despite the gray overcast outside, life is bright and shiny for me today.

Because I'm *alive…* and not just kickin', but given official orders to kick as long and hard as I can for many years to come.

See, I just got back from going under the surgeon's knife again -- second outpatient surgery in a month, all because I got sunburned too many times as a kid. (We started our tans every summer by getting burnt to a crisp. Then we'd slough off dead skin like a molting snake, and *voila!* Nice brown tan underneath. Apparently that was a bad idea, and now everyone my age is paying the price.)

I'm fine, and don't expect further problems, though I will be watchful.

It didn't even seem like that big of a deal to me -- nothing I couldn't handle myself with a mirror, a rusty razor blade, and a shot of whiskey. (Or, as my friend Renae suggested, just taking the car cigarette lighter to the offending spot until I burned down to bone.)

But no, the doc *insisted* on all this sterile crap, shots of numb-o-caine, expert stitching, the works. Leave no scar, he said.

Hey, I *wanted* the scar. Make a good story about surviving a knife fight or something.

I'm joking about this because I know how much of a bullet I dodged. I can't count the number of friends I have suffering more serious problems, but I do count my blessings.

If I'm still ridiculously healthy (in spite of this one minor setback) it isn't because of anything I've ever *done* to create health.

In fact, I've logged many, many years in a self-destructive daze, daring the worst.

That's why I suspect I'm being spared a horrible illness only if I agree to continue to help others -- which is why starting this chapter seems like a front-burner project, even while the bandages are still on.

I actually *crave* the privilege of telling you another story with a lesson. Of all the desires that crossed my mind on the ride home, doing this was astonishingly high on the list.

You may not be aware of it, but there's a spiritual fulfillment on my end when I write this swill. I normally ignore it myself…

… but today, it's loud and clear.

Mark Twain famously suggested that even the most responsible man, having died and then given another day to spend on earth, would immediately secure a bottle of rot-gut whiskey and a hooker.

I'm not ruling those options out if things ever get worse, but for now I'm enjoying the lure of my work. (It's like I've been poisoned with a sudden dose of maturity, late in life.)

If you've ever been swabbed and butchered on an examining table, you know it's true there are no atheists in foxholes or doctors' offices.

You just get the feeling there's something... *more*... going on. And big damn mysterious reasons behind it all.

It's as close as I ever get to feeling religious.

But that's not why I bring this up. (Is there anything more boring than a conversation that begins "I just had surgery, and..."?)

No.

What's more relevant here is the feeling of *aliveness* I'm experiencing.

It's better than drugs or sex. Everything I see is a visual delight, every sound a symphony, every surface a tactile wonderland. Those shadowy mountains are just stunningly gorgeous. The hum of traffic is as soothing as spring bees attending their flowers. My mutt terrier's bristly fur feels like mink.

Mind you, this was *not* a near-death experience I had. Routine stuff, and the doctor and I joked and discussed art and movies throughout the procedure.

I was, however, still more or less lying on a slab. Being filleted like a fish. My jokes were a little forced, more bravura than wit.

It's not a pretty view, having people with surgical splatter-guards bending over your chest, fussing with blades and needles and bloody gauze. (I had flashbacks to Ken Burns-style scenes of Civil War era field hospitals, long before the niceties of anesthesia and antibacterial agents. We got *nothing* to complain about today.)

And, simple procedure or not, I still experienced the amazing "second chance" thrill that is so familiar to anyone who's brushed up against their own mortality.

One of my long-term goals is to live in this bright state most of the time, and not just on special occasions.

It's a Zen thing, and doable.

But I have to *want* it, and I have to *do* the things required in order to attain it.

And this -- short drum roll -- is the perfect segue into what I wanted to talk about here. I call it…

**"Goal Setting 101 And
The January 15th Letter"**

Yeah, yeah, I know that a chat about goals can quickly turn into a boring, pedantic lecture.

But then, so can a chat about space flight.

And, in reality, both space flight and your goals are VERY exciting things. Or should be.

It's all in the telling.

What I'm *not* going to discuss are "resolutions". Those are bogus pseudo-goals that have the staying power of pudding in a microwave.
No. It's merely a coincidence that I'm suggesting a review of your goals in January, just after the New Year's supposed fresh start.

I mean… there's not much *else* to do, so why not sit down and plan out the rest of your life.

This is, of course, a very damp, cold, and bleak time of year.

The depths of winter and discontent.

A good percentage of the population suffers fleeting depression because of lack of sunlight… thanks to the geniuses behind Daylight Savings Time, who arrange for dusk to arrive around 2:30 in the afternoon in these parts.

We also just got slammed with back-to-back-to-*back* "Storms of the Century", each one dumping a record load of snow on us. I sent photos to friends, and many emailed back wondering when I'd gone to Antarctica to live.

We had a little cabin fever brewing. Didn't help when the local PBS channel ran a special on the Donner Party, either. Three feet of snow drifting down, the lights flickering, enough ice on the road to make the SUV sidle like a Red Wing goon slamming someone into the boards.

The safest place was home… but man, the walls start to close in after a few days.

I'm telling you, I had excuses up the yin-yang for allowing my senses to get a little dulled. The natural response is to turn your mind off, and *hibernate* until March.

And I succumbed, until the surgery. Started moping around, watching CSI: Miami reruns instead of reading a book, surfing the Net for stuff I didn't care about… you know the drill.

I'm sure you've done your own version of it now and again.

And I'm also sure you already know that no amount of "buck up" happy talk will mitigate the gloom.

In fact, there are a few enlightened health pro's who say we *should* let our bodies wind down every year or so. Get a full system-flush type of bad cold, crawl under the covers for a few days and let the demons and other bad stuff bubble to the surface.

So you can *purge* the crud. Evacuate the used-up bacteria and tube-clogs out of your pipes, physically. And shoo the whispering monsters out of your head.

We're not perfect creatures. We need to sleep, we need to recharge our batteries, and we need to stop and get our bearings. At least once a year.

So don't beat yourself up for the occasional down period. We all have them, and the healthiest folks just roll with it.

It's not good to repress this stuff.

It only becomes a problem when you sink into clinical depression. That's the cold, empty state where nothing looks good, and hope is an absurd memory.

I've been there.

Several times.

The year I turned 30 (for example) I lost my job, my girlfriend and my place to live… all within a 45-day stretch.

That shit can wear you down.

Now, I have two things to say about this:

Thing Numero Uno: If you think you're losing a grip on your mental state, seek professional help. (I'm not a doctor, but I feel pretty safe recommending this. And if it's *really* bad this time, don't hesitate to call The **National Suicide Prevention Lifeline** (1-800-273-TALK [8255].)

If it's just a normal funk that's got you down, though, give "talk therapy" a try with a real, qualified psychotherapist.

Choose this therapist carefully. You're going to dump every secret you have on him, and examine the dark corners of your mind. (I've been doing this regularly over the years, going in for a check-up visit or two when needed – sometimes every year, sometimes not for years at a time… and it's *very* effective… especially for creative types working through down periods.)

Keep in mind the fact that *everyone* goes through bumpy emotional states. And that the percentage of people who actually do lose it every year is rather small.

That's why *talking* about your problems with someone who has perspective can be so beneficial -- the first thing you learn is that *you aren't alone.*

And what you're going through is *not* abnormal.

Most of the time, you're gonna be fine. Even when your problems seem overwhelming at first.

There are tools available to help cope. You don't often come across these tools on your own. This is one of the few times that the "science" of psychology earns its keep -- finding out how *others* successfully dealt with the same nonsense you're suffering through can change everything.

A good book to read (while you're waiting for the spring thaw) is **"Learned Optimism"** by Martin Seligman. I've recommended it before, and it deserves another nod. (The blurb on the back cover, from the New York Times Book Review, starts with "Vaulted me out of my funk…")

I haven't read the book in ten years, but I remember the main lesson well. A study, explained up front, stands out: Someone tested the "happiness" quotient of a vast sample of people, including Holocaust survivors.

And it turns out that, at some point in your life, Abraham Lincoln was right -- you are as happy as you *decide* to be.

This is startling news to anyone lost in despair. Because it seems like you've been *forced* to feel that way. With no choice.

But it's not the case. The happiness study revealed that you can *not* tell from a person's current attitude what sort of trauma they had gone through earlier in life. People who had suffered horribly could be happy as larks, while silver-spoon never-stubbed-a-toe folks were miserable.
The difference?

Attitude.

Optimistic people work through setbacks and trauma… while pessimists settle into a funk that can't be budged.

And it's a CHOICE. At some point in your life, you *choose* to either live in gloom or sunlight.

This realization rocks many folks' boats. Especially the pessimists. They dominate society, politics, business, everything.

And they are *very* protective of their gloom and doom outlook. Invested, heavily, in proving themselves right about the inherent nastiness of life.

Maybe you're one of 'em.

If you are, you're *killing* yourself, dude.

Current studies show that heart disease rates are HALF for optimists over pessimists. So, even if you doubt the ability to measure "happiness" -- it is a rather rocky science -- you still can't deny the stats on dropping dead from a gloomy ticker.

Now, I am most assuredly NOT a clear-eyed optimist. I get creepy feelings around people who are too happy all the time.

But I do prefer *having* a good time, and appreciating the finer things in life (like a deep breath of cold alpine air, or the salty whip of an ocean wave around my ankles, or a secret smile from the wonderful woman I live with).

I'm just adept at balancing out the bad with the good.

Being in direct response helps. Lord knows, there's a LOT of bad with every piece of good news in this wacky biz.

Gary Halbert and I had a term we used for years: We were **"pessimistic optimists"**. (Or maybe we were optimistic pessimists. Same thing.)

How does that work? Easy.

We *expect* horrible atrocities at every turn…

… and *rejoice* when we defy Fate and unreasonable success rains down on our undeserving heads.

We groove on the good stuff in life… and just nod sagely at the bad stuff and *move past it* as quickly as possible. Learn our lesson, if there is one. And move along.

If you focus on the bad things that can go wrong, you'll never crawl out of bed in the morning.

When you finally realize that -- not counting health problems -- pretty much everything bad that business, or relationships, or politics can throw at you will *not* kill you…

… then you relax.

And eagerly court the Unknown by starting another project.

Have you ever had your heart broken? Hurts like hell, doesn't it. Feels like your life is over.

Well, from my perspective, sitting here at "the far end of middle age" and pretty darned happy, all those women who broke my heart long ago look just plain silly now.

And my resulting deep depressions -- where I was *sure* life was over -- are just tiresome lessons I had to get through.

Not a one of those ladies was worth a burp of angst. They were fine people, I'll agree to that. A few were exceptional (and very skilled at certain man-pleasing arts).

But worth a Shakespearean suicide?

No way.

It's taken me a while, but I'm now a certified **realist**. My youthful idealism has drained away, and my brushes with hate-everything dogma never took.

And guess what? Contrary to what an embarrassing huge number of self-righteous folks would have you believe… being a realist has *not* dented my passion for life one little bit.

In fact, it has opened up a whole new world of unexplainable spirituality (which cannot be contained within any formal religion).

I'm not against religion. Let's have no "save my soul" emails here. One of my good friends is an ordained minister with a doctorate in theology. And I have other friends committed to various belief systems ranging from fundamentalist to Buddhist to humanist.

We get along because, on a deep level, we understand that true spirituality *transcends* whatever way you choose to express it or appreciate it.

I loathe black-and-white views of the world. It's a shame that our great country has descended to this "you're nuts if you don't agree with me" mentality… but it's part of the pendulum that's been swinging back and forth ever since we left the jungle.

The far edges of our institutions -- political, religious, cultural, all of it -- are in spiritual and emotional "lock down". They're sure they're right, they're positive you're wrong, and neither facts nor logic will sway their position.

I have no use for dogma, or idealism, or punishingly-harsh rules that have been cooked up by hypocrites.

Hey -- I'm in no position to tell anyone how to live their life. I've screwed up plenty, and if I have any wisdom at all, it's only because I've survived some truly hairy situations.

But I don't believe anyone *else* is in a position to tell you how to live, either. That's gotta be *your* decision.

And it's a damn hard one to make.

Fortunately, while I can't tell you how to live, I *can* move some smooth (and proven) advice in your direction.

Take it or leave it… but give it a listen anyway, cuz my track record on successful advice-giving is fairly impressive.

And I'm telling you that having a hateful, brooding attitude will stunt your growth. It will make you a smaller person, a less-wise person, an older and feebler person.

And you won't *grow*. Not spiritually, not physically, not emotionally. Not in your business life, either.

Most people don't *want* to grow, anyway. Growth only comes from movement and change… and the vast majority of the folks walking the earth with us today are *terrified* of change.

You can't blame them, really. Change is a form of death. Whatever was before, dies. And whatever comes next must be nurtured with devotion and sacrifice.

That's hard. That's a hard way to live, always dying and being reborn.

And because it's hard, it's avoided.

Well, screw that.

I suspect, if you're reading this, you are *not* afraid of change.

After all, you had to change your bank account by a few bucks in order to buy this book -- you took a shot, and gave me the opportunity to prove to you that I could change your bottom line. And make the pittance you shelled out a small detail, as you get paid *back* many times over with results.

But you may not yet understand the *power* that REALLY giving yourself to change offers.

And that brings us to…

Thing Numero Dos: Goals are all *about* change.

That's a subtle point many people gloss over. Rookie goal-setters often get stuck on stuff like quitting smoking, or vague concepts like "become a better person".

Or "get rich".

That seldom works. Goals need to be specific…

… and they need to involve *profound change* in order to take hold.

Halbert often talked about "image suicide" -- the necessity of killing and burying the "self" you are so heavily invested in, before you can move to a new level of success.

I see this all the time in my consultations. Biz owners refuse to do even slightly risky marketing, for fear of damaging their "reputations."

And my question to them is: *What* reputation?

Unless you're the top dog in your niche, no one gives a rat's ass about what you think or do. No one is looking at your marketing for inspiration or condemnation, because you aren't the guy to look at.

No. What these scaredy-cats are talking about when they say "reputation" is what their *family and friends* think of them.

And that's a sure sign of a losing attitude. That ain't Operation MoneySuck.

My colleague Ron LeGrand, the real estate guru, is one of the best natural salesmen I've ever met. The guy understands the fundamental motivating psychology of a prospect at a master's level.

And he knows that one of the major obstacles he faces in every sale... is what the prospect's *spouse* (usually the wife) will say.

She can nix the sale with a sneer. Or she can nix it in the prospect's head, as he *imagines* that sneer.

Ron counters both sides of the objection expertly. He encourages the prospect to get his spouse involved in the decision, so she becomes *invested* in it.

Or, he suggests waiting until the first big check comes in... and letting the *money* explain to her about what you're up to.

This is the reality of most people's lives. As much as they want what you offer... they are *terrified* of making a mistake. Cuz they'll pay dearly for it at home.

It's a *huge* deal-nixer.

That's why you include lots of "reason why" copy in your pitch -- to give your buyer ammunition for explaining his decision to the doubters in his life.

However, as Ron knows, the best (and simplest) "reason why" is *results*.

Money, as they say, talks.

The top marketers seldom give a moment's thought to what a risky tactic might do to their "reputation". They don't really *care* what people think about them.

You can't bank criticism.

I know many marketers who are involved in projects they are passionate about… but which bore their spouses to tears. Some (like Howard Stern's former wife) are even deeply embarrassed.

But they don't *complain* much. Because the money's so good.

Aw, heck. I could go on and on about this. The story of Rodale's shock and dismay at the brutally-honest ad I wrote for their timid "sex book" is a great example. They refused to mail it, because of their "reputation".

Yet, after it accidentally *did* mail, and became a wildly-successful control for 5 years, they suddenly decided their reputation could handle it after all.

The people who get the most done in life are all *extreme* risk-takers. They embrace change, because growth is impossible without it.

But you don't go out and start changing things willy-nilly.

You need a plan.

You need goals.

Now, there are lots of books out there that tell you how to set goals. I recently found, in a moldy banker's box, the ad for Joe Karbo's book "The Lazy Man's Way To Riches" that I'd responded to back in 1982. *The exact ad!* With the order form torn out… it was the first direct mail pitch I'd ever encountered, and it changed my life forever. Joe's book was essentially a treatise on setting goals.

And it's good.

It was a wake-up call for me.

I'm having that crinkly old ad framed. Can't imagine why I kept it, but I did. Pack-rat riches.

If you can't find that particular book, there are dozens of newer goal-setting guides on the shelves.

But they're all based on the same formula: Decide what you want. Write it down, and be specific. Read the list often, imagining as you read that you have *already* achieved each goal.

What this does is alter the underpinnings of your unconscious. When one of your goals is to earn a million bucks this year, and that goal burns bright in the back of your mind, each decision you make will be influenced.

So, for example, you won't accept a permanent job somewhere that pays $50,000 a year. Cuz that isn't going to help you attain your goal.

The problem is, to earn a mil in a year, you need to average around $50,000 every two *weeks*. This is why it can take a while to get your goal-setting chops honed. As I've said many times, most folks don't know *what* they want.

And they aren't prepared for the changes necessary to *get* what they want, once they do decide on a goal.

What kind of guy earns $50,000 every two weeks, like clockwork?

It takes a certain level of business savvy to create that kind of steady wealth. It doesn't fall into your lap.

What kind of guy makes a windfall of a million bucks in *one chunk?*

That's *another* kind of savvy altogether.

In that same moldy banker's box, I also found a bunch of my early goal lists. And I'm shocked at how modest my aims were.

At the time -- I was in the first months of going out on my own, a totally pathetic and clueless rookie -- I couldn't even *imagine* earning fifty K a year.

My first goal was $24,000 as a freelancer. And to score a better rental to live in. Find a date for New Year's. Maybe buy a new used car.

Listen carefully: I *met* those goals. As modest as they were, it would have been hard not to. I *needed* them to be modest, because I was just getting my goal-setting chops together.

And I wasn't sure if I was wasting my time even bothering to set goals.

Let me assure you, it was NOT a waste of time.

The lists I found covered several later years, too. And what's fascinating is that many of the more specific goals I set down were crossed out -- I wanted those goals, but didn't feel confident about obtaining them.

So I crossed them out, and forgot about them.

A couple of decades later, I realize that I've attained *every single one* of those "forgotten" goals. The big damn house, the love of my life, the professional success, even the hobbies and the guitars and the sports car.

I'm stunned. **This is *powerful* voodoo here.**

The universe works in mysterious ways, and you don't have to belong to a religion to realize this. The whole concept of "ask and you shall receive, seek and you shall find, knock and the door will be opened" was well-known by successful people long before Luke and Matthew wrote it down.

The keys are *action. Movement.*

Ask, seek, knock.

These simple actions will change your life forever.

Back to making a million in a year: Some guys *know* what they need to do to make this goal real. They've done it before, or they've come close.

Setting the goal is serious business for them… because they are well aware of the tasks they've assigned themselves. Take on partners, put on seminars, create ad campaigns, build new products. Get moving on that familiar path.

I've known many people who started the year with such a goal… who quickly modified it *downward* as the reality of the task became a burden. Turns out they didn't really want the whole million after all.

Half of that would suffice just fine.

To hell with the work required for the full bag of swag.

Other guys *don't* know what they need to do to earn a mil. So their first big goal really is: *Find out what I need to do to earn a million bucks.*

Their initial tasks are to ask, seek, and knock like crazy.

And change the way they move and act in the world. Because they must *transform* themselves into the kind of guy who earns a million bucks in one year.

Right now, they aren't that guy.

So, for example, reading "**The 7 Habits Of Highly Effective People**" suddenly becomes an "A" task, while remodeling the kitchen gets moved to the back burner.

Sharpening your ability to craft a killer sales pitch becomes more important than test-driving the new Porsche.

More important, even, than dating Little Miss Perfect. And test-driving her new accessories.

Tough choice? Nope. When you get hip to the glory of focused change, you *never* lament leaving the "old" you behind.

It will be hard, sometimes, no doubt about it.

Especially when you discover your old gang no longer understands you, or mocks your ambition. They *liked* the old, non-threatening you. They want him to come back.

But you've changed. And hot new adventures are going to take up a *lot* more of your time now.

My trick to setting goals is very simple:

Every January 15th, I sit down and write myself a letter, dated exactly one year ahead.

And I describe, in that letter, what my life is like a year hence. (So, for example, in 2017, I dated the letter to myself as January 15, 2018.)

It's a subtle difference to the way other people set goals. Took me a long time to figure it out, too.

For many years, I wrote out goals like "I live in a house on the ocean", and "I earn $90,000 a year".

And that worked. But it was like *pushing* my goals.

Writing this letter to myself is more like *pulling* my goals.

For me, this works even better. Every decision I make throughout the year is *unconsciously influenced*, as I am pulled toward becoming the person I've described.

But here's where I do it *very* differently: My goals are deliberately in the "*whew*" to "*no friggin' way*" range. Mega-ambitious, to downright greedy.

There's a sweet spot in there -- doable, if I commit myself, but not so outrageous that I lose interest because the required change is too radical.

I'm pretty happy with myself these days. Took me a long, hard slog to get here, and I earned every step.

And I want to continue changing, because I enjoy change. But I don't need to reinvent myself entirely anymore.

So here's what makes this ambitious goal-setting so effective: **I don't expect to REACH most of them.**

In fact, I'm happy to get *half* of what I wanted.

There's a ton of psychology at work there.

The person I describe a year away often resembles James Bond more than the real me. Suave, debonair, flush, famous, well-traveled… and in peak health.

I hit all the big ones.

However, long ago I realized that trying to be perfect was a sure way to *sabotage* any goal I set. Perfectionists rarely attain anything, because they get hung up on the first detail that doesn't go right.

Being a good goal-setter is more like successful *boxing* -- you learn to roll with the punches, cuz you're gonna get hit.

You just stay focused on the Big Goal. And you get there however you can.

I'm looking at last year's letter. I was a greedy bastard when I wrote it, and I didn't come close to earning the income figure I set down.

Yet, I *still* had one of my best years ever.

And -- here's the kicker -- I would NOT have had such a great year, if I wasn't being *pulled* ahead by that letter.

There were numerous small and grand decisions I made that would have gone another way without the influence of what I had set down.

I didn't travel to the places I had listed. But I did travel to other, equally-fun places. I didn't finish that third novel. But I did position it in my head, and found the voice I want for narration. That's a biggie. That was a sticking point that would have kept the novel from ever getting finished.

Now, it's on power-glide.

There's another "hidden" benefit to doing this year-ahead letter: *It forces you to look into the future.*

A lot of people make their living peering ahead and telling everyone else what to expect. Most do a piss-poor job of it -- weathermen are notorious for getting it wrong, as are stock market analysts, wannabe trend-setters, and political prognosticators.

Yet, they stay in business.

Why? Because the rest of the population is *terrified* of looking into the future. That would require some sincere honesty about their current actions…

… since what the future holds is often the *consequence* of what you're doing right now.

If you're chain-smoking, chasing street hookers, and living on doughnuts, your future isn't pretty. For example.

Or if you've maxed out all your credit cards, and haven't done your due diligence to start bringing in moolah, your future isn't nice, either.

No one can "see" into the future for real.

But that doesn't mean you shouldn't *try*.

In fact, it's *easy*, when you have a little experience in life.

Things you do today will have consequences tomorrow. If you put up a website today for a product, and you do everything you can to bring traffic to it and capture orders…

… your consequences can be pretty and nice.

Sure, you may get hit by a bus while fetching the morning paper… but letting that possibility scare you away from trying for something better is for pessimists (who are scheduled for early checkout).

You have *enormous* control over your future.

And once you realize that, you can set out to start *shaping* it.

<u>Chapter Four:</u>

Quick-Start Mentoring List

Why you're sabotaging your own show, the simple "rule to live by" that solves all professional problems, and the Magic Key on your computer keyboard that solves most of the other stuff...

S ometimes, good advice doesn't come in nice tidy packages.

Okay, *most* of the time it doesn't come that way.

If you've ever been fortunate enough to have a mentor who really got in your face with the good lessons, then you know much of it comes in haphazard tidbits, not always directly connected to what's going on around you at the moment.

Still, good advice is good advice...

... and here's a nice list of fundamentally solid tactics, advice and insight that any decent teacher would make sure you received early in your mentoring.

The kind of stuff you can build a career or an entire business on, and know you've got a foundation that cannot be easily toppled.

Let's just dive in:

Fundamental Lesson #1: One of the main tricks to getting anywhere in life... *is to let the curtain go up on your act.*

Too many people sit around wringing their hands, doing *anything* they can -- both consciously and unconsciously -- to keep the show from going on. Because they're terrified of what might happen.

And here is your reality check: *Everyone* gets scared when they do something new. Almost every single one of us.

Many of the biggest stars on Broadway ritually have to bounce off the walls, threaten to bolt, and toss their cookies in the wings... before stepping out on the stage.

It's such a common occurrence, it seldom even makes the gossip columns.

Everybody backstage *understands* the butterflies. Nobody mocks the guy blowing lunch just behind the scenery.

Same with sports. You don't talk to a pitcher who's tossing a perfect game, because you don't wanna jinx him... or make him nervous. He's sitting at the far end of the bench between innings, staring into space and desperately avoiding any thoughts at all. His nerves are ready to ignite at the slightest startle reflex.

Leave him alone.

Business, too. The cool advice is "never let 'em see you sweat" when you're swimming with the sharks...

… but inside, all but the most pathological among us are ready to jump out of our skins.

When money, prestige and the future of your business is on the line, yeah, you get a little skittish and queasy.

I go through this every time I'm about to speak in front a huge audience of marketers, copywriters, business mavens and movers-and-shakers. I plan extensively, get my PowerPoint down cold, know what I'm gonna wear and what attitude I'm going to take. (Those of you who've seen me speak know I can dominate the room with an aggressive glee, despite being a stone-cold introvert.)

(**Odd side fact:** Most of the best speakers on the circuit are introverts. We just pretend to be extroverted for the length of a speech.)

I'm focused and somewhat relaxed, when prepared... but I'll *still* be nervous about things right up to the point that I go to the front of the room, clear my throat and start talking.

And then... like the actor, the pitcher and the businessman...

... once the curtain comes up, *I will be just fine.*

The "pain" of not dealing with the fears is like metaphorically standing on the edge of a pool, and refusing to jump in, no matter how much fun everyone seems to be having.

You're just too terrified of that moment when you hit the water. Will it be cold? Will I get water in my nose? What if I look silly with wet hair?

And yet the simple fact is: Once immersed, you relax, forget all those fears, adjust to the temperature and just get on with *being in the pool*.

And that's the *key* to succeeding with anything when you're nervous or afraid: **Just do it anyway**.

Carl Jung, the great early psychologist, urged people having recurring nightmares to just turn and "face the beast". The horror you're running away from is almost always much *less* horrible than your imagination would have you believe. Nightmares dissolve into realizations.

In waking life, the most successful people *never hesitate* to "face the beast".

They know that the real problem is *avoidance* of the showdown.

You got a big deadline coming up... or your family will be in the audience on opening night... or you're taking the mound with the season on the line...

… well, you got a choice.

You can hide under the covers and work yourself into a frenzy of fear... or...

… you can get to work, *preparing* yourself for the ordeal.

Yes, I know you're afraid to get out there and take a chance. *Do it anyway.*

Yes, I know you may fail, and that will hurt like the dickens if it happens.

Do it anyway.

And yes, I know there are a thousand reasons... *damn good* reasons, too... why you should just give up, or put it off again.

Do it anyway.

Movement *solves* the problems that hand-wringing inaction creates.

Decide what you want to do, and then go *do* it. No one else is gonna do it for you.

Your life is a precious thing... and if you're wasting it, lollygagging around and never risking anything to get what you want... *then shame on you.*

***Shame* on you.** I can name several close friends who died, too young and completely unexpectedly, over the last couple of years... who wouldn't hesitate to trade places with you right now.

Yes, even with all your grand problems and your fear of risk and your crippling worries.

Because you're *alive*. That's all that counts. You've got more at-bats coming.

But don't just run out the door and blindly start risking everything on wild-ass notions.

Commit, and commit *100%* to what you're doing. Pour discipline, passionate preparation and all the problem-solving skills you can muster into the effort.

And wake up your Inner Salesman.

Get that bad boy all hot and bothered about moving ahead in life, and get him on the program. He'll know what you have to do. He's the best darn guide you'll ever have... and he's inside you, *right now*, snoring away.

Don't get me wrong -- failure *sucks*. It's humiliating, and it can stay with you for years if you're the type to obsess (like I am).

I've been on losing teams. Had projects go sideways. And I've been involved in band gigs where we cleared the room because we sucked so bad.

And I've learned to just dust myself off, absorb the excellent lessons offered...

… and look around to see who my friends are, and who I now know I *can't* count on in the clutch.

Those are damn good lessons that occur *only* from failure, and *never* from constant success.

I also learned to say *"so what?"*

So I flopped, so what? You know what the worst thing that happens is? Somebody gets physically hurt. *That's* hard to take. That truly is a different story.

Other than that, though, *you can handle whatever -happens.*

Your spouse leaves, your best friend abandons you (maybe *with* your spouse, I dunno), your business goes into a death spiral, you lose your precious collection of gold coins, the tabloids print photos of you and the goat (from that wild night in Greece last summer, remember?)...
So what? The great thing about living in America is... we ALL get a shot at a come-back.

There are *no rules* that say once you fail, you're done.

In this country, you're never done until you say "I quit."

Learn the basics of great salesmanship, learn how to craft ads, how to create valuable products, how to reach people who want (and will pay for) what you have. Everything else in your life (almost) can be *replaced.*

And as long as you've got enough gumption left to pick yourself up and get back in the ring, the world will welcome you with open arms.

And give you the *same identical chance* that everyone else (who can commit and get past the butterflies) has to succeed.

Nike may have snagged it as an empty slogan... but "**just do it**" has been around for a very long time.

If I were the type to get a tattoo, that's probably what I'd have on my arm.

Fundamental Lesson #2: Here's an advanced lesson on the same subject.

It, too, is a cliché... but so what. Most people have heard it, but don't really understand how it applies to them.

Here it is: **You gotta stay *hungry* to succeed**.

It's easy to identify with being hungry when you really *are* starving -- as I was when I went solo as a freelancer. There were dozens of fat, lazy, self-satisfied copywriters in Los Angeles back then... and they soon learned not to try to compete with me.

Cuz I was like a ravenous wolf, willing to do anything to make my ads beat the other guy's.

Anything. Including doing the really hard work of digging for hidden hooks and sweating out the bullets and finessing the greased chute of a pitch that could not be ignored.

Edit after edit after edit, into the night.

Eventually, of course, I wasn't physically deprived anymore. In fact, I got a little fat and lazy myself, after a year or so of consistently winning.

So I kept the pressure on to *act* like I was hungry.

I searched for ways to stay hungry even when I was well-fed.

There's a secret to it. The Beatles knew this secret, and it kept them sharp for years.

Listen: There's a cool story about John Lennon and Paul McCartney sitting around one day during the early curve of their success. Wealth was starting to pour in along with the fame.

They had just bought new houses -- the first big purchases of their lives. They would have been excused if they sat back and savored the victory of rising above their working-class roots so quickly and dramatically.

But they didn't.

Instead, John turns to Paul and says "Hey, let's write a song that will pay for *pools* at our houses!"

This is pure genius. If and when you ever hit it big, and the money starts pouring in fast and furious... you'll start to *lose track* of it all.

When you're poor, you know down to the penny how much money is in your checking account. And how much a quart of milk costs.

But suddenly, there comes a day when you have so much money, you *forget* about an account stuffed with cash over at another bank. You just blank out on it, because you don't need it.

This is dangerous. Not because you might actually forget about cash you have somewhere...

... but because you're gonna lose your *edge*.

Don't ever put yourself into the position where your next big hit will just be adding a few zeroes to an already-bursting bank account.

That's a dumb way to go about your business... because the money won't *mean* anything to you.

And that robs you of your necessary hunger.

So... stay focused on what that money can **DO** for you.

Over the past year, I took on one job not because I needed the bread... but because I wanted a new car. I got all excited about the new car, and every time I went to work on that project, I knew it was all about me getting that car.
The money *meant* something. It had a purpose. It was ear-marked in my life.

Sure, I could have bought the car out of existing funds. But that dilutes my focus. I did a great job on that project, because I was committed to the money that came from it paying for my spiffy new ride.

I've done the same thing with musical instruments, the down payment for our big damn new house, our upcoming week in Italy, a nice donation to the local Food Bank, and on and on.

You don't win in life by becoming fat and rich and sleepy.

Nope. You win by *staying involved.*

Use these little tricks. They work.

Fundamental Lesson #3: Learn to *be* that guy who is *where* he said he'll be, *when* he said he'll be there… having *done* what he said he'd do.

Got that?

It's simple professionalism... and it's a *dying habit* in the business world.

I've just gone through a nightmare with a contractor here at the house. (Yes, I know you, too, have a good contractor horror story. We all do. They're all the *same story*, more or less. That's why we call our homes "money pits".)

I won't bore you with the details... but it was upsetting enough that I found myself talking to my buddy Stan about it.

Stan, it turns out, comes from a New Jersey town stuffed with contractors. (Yes, including a few Soprano types who fill their homes with stuff that "fell off a truck".) He understands them, and he enlightened me.

Contractors live in a different culture than we do. They are closer to carnival workers than they are to anyone working in a cubicle at IBM.
They don't hate you, the customer. They just don't consider you *worthy of the truth*.

They will say "yes" to every question you ask, automatically. They are experts at soothing your worries and overcoming your objections to starting a job. You feel safe with them, you feel they understand what you want, and you feel you're gonna get a great job out of them.
Hah!

Most of them (not all, but most) see you, the customer, as a "rube".

You have money that rightfully *belongs* to them, and they feel completely justified in telling you *whatever you want to hear*, so you will part with said money.

And then, of course... **the contractor just does whatever the hell he wants.**

Violates every agreement made on quality, time and craftsmanship, and will cop an attitude if you so much as bring up the fact he just took another four-hour lunch break. Piss him off, and he just won't show up for the next three weeks. Or return phone calls.

Heck, he may just not show up anyway. Just for the sake of principle.

This is vice squad knowledge, so listen up: The next time you have to deal with a contractor...

... **USE YOUR *OWN* FRIGGIN' CONTRACT!** Because, if you sign the one he gives you, you will be wrong, wrong, *wrong* in the law's eyes no matter how shabbily he treats you.

He may knock out the back wall of your house... and then not show up for six months while you battle the snows of winter piling up in your front room... and, once it goes to court, you will *still* have to pay him for the work he did knocking the wall down.

Do not expect logic or compassion from the justice system, should you end up in court.

Instead, use your smarts. Write your own contract. Put the money for the job into an **escrow account**, to be paid out when the contractor fulfills his promises.

Put in the contract when the job will start, what hours the crew will work, how much materials will be... and... when the job will END.

Put in penalties for every day past that date the job isn't done.

The contractor you want to use may tell you to go take a hike after reading this contract.

Guess what? You've just identified a guy who *intended* to screw you the second it became convenient for him to do so.

Yes, it will be hard to find a contractor who will look at your logical, fair and straightforward contract and say "Sure, we can do that." There may not even be one in your town -- you may have to cross state lines to find him.

But he's out there. My father worked construction all his life, as a foreman and teacher of apprentices. He is ashamed at what has happened to the "code of honor" among so-called craftsmen in the building trade.

But his ilk are still out there. They know their craft, and they treat people the way they want people to treat *them*. With respect for their time, and value for their money.

I've said before that I often work on a handshake with clients, and eschew contracts.

But I learned long ago to spot the bad apples, and avoid them. Besides, I get half my fee up front... and the client is usually *very* interested in keeping me happy, since there's always more work down the line.

And good writers are oh, so hard to find.

But I, too, am ashamed of some of my colleagues.

They take money for jobs, and then don't deliver. Or miss deadlines. Or just do shitty jobs once they have the cash in hand.

That gives us all a bad name.

One of the reasons I can work on a handshake is my reputation.

And guess what? *One* bad screw-up on my part can damage that reputation beyond easy repair.

The contractor that screwed us still doesn't know what hit him. If he had considered for even a second how well-connected we are in town, he would have changed his tune in a heartbeat.

His name is now *mud* in every major word-of-mouth circle. I know he's lost at least three referrals, just from us alone. And, our eloquent story of his treachery has lost him bids at other developments worth a fortune.

I have no sympathy for him at all. I'm sure he has a long string of victims behind him... people without the connections or wherewithal to do anything about it.

Most folks get real mad... but are ineffective at revenge.

So he got cocky, thinking he would *never* be held to account for his rude and unprofessional (and property-damaging) behavior.

That's *always* a mistake. After years of dealing with street fighters and Special Operations soldiers, I know one thing for certain: **You can NEVER TELL whether the guy next to you can kick your ass or not** (figuratively or literally).

Some of the nastiest and most effective fighters are small and skinny, I kid you not.

You may think you can knock them down with a casual brush-off...

… and you would be wrong.

Until you know your enemy inside and out... you don't know him at *all*. Cocky guys get hurt.

I'm not gonna resort to violence, of course. But I am enjoying surprising this guy with a little street-level justice.

Fundamental Lesson #4: Let's stick with the Vice Squad stuff.

I just heard a story about a divorce settlement that made my day.

Brilliant problem-solving -- and I want to share it with you, because THIS is how great *salesmen* think, too.

It's the wisdom of Solomon.

Here's the story: A woman was married for half her life to a cad who treated her shabbily and without respect. Screwed around on her, made her miserable. Kept the finances secret, too.

So she finally filed for divorce.

She shows up in court with her lawyer... and hubby shows up with his *battery* of lawyers, all snarling and uppity.

But the judge turns out to be the guy I want, if I ever need to rely on the justice system.

His Honor orders everyone to listen carefully, and tells all parties that he will not tolerate *any* lying.

"You lie to me, and you will do jail time. Lots of it. I don't care who you are, lawyer, secretary, plaintiff or defendant. You lie to me, and I find out... you're wearing pinstripes."

He stares around the room for a few seconds, and then raps his gavel. Let's get on with it then, he says.

It was a short proceeding.

The husband agreed to split everything 50/50, which is what she wanted. There was a lot of property in their portfolio, and the judge ordered the husband to divvy it up fairly.

Hubby and lawyers show up the next day with two sheets of paper. These are her properties, and here are his.

Now, the wife has been in the dark about these properties for years. She can't tell if it's truly a fair split or not.

But she knows her husband. So she leans over and whispers to her attorney: "Switch the papers."

"Huh?"

"Switch the papers. If he was so fair, let me keep the ones on *his* list, and he can have the ones he wanted to give to me."

The lawyer smiles, and asks the judge if they can swap the sheets of paper.

The judge laughs. He *loves* the idea -- it's the only fair thing to do.

And the hubby -- the rat who betrayed her for years and rubbed her nose in it -- turns white and starts gurgling.

His pit bull attorneys look at each other, helpless. They can't say a thing... if they object, it proves they were lying.

And none of them want to spend a second behind bars.

After the decision, the suddenly humble hubby comes over to the now ex-wife and BEGS her not to do this.

Why? Because it will *ruin* him.

That's the kind of bastard he was. He fully intended to screw her over...

... and when the tables were turned, wanted her to sacrifice for *him* one last time.

What do you think she did?

Yep, that's *exactly* what she did.

Smiled and wished him luck with his batch of rotten properties.

Sweet. Don't underestimate your competition.

Fundamental Lesson #5: I want to now reveal to you the "Magic Button" on your desk that will erase much of the B.S. in your life. *Instantly.*

It's the "**delete**" key.

At this stage of my career, about half of the email I get is important. The other half is a mix of the bizarre, the unimportant... and the downright offensive.

All of which wastes my time.

I've had to learn this lesson over and over again. I hope it's stuck by now. But if it hasn't, I'll keep re-learning it. It's worth the trouble.

You know, my general attitude is one of benign helpfulness. I'm a generous guy, and I have stayed in tune with what it's like to be starting out and need a word or two of advice.

Lord knows, I'm not stingy with the advice.

But I have my limits.

The people who really need advice, because they're moving ahead with their career, don't *ever* waste my time. They have specific intelligent questions, are very grateful for any help I can offer, and then move on.
I wish they were the majority. They ain't.

Nope. My email often is stuffed with poorly-thought-out ramblings that I have to read three times to even begin to understand.

This is unfair to the people who respect my time. Because, by the third reading, I'm pissed off. The writer has been too lazy to make his point clearly... or has no real point to make. No actual question.

And then I'm pissed that I wasted the time reading his drivel, and the next guy -- who is respectful and careful to be clear and concise -- doesn't get my full attention. Cuz I'm still mad at the time-waster.

Side story: Back when I was in the corporate world, I struggled for a year as a production manager for a catalog.

I was so overwhelmed with my basic duties, that I developed a tactic for dealing with all new shit coming at me.

I called it the "**3 Memo Rule**".

Whenever I received a memo from anyone but my direct boss... I *tossed* it.

I figured if it was important enough, I'd get a *second* memo. Which, usually, I would *also* toss in the trash can.

If I ever got a *third* memo on the subject, then I knew I was facing matters of real importance.

I don't recommend this tactic -- I missed a few semi-critical meetings here and there, and when people caught on they became apoplectic with rage at my impertinence.

But it worked for me at the time. I was drowning. I was essentially performing three jobs, and most memos were the equivalent, to me, of rearranging the deck chairs on the Titanic as she went down. Just not all that damned important in the overall scheme.

But the "3 Memo" *principle* has stayed with me.

I've shared my discovery of the "delete" key with many other businessmen... and the odd thing is how *hard* it is to get into the frame of mind where you can actually USE it.

These days, I'm ruthless.

And you know what? It feels **GOOD**.

I just saw (twenty minutes ago) the first sentence of another email that went like this: "Why should I spend any money with *you* instead of..." Insert any name there: Dan Kennedy, Gary Halbert, whoever. Many times, I don't even recognize the expert they're taunting me with.
Now, I used to pen answers to these Bozos. Because I wanted to know how the *hell* anyone could plow through my 20-page super-detailed sales pitch... and have the nerve to ask for *more* info.

You need me to craft a *separate* pitch, just for you?

Are you imagining me wringing my hands and wailing in fear over the prospect of you passing my stuff up for someone else's?

"Ooooooh, no, please please *please* buy my stuff! Here, let me try again, with a customized sales pitch *just for you*, and accept my apologies for forcing you to even have to ask, while I grovel and beg for your order..."

Horseshit. The very first time that kind of email appeared, I wrote a short email back, suggesting tactfully that they reread the guarantee, the testimonials, and the very generous details of the offer in the original pitch.

The second time I got a similar email, I just flat out urged them NOT to buy from me.

Please, I wrote, go bother Dan or Gary.

And when they wrote *back*, taunting me with the idea that they DID spend their funds elsewhere, thanking me for being so rude that I made up their mind for them... I replied with a two-word email: **You're welcome**.

Well, guess what? They wrote back *again*.

And I snapped. And hit the delete key. I have no guess at all what that last email was about.

Click. *Gone.*

When you have a public email address, like I do, you are fair game for a lot of people who desperately need a hobby. Or a pen pal.

And they are welcome to write to me. Type away, you scary little losers.

I have the right to *skip* your nonsense. Even the few minutes it takes to craft a sarcastic reply robs me. And irks me, and unsettles my good mood.

What a relief to realize... *I don't have to do it.*

Click. *Gone.*

I only wish I had a delete key in my car, so I could make the idiots in the Caddy ahead of me driving twenty miles under the speed limit disappear.

Fundamental Lesson #6: I have several clients who marvel at the fact that I've co-produced a couple of dozen big honkin' seminars. I tell them, yes, they're huge, gonzo events and they take a lot of time and energy to produce...

... but it's not so hard you can't figure it out.

Oh, no, they say. We tried it once, and it was a *nightmare*. We're *still shaking* from the experience.

I don't even have to ask what went wrong. I know, because I made the same rookie mistakes everyone suffers while hosting my first few seminars.

Here's what I tell them: Make a long list of everything you DON'T want to do or have happen at your dream seminar.

Then... ***don't DO any of that.***

Make it part of your pitch. If you don't wanna feed the audience, don't do it. It's a pain, it's expensive, and no one's ever happy about the meal.

If you don't want to be stuck with a "tail"... meaning, having to provide anything to the attendees after the seminar is over...
... then *don't offer* a tail.

I learned this the hard way -- when my very first big seminar was over, I still had *months* of work to do...

... and it was all an un-funded obligation, and it sucked the life out of me.

So simply make all your obligations *end* at the end of the seminar.

And eliminate the urge to offer anything after the last day.

So when it's over... it's *over*.

Hey, I don't want to start my own seminars too *early* (most events begin at 8 am, when I'm still half-asleep)... so I've occasionally set the start time at 10 am.

And the roof didn't fall in. *No one squawked.*

Again, this ain't rocket science.

It's just simple problem-solving.

If something is keeping you from going ahead with things you SHOULD be going ahead with...

... just make a list of the stuff you don't want to deal with...

... *and then arrange things so you don't need to deal with it.*

Set it up so it isn't necessary.

Hell, rip the phone out of the wall if it bugs you so much. Just stop bitching about incoming calls.

Okay, I'm done. That was fun.

Chapter Five:

How To Murder Stress While Goosing Your Salesmanship Chops.

Remembering why you became an entrepreneur in the first place... squeezing fun back into your life... and sliding into the best possible groove for maximum wealth and happiness.

A h, the California coast. Especially the northern part of Highway 1, where cell phones don't work much of the time, the air smells of pine and brine, and the loudest noise is the crashing of surf.

Heaven.

However, getting away from our day-to-day lives this time for an extended weekend was like trying to extract ourselves from a glob of glue. Job emergencies exploded, pet sitters got sick, storms threatened and events from all sides converged in an evil plan to keep us from leaving.

The responsible part of my brain whispered *"you can't leave"* over and over. *"There's too much work to do."*

We split anyway.

Did some lifestyle triage -- band aids on the work crises, back-up help from friends, charted a path over the Donner Pass during a lull in the wintry *Sturm und Drang,* packed up the dogs and suitcases, and headed for the coast.

You gotta do it. I know that you -- like me -- have so much urgent work to get done that there is *no possible way* you can take any time off.

Why, the world might implode, civilizations topple, and the space/time continuum warp beyond repair if you so much as *think* about a real vacation!

Can't be done! No possible way!

It's all nonsense, of course. While the difference between success and failure in America often rests on your ability to spot and grab opportunity…

… that doesn't mean you have to grab *every* opportunity that comes into view. One slips by, you'll still be okay.

You gotta remember why you became an entrepreneur in the first place.

And if you aren't doing it so you can have a better life, *then you need to readjust your priorities.*

Most businessmen live like junkies -- the game just completely and utterly absorbs them, to the exclusion of everything else life offers.

I've known several older men (women seem to escape this trap) who never cultivated any hobbies or interests outside of work… and they *all* dropped dead soon after retirement.

There was nothing of substance to their existence -- when the job ended, their reason for getting out of bed was gone, and all they had left was a stare-down with eternity.

My father was a great example of how to do it right. He waltzed into his ninth decade still leading a lifestyle that would exhaust most men half his age (and made it to 95 sharp as a tack).

He and his wonderful wife (having remarried after Mom passed cuz he enjoyed nuptial bliss so much) went out dancing several nights each week, worked hard in the garden, and wandered off on multiple globe-hopping adventures while in their eighties.

China, Central America, Australia, Europe, Alaska… I wouldn't have been surprised if they'd decided to climb Everest on one of their jaunts to the Orient.

He carried a 175 bowling average, too, right up until he could barely lift the ball anymore. And had the occasional over-200 game when it counted in team leagues.

He was fit, curious, interested and interesting. Every day was precious, and not to be wasted.

No one *taught* him how to grab life by the horns like that. Most of the friends he grew old with never found the groove after retiring, and every time we talked it seemed another of his current crowd had passed on.

Sure, many of them raised fine families, put kids through college, met the mortgage and paid their taxes. Did their duty. They grew up in tough times, and vowed to never let the poorhouse come in sight again…

… so they kept their nose to the grindstone.

Must… keep… working. No… time… to… play…

Look, I am not an advocate of goofing off your entire life. "Work hard, play hard" is a darn good slogan to go by.

But you need to *play* even if you have to work at learning how to do it.

When I hear people insist they simply *cannot* afford any time off, or can't fit the kid's soccer game into their schedule, or feel guilty kicking back...

... I think about all the poor slobs around the world who really *do* have to work all the time to scratch out a living.

It's not hard to imagine some Third World dirt farmer dreaming of coming to America... *where we already are...* so he can finally relax, because the Gestapo aren't gonna bust the door in, roaming gangs aren't gonna burn his crops, and water from the tap doesn't need to be boiled before drinking.

Just for starters.

You know what that farmer would say to us if we complained about how overwhelming our workload is?

"But you have so *much* -- why are you not happy, and why do you not *enjoy* it?"

Now, it's true that some Americans enjoy kicking back a little *too* much. We have no shortage of goof-offs in the workforce.

However, if you're reading this, you're probably an entrepreneur or business owner. And you ain't no slouch, cuz being at the top of the food chain really *is* a tough job.

But that doesn't mean you can't still partake of the feast of life out there. Running the show doesn't mean you can't *enjoy* the show, too.

Dude -- you *owe* it to that poor guy slaving in the muddy fields to live the dream America offers. Give generously of your time and money to good causes, and pay attention to the footprint you leave -- in other words, pick a good charity, and don't start hunting endangered species.

But then... *go out and smell the damn roses once in a while.* Look around at the banquet life offers, and *sample* a few things. That's what all this struggle to civilize and tame the wild world was about.

Do it now, while you're young and healthy.

Don't put it off. If you've been practicing "Operation Moneysuck" like a good capitalist, you can afford to leave the office every now and then. The biz will survive your brief absence.

Don't put it off.

I see this soul-killing "deferred gratification" habit in too many of my same-age friends. They work like demons, with their eye on the "prize" of early retirement. Retirement, somehow, will be their reward for a life of brutal hours in the office.

But they can never adequately answer the question "And *then* what?" To them, retirement is a hazy paradise that will take care of itself. All they focus on is finally being able to quit working so damn hard.

That ain't living.

That's self-enforced slavery.

And it sets you up for an early post in the obituary pages. Because about a week after you get used to not working so damn hard... you're gonna be bored to tears. And that's a shameful legacy you very much want to avoid.

Listen: I have heard two excellent pieces of advice regarding this matter, and I've done my best to follow both of them.

The first piece of advice arrived via the Travis McGee novels by John D. MacDonald. (If you haven't read this series, you've been cheating yourself. It spans the late-fifties to the late-seventies, but the stories remain fresh and fascinating, and it's addictive writing.)

Travis was one of the last Renaissance men in America -- excellent taste in music, art and women, with an appetite for raw adventure that tested his wits and his street-fighter skills.

But the one thing that stuck with me was his attitude about retirement: **He took it in *installments*, while he was young.**

Whenever he got a little cash together, he would *temporarily* retire, and live a life of luxury and fun. When the coffers got low, he would simply get back in the game.

This appealed to me immensely. And for over a decade, I was able to do my own version of it. I took *three to six months off every year* and did whatever I damn well pleased.

Sometimes I would work just a little as I went along, so I could string out each mini-retirement. But mostly I put my working mind in limbo.

Because I had a *lot* I wanted to do. I formed a power rock trio in my forties, and played the biker bar scene here in Northern Nevada. (God, that was fun.) I wrote a couple of novels while house-sitting in amazing places, soaking up local vibes. I traveled to Europe, and scuba'd in the Caribbean, and golf-bummed my way along the coasts of California and Florida.

And you know what?

I *never* had to be spurred back into work by low bank accounts. Nope. After a certain time, I would just feel that *hunger for the game* coming back.

I *like* to work. I like to play, too.

But I don't ever want to feel that I HAVE to do either. I want options. That's what I'm always working toward. That's my overall goal.

This is also why I distrust the sort of retirement most Americans lust for. It's like eating steak and cake for every meal -- it gets boring and unsustainable very quickly, no matter how good it sounds while your belly's growling.

I mean... how the hell do you even know if you'll *like* being retired, if you've never tried it before?

I've met a few guys who earned enough to quit working for good... and went to live in certain foreign countries where young women lavish attention on financially-set *yanquis*.

This attention is very startling to most American men, who have been walking on eggshells their entire lives in our *uber*-confusing politically correct world of "*no means no except when it doesn't*" neo-feminism.

Both genders are having their belief systems wrenched beyond recognition during this post-equality shake out, and yeah, romance is a little tense and chaotic in the States these days.

So these ex-patriots skedaddled to foreign shores for relief, and suddenly find themselves in a real-life porn fantasy. At first, they can't believe their good fortune.

Then, they wake up one sodden morning. A year or two has passed, and they start to panic. Their lives have become a dazed jumble.

What the heck does it all *mean*, they ask, desperate and adrift.

Because being spoiled only looks good to outsiders.

Self-actualized men and women *work*, and work with a purpose. For the best of us, being deprived of meaningful work is the worst punishment there is.

The pampered royalty of every kingdom that has ever existed has resorted to war and conquest -- risking the whole enchilada -- just to relieve the *boredom* of getting everything you want, all the time.

This is why taking chunks of your retirement as you go makes such good sense.

Everyone is different… but for me, half a year off is about all I can take before I get antsy. But, my oh my, those few months sure are a blast.

Yeah, I know you can't possibly do something like that.

It's just too radical a lifestyle change.

So don't worry about it right now.

Just tuck the notion away in your head somewhere -- the concept that, if you arrange it right, you really can just take off for a while and do whatever your little heart desires.

And, when you've recharged your batteries… *you can come back.*

And repeat as necessary.

Maybe you really can't do it… but then, maybe, down the road, you might realize you *can*. It doesn't hurt to let the idea rattle around innocently in your brain.

Doesn't hurt at all.

Second piece of advice: When I took on the responsibilities of a guru a few years ago (committed to coaching and helping folks like you get their act together)… it meant I had to forgo taking off so much time all at once. At least for a while.

I consciously made that decision. I have a back-log of stuff I've learned in my career that I want to share, and I'm getting serious jollies giving something back to the industry that saved my own life.

However, this doesn't mean I have to stop taking bitchin' vacations. I still have the *option* for taking longer-than-usual amounts of time off, whenever I need it.

It's a slightly different concept.

About ten years ago, I had a client who specialized in "coaching" doctors whose lives were in turmoil.

Part of the coaching for his health care clients was about setting up automatic streams of incoming patients… part was learning to manage the office on autopilot…

… and a *huge* part was getting their personal life in order.

This meant putting money aside for retirement, investment, and fun. Most doctors do not have fun. They work until they, literally, drop. And their marriages fall apart along with their practice, and they are prey to the worst sort of investment scams out there.

(Why are health care professionals so vulnerable? In many ways, their long education disconnects them from the maturing process -- so while they are respected for their ability to heal, *emotionally* they're often still teenagers. And never realize it, since they live in the rarified world of medicine, where everyone is either a peer and in the same boat, or sick. Doctors are notoriously susceptible to financial disaster, because they just cannot believe that a smart guy like themselves could not *naturally* understand economics. They *fool* themselves.)

This coach's simple plan for a better ride was life-changing stuff, and I enjoyed helping him sell it.

But there was one piece of advice he gave out that stuck with me all these years.

Here it is: **You gotta take at least one vacation *every month*.** No exceptions. It can be a weekend, but it's better if it's four days or longer.

Every month.

You just build it into your schedule, giving it even *more* weight than many other parts of your job.

So if it comes down to, say, having a meeting with someone about an important project, or making the plane to Barbados, *you re-schedule the meeting*. Without a second thought.

Why?

Because these frequent vacations will keep you sharp, interested and interesting. Dull boys do not perform well. Happy, refreshed boys kick their ass every time.

It is vital that you recharge your batteries on a regular basis.
It's even MORE important than making a few more bucks each
month.

However, there are very specific rules for these monthly vacations.
Like:

You must *leave town*, or at least leave your same-old, same-old
environment and habits.

You cannot go to some place where all there is to do is lie on the
beach and drink beer. (Many beer commercials argue that this is an
excellent way to spend time off… and only people who haven't
done it believe that story. In reality, it sucks.)

Instead, you need to take "**active**" vacations. Go to a foreign
country where you must learn some new language skills, new
money denominations, new customs. Take some classes
somewhere -- classes in something *utterly outside* your area of
expertise, so you're a complete rookie. Try some new, and even
frightening, sport. Get out of your rut.

Wherever you go, whatever you do, spend time *learning* about it.
Read books, travel literature, web sites, whatever you can get your
hands on. So you're never a rube wandering around lost, and you
have some *insight* to your surroundings. And maybe a list of places
or events or activities you want to sample. You gotta *live* the
experience.

This coach actually flew to Europe, even if he only had *two days* to
enjoy there. He knew how to spend "down" time in airplanes and
airports -- always learning new things, thrilling his mind with good
literature, relishing the adventure he was embarking on. He had it
down.

The key is to do *active* vacationing. Engage your brain and your nervous system. Don't just blunder off in your car. *Learn* something about a new place. Then *go* there.

When you get back to work, you will be refreshed and alert and more alive. And even those few days will seem like a full week... because you fit so much into each hour.

You go to Puerto Vallarta and drink yourself into a stupor every night, and you're gonna return in a daze. More tired than when you left. This isn't what you want.

It's all about living life deep.

And guess what?

There's a *marketing* lesson in it!

Yes, there is.

I realized this after our second day in Mendocino. The three basic ways you can get to know a town... are *identical* to the three ways you can get to know a *market*.

First Way: *Shallow blundering.*

You can go into a town -- or a market -- without really knowing a thing about it. And you'll probably survive to a degree, if you know enough to stay out of harm's way.

If you insist on not being at least a *little* cautious, however, you can get hurt.

I know a number of novice marketers who thought they were ready to take on the diet market, for example. It seemed so obvious -- just find a pill, or a method to lose weight, and send out a killer ad.

Imagine their surprise when (a) their killer ad contained *verboten* claims that aroused the scrutiny of the federal government and (b) the amazing weight loss secret they tried to sell elicited nothing but *yawns* from the jaded "seen it all before" market.

Just like traipsing down an unfamiliar street into a dark alley full of crackheads, oblivious and asking for it.

In most cases, you even have to be careful who you ask for help or directions. There are clueless "experts" in marketing who will lead you into bankruptcy just as readily as trawling street hustlers will happily herd you into a mugging.

Second Way: *You can prepare yourself for the adventure.*

By reading, by asking experienced people you trust for insight (but not accepting anything blindly), by doing a little detective work and research with a critical and skeptical mind, you can become a quasi-expert in a very short time on any place.

Get a map and a travel guide… or check out existing data online, see what lists are available, and what people have bought, for what amount, in what quantity. Learn the language and customs of the city… or the buying habits of the market.

This ain't rocket science.

Since the advent of the Web, it's easier than ever. Maps are free. Even small towns have websites with good info.

And there may not be any markets left that someone hasn't already tried to conquer… and you can *learn* from their mistakes and successes. Critically examining how others have done what you're about to attempt can shortcut the success curve by years, while helping you avoid the mistakes that shut down others.

Last Way: *Go deep.*

This is my favorite.

After dinner each night, we popped into a local watering hole for a drink before bed. But we didn't sit at a table. Nope. We bellied up to the bar -- where the action was.

And you know what? Because we knew the history of the town… and some of the legends and myths… and had some personal observations to make, as eager tourists from another state… and because we are smart, witty and interesting people…

… we were embraced by the locals.

And they proceeded to share some very fascinating secrets about life in Mendocino.

Yeah, yeah, I know that I've previously warned you away from making deals in bars. That's still valid. A boozy agreement isn't worth the breath wasted making it.

This was different. It wasn't business, it was practicing our *bonding skills*, and getting the inside scuttlebutt on something we were interested in. We didn't get roaring drunk, and we didn't try to make lifelong friends.

No. We just tapped into the passion that already existed -- the locals' love/hate relationship with their odd little town.

Longtime readers of my stuff will recognize this tactic as "going deep". We did our research, our get-up-to-speed reading, and we melted into the area for a couple of heady days.

So, when the opportunity to talk to a resident, or the bartender, arrived, we were right there in their *passionate sweet spot.*

Not clueless tourists, looking for cheap thrills and complaining about the weather.

Rather, we brought up subjects and questions that allowed the locals to do something they weren't able to do even with other locals -- *talk about their own experience living there.*

Everybody's got a story to tell, and they're dying to tell it.

Each night, we learned fascinating things, ranging from gossip to lore to recent events to short cuts and insider tips on the best places to eat. Not the cheat-joints where they send the loud, obnoxious tourists. No, they sent us where the *locals* go to eat.

In marketing, this is akin to getting past the business owner, and doing some serious research among the engineers, "feet in the street" sales staff, warehouse workers and secretaries... to get the stories (and the gossip and rumors and tall tales) the owner almost never knows about.

This is where your world-class hooks always come from. As a writer, you can usually throw away the standard "company line" on any product or service...

... because it will be mostly fantasy, or empty slogans about what the client *believes* his prospects want to hear.

Screw that nonsense.

The really good stuff comes from real people, who have to wrangle over the product with actual customers...

... people who know how much it weighs when you lift it, how long it lasts when you mistreat it, and all the ways you can use it that aren't in the official manual.

I had to learn how be a sales detective, and it paid off in spades for my career.

Transferring the same skills to traveling has made each trip a true adventure that leaves me invigorated and recharged.

But I had to *learn*.

You know, if I hadn't been with a well-traveled friend, I would *still* be lost in the Paris Metro system, ten years after wandering into it. Because I was clueless back then. I couldn't tell you which way was north, let alone where in the city we were. I'd never looked at a map of the place, and never got my bearings.

It was still fun… but next time, it will be *more* so, by a thousand percent.

Because I will have gone deep. And the city will be mine.

This one tactic, of going deep, will be your new favorite tool as you get busy tackling the good stuff in life and business.

Salesmanship 101

Too many folks out there think great salesmanship is all about tricks and bludgeoning the prospect over the head with the power of your facts and personality and charm.

It ain't so.

In fact, the most important thing you can cultivate to become a world-class salesman…

… is to learn how to *bond* with people.

There is a whole school of thought behind this skill, and someday I'll write the book. And, yes, some of it involves Vice Squad knowledge, and doesn't necessarily require sincerity.

That's because the basics of bonding are very simple: *Learn to smile and listen.*

This alone will get you farther than you can imagine.

Add the Psych 1A technique of *repeating back* what you hear in an interested but non-judgmental way ("So you're saying that UFOs have taken over the White House? That's fascinating…") and you will open a serious crack in the floodgates of incoming information.

But these behaviors will only take you so far, and you cannot really *control* what information you receive.

In sales, control is important.

The slightly advanced class in bonding starts with **knowing something about who you're talking to.**

For example: When I was a young and dumb freelancer, I just naturally enjoyed chatting up the receptionists at the agencies I worked with. Usually a young woman, she was bored to tears, sitting alone and lonely in an empty room with a phone that never stopped ringing.

So I would casually bond with her, starting with "I'll bet it gets lonely out here, with just the phone and this big old empty lobby." If she had a photo on her desk, I might say something pleasant about the person in it.

By my second visit, I would greet her by her first name, ask her about her kid if she had one (or some other casual event I had learned about in our brief first conversation), maybe have a wise-ass comment or two on how clueless the executives were… and I would have a stick of gum for her.

That's it.

I didn't hit on her, didn't push for personal info, and always smiled and waited patiently when the phone rang to interrupt.

Yet, just those few minutes (and sometimes seconds, if I was ushered in to my meeting immediately) paid off in unexpected ways. I became a small bright spot in her day -- no one else ever cared if she wanted a stick of gum, or how her cough was doing, or if her kid had won the soccer game. To all the busy executives in the building, she was furniture.

To me, she was another human being, with stories to tell and a need for recognition.

Here's one unintended way it paid off: Whenever I came in to this one agency, the receptionist immediately and happily tracked down the guy I was meeting with, taking extra steps she wouldn't take with anyone else. (She admitted this to me.)

And when I called, she would put me through to vice presidents *even when they were in meetings.* They were astonished that I'd reached them. They couldn't believe I had that kind of mojo.

In fact, I had better access to the inside of that agency than some of the preening executives who *worked* there.

And get this: Several times, the receptionist at an agency would personally introduce me to the accountant who cut the freelance checks…

… and when I then bonded with *him,* I ended up getting paid for my work even before the vice prez of marketing had signed off on my invoice.

This is powerful stuff.

When I'm digging for information on a project, I follow those three basic tactics every time: Be pleasant… listen and *show* him I'm listening by repeating back what he says… and have some inside information to share that lets him know I'm hip to what's going on.
For example:

Me: "So, is it true that the town founder was a transsexual logger?"
Bartender: "Oh, so you know about that, huh? Well, did you know he also…" Yadda yadda.

Or:

Me: "I heard you hit a golf ball 432 yards at the Max Flite competition last year -- how the heck did *that* feel?"

Him: "Are you kidding? It was great. But I couldn't have done it if I hadn't…" and so on, spilling every secret in his bag.

Me: "I once hit a 437 yard drive. Hooked it thirty yards into a tree, and it dropped into the cart path and rolled 407 yards downhill. Birdie."

Him: "That's funny. I once…" And *here* is where the brilliant hooks start to surface.

You get the idea. (And yes, I really did birdie that hole, at the Lakeridge par five eighth here in Reno. My buddy still hates the fact it was, technically, a legal drive.)

And that bartender in the first example wouldn't have revealed the true inside story of the town if I hadn't shown him I *already* knew some juicy stuff.

Often, when you have the luxury of time, you can parlay info you learn into each *new* conversation... essentially becoming one of the most knowledgeable people around. Each tidbit you learn *multiplies* itself many times over, as you use it to gain access to more hidden stuff.

And the golf genius wouldn't have started telling me his own stories if I hadn't evidenced a real, tangible interest in the sport. I'd learned about that one specific long drive from someone else, and knowing the exact distance *meant* something to him.

The gossip and inside stories he told me became the crux of my *hook* in the magazine ad I wrote. (That ad is still running almost 20 years later, now online as a video sales letter, with barely a word change.)

Now, I don't know why these simple tactics aren't known and used by everyone.

Okay, wait, I *do* know -- most people are just too self-involved to allow themselves to listen.

And, jeez, it's just too *hard* to do any prior research.

During consultations, I see copy come across my desk all the time that reeks of ignorance of the very subject it is supposed to be revealing inside secrets about.

Often, *zero* research has been done, let alone any decent sales detective work.

And, without serious rewriting, I would probably be the *only* person, besides the writer, who would ever read these ads. The target market certainly won't waste any time reading them.

Do your detective work.

At the last bar in Mendocino we went to, there were two locals and three tourist couples. I got them all riled up and talking, and for all but two of us, it was a lively conversation.

You know what good conversation is, don't you?

It's give-and-take, short witty repartee with pauses for someone else's clever reply or addition. It's teamwork.

And it's a lost art, mostly.

One couple just didn't get it. They were incapable of listening to anyone else, and would interrupt to make their point... when they *had* a point. It was never a very good point, but it was theirs, and they felt everyone should hear it.

Mostly, though, they just interrupted in an attempt to dominate the conversation. They never listened... only watched for a pause they could leap into and have their say.

I'm sure they came away thinking they'd sure impressed the rest of us. Which they most assuredly did not. They knew nothing of the town they were in, and weren't interested in learning anything about it. They might as well not have bothered coming at all.

Don't be a putz like them. Practice listening. Confident professionals have no need whatsoever to impress anyone with anything.

For example: There aren't more than two or three people in Reno who have a *clue* what I do for a living -- I've never had the need to tell them. They suspect I may have some influence in some endeavor or another... but they couldn't describe it if their lives depended on it.

I don't need the limelight. Don't get me wrong -- under the right circumstances, I love a knock-down, drag-out argument on the things I'm passionate about -- music, art, writing, politics, history, etc. I can be one opinionated bastard, and (mostly) I have the chops to back it up.

But I don't mind being underestimated.

In fact, when I'm doing my research, I *prefer* it. I want to be a cipher, a blank slate to the person I'm talking to. They can fit me into whatever category in their belief system they like, as long as it's a category they feel comfortable spilling their guts to.

Coaches Corner

Okay, one final story on this subject. (And, in case you care, I'm back in Reno. Still glowing from the wonderful trip to the coast. This chapter took several days to write.)

I was on a conference call recently with Dan Kennedy, which was going out to his super-insider people.

Now, I dearly love sharing the stage with Dan, cuz he's smart, funny, and a world-class salesman. I always learn something new, and I think Dan would agree he does, too.

Anyway, we fielded some questions, and one stood out: "What do I do if I have a boring product, like insurance… and I'm essentially a boring guy?"

Don't laugh. I get asked this all the time.

And the answer is always the same: First, if you truly believe your product is boring, *you need to get out of that biz.*

Or step back, and readjust yourself -- what, for example, is so boring about making good investments that guarantee wealth?

The real problem, of course, is your view of yourself. As a marketer, you MUST find your own sweet spot of passion.

We all have it. It may be hidden under a ton of repressed feelings and denial... but it's there. Start reading emotional literature. Danielle Steel novels, bodice-buster romances, Cosmo magazine. Get the DVDs of "Sex And The City" and study them.

More important... *kickstart your heart.*

As Dan put it, get a date.

As I put it, go get *laid* -- either physically or metaphorically. If you're running around so obsessed with being boring that you are annoyed at gorgeous sunsets, or never play the radio because music bugs you, or hate to touch or be touched by another human being...

... do the right thing and get thee into therapy post haste.

As a marketer, you have a grand opportunity to go deep in life -- an opportunity the majority of sleep-walking people out there will never enjoy.

Embrace your specialness.

Now, get out there and chew up some scenery. Your bank account will thank you.

Chapter Six:

The Conspiracy To Eat Your Productivity Alive.

Why the "D" word is like battery acid on your brain... where your concentration goes to die... and how to clear the pipes when your thinking is clogged up.

My Dad, when he was vigorously coming up on 94 years old, swore to me that time just goes by faster and faster as you age...

... but I shudder to imagine it rushing by any quicker than it is now.

Last winter? Zoom. Spring? Zzzzip. Summer? Blinked and it was gone.

I swear to you, just yesterday it was a nice fall day in early November, and I was calmly considering how I wanted to spend the holidays.

Short pause. Flurry of action around me.

Boing. Suddenly it's several days into January, and I wanna know who the hell I have to talk to about getting December back.

Something's broken here. And it's starting to piss me off.

Deep breath. Slow exhale...

Okay, I know what's wrong.

It's me. Goddammit.

I have no one else to blame (and believe me, I've tried to find someone else to take the heat).

See, I KNOW how to slow time down.

And the kind of mega-distracted "ooh, look, a shiny object!" behavior I've been indulging in ain't the answer.

No. There's a very simple and easy trick to putting the brakes on the clock that I've been ignoring: **Disciplined concentration**.

Which is, of course, like flashing a cross to a vampire, as far as multi-tasking addicts go. ("Children of the night, what sweet music they… aaargh!")

Just the word "discipline" is like battery acid on the brain to anyone who seeks out unrelenting multi-sensory bombardment.

But it needs to be said, and heard, and acted upon… if you value high productivity.

Because the culture is conspiring to eat your brain, you know.

It's just so easy to act like a hungry kid in a candy store these days…

… with every scrap of human knowledge, past and present, available online, along with hour-devouring escapes like YouTube and the moment-by-moment adventure of instant-messaging and posting to social media every empty thought that pops into your brain to every "friend" you have.

And I can't be the first person to notice that the more "connected" we get through the Web…

… the less time we actually spend with real people.

We're in the middle of a hellish social experiment, and nobody's in control.

Forced isolation is considered almost a cruel and unusual punishment for criminals…

… because humans are so hard-wired for social interaction.

Even sitting quietly in the corner is torture. Ask a kid who misbehaved.

And yet…

… certain kinds of self-imposed isolation are the ONLY way to occasionally hop off the hamster-wheel of life and **get stuff done**.

The "old school" trick of slowing time down was to learn something new -- like a language. Or travel to strange places. Or read a good book in silence. Or (I can hear the shocked gasps of all the folks Web-surfing while they distractedly read this) sit quietly and meditate.

Somewhere along the line, we all have just forgotten how to zone in. For too many folks, zoning out is actually a forgivable excuse for screwing up. It's the new plague.

And if I could find the son of a bitch who first introduced the idea of "multi-tasking" as a good thing, I'd strangle him.

Most people I know rush through life believing the more crap they cram into each minute, the more they're "living".

And it's not just the bobble-heads trying to steer a lumbering SUV through traffic, dial a number on their cell phone, eat tacos, and keep the dog from leaping out of the window all at the same time.

I mean… heck, I do that sometimes. So it can't be all that bad.

Or maybe it IS that bad.

I have copywriting students and rookie entrepreneurs coming to me in droves these days, baffled that they can't seem to shake the angst-ridden feeling of being **overwhelmed**.

"How can I be expected to write copy or plan for success, when I've got so much ELSE to accomplish at the SAME TIME?" they ask, eyes starting to roll back into their skull.

You're snickering, aren't you.

You know the answer: Prioritize your projects, set aside time to do the most important ones, take the phone off the hook, yadda yadda yadda.

But do you DO this?

Most people don't. Like me, you KNOW the answer is all about discipline…

… but getting your ass to follow your own advice is just ridiculously hard.

Because it's too friggin' NOISY to think clearly.

So here's something I've rediscovered for myself. Maybe it can help you, too.

Are you ready?

Here it is: **Do one thing at a time.**

Shocking, I know.

Just try it for a week.

When you sit down to a meal, don't check email or do the crossword puzzle (or see if your dreaded opponent made a move in Words With Friends).

Just eat.

Taste your food. People are starving all over the world, and you're treating your meal like an interruption in your quest for maximum stimulation.

When you're done eating, open a good novel, and just read in silence for an hour…

… solely for the pleasure of melting into the story. You can still blow through your business reports, skim your memories of high school romance, and get some phone calls in… after your hour is up.

But, just for a week, set aside that single measly quiet hour a day to really read.

People have died to give you this privilege. Give it some respect.

And if you want to watch TV, fine.

But sit down and watch.

Don't surf the Web.

Don't talk on the phone.

Don't try to have a meaningful moment with your significant other.

Just click on the program you want to watch, and WATCH it.

What? You don't have a specific program you want to watch?

Then don't turn the boob tube on.

Radical concept, I know.

I mean… 500 channels. There's gotta be something on. Somewhere.

Of course, that's what's fueling the hard-to-grasp growth of YouTube and Facebook and everything else on the Web -- like true junkies, the old levels of stimulation that TV and other "old media" used to provide aren't hitting the spot anymore.

Gotta jack up the dose.

But I'll tell you what -- it doesn't take an anthropologist to see how screwed up a person can get with too much gadgetry in their lives, all bleeping and blurping at the same time.

Maybe you enjoy being a Space Cadet. That's fine.

But don't expect good things to happen in your life.

Instead, expect to wake up one day and wonder what the HELL just happened to your youth, your dreams, your business, and your vitality.

There's no need to be a hard-ass about any of this. I'm a lazy guy, and I love to dink around with technological gadgets and waste time in all sorts of non-productive play, just like you.

In fact, I wouldn't want to spend five seconds in the skin of some of my colleagues -- especially the guys who start work at dawn and don't quit until there isn't a drop of brain juice (or daylight) left.

Naw... life isn't about 24/7 productivity.

Nobody ever wished, on their deathbed, that they'd spent more time at the office.

But life isn't about distraction, either.

Work hard, then play hard is damn good advice. And you'll notice that phrase omits any reference to "distract hard".

Now, I will grant you that, for some people, doing TWO things at once can be a boon to getting serious work done.

Stephen King listened to AC/DC tunes while he pounded out very coherent novels, for example.

And I know that Gary Halbert used to write killer ad copy while sitting in airports, surrounded by chaos.

But that kind of split-brain activity is actually a forced form of concentration... and it requires discipline.

With practice, some sets of incoming aural data -- including music and the antic shuffle of travel -- can be processed as "white noise", which occupies a part of your brain in a way that is actually calming.

And that frees the creative side of your noggin to work very efficiently.

But you're not listening to Angus's ball-busting guitar licks...

… and you're not hearing the urgent "white telephone" announcement as all your fellow waiting passengers discover your gate's been changed and begin to leave.

(King, who always wished he could have been a rock star, still can't sing a note from even his favorite songs… and Halbert was known to miss a few flights in his time.)

In other words -- writers who use sound while writing are not listening. They're using white noise to NOT listen, while they go deep into their minds. Same with entrepreneurs plotting the next assault on their niche.

And it's a big difference.

If you're trying to write while singing along to Justine or Britney or Beyoncé, or allowing every sudden movement around you to break your concentration…

… then your writing will come out shallow and weak.

So, if you can't do other things while you're writing the most important stuff in your life…

… **then don't DO other things.**

I can't.

Most writers I know can't.

So stop it…

… unless you can PROVE, with results, you're part of that brilliant minority who can get away with it.

And it's not just writing this applies to. It's EVERYTHING that's important in your life.

The concept of cramming your senses with experience and pleasure and distraction, in an attempt to "have it all", is almost always misguided.

It's living life SHALLOW, not deep.

I mean, you may be able to fold laundry while chatting with a friend on the phone about inconsequential things.

But you won't be doing anyone any favors trying to have a serious discussion while doing any other task at the same time.

The serious stuff in your life demands concentration.

And -- increasingly -- many people just are not able to pull it off anymore.

Recently, I've started asking some students how they've written the lame-ass copy they've sent in for critique.

After carping incessantly on the need to go deep with your writing, I sometimes lapse into the delusion that people actually follow my advice.

And delusion is the right word.

Many folks are still operating under Fantasy Rules Writing -- they believe they can perform their same-old distracted dance and still somehow get the most important thing in their life done in the seconds-long periods they gain clarity each hour or so.

So, once again, let's get this straight: I don't care how you choose to live the rest of your life.

But when you're writing or working on your business…

… that is ALL you are doing.

No TV in the background, no phone ringing nearby, no conversations or interruptions of ANY kind while you're writing the ads (or plotting the marketing) that is the rocket-fuel of your destiny.

You cannot look to the rest of the world for advice on this matter.

The rest of the world is half-asleep, and would FREAK OUT if forced to actually concentrate on something for five minutes.

They're living life in a vacuum… so they don't notice that Ms. Reality Star is an utter moron with nothing to say… they don't notice that professional sports actually has no real impact on their lives… they don't notice that they've never had a significant conversation with their children or spouse…

… and they don't notice that vast stretches of time are vanishing while they snooze.

Yes, time is fleeting…

… but even the goofballs doing the Time Warp were at least totally absorbed in that single act of synchronized dancing. (Rocky Horror Picture Show reference. Never mind.)

Living life DEEP means total immersion. You can't do that in the shallow end of the pool.

And it means you strive to not get distracted by all the shiny objects vying for your attention.

Discussions of "clinical Web addiction" are getting serious…

… because the Web is a pretty serious source of bright, shiny objects. And God forbid I should recommend that you turn off your Internet connection and go outside to play.

Well, okay, I do recommend that you do that, at least once a day.

But for most of us, the Web has become a critical part of our livelihood. We have to wander the online jungle, or risk becoming irrelevant.

So here's a simple proposal: Just experiment with the concept of scheduling your time online.

You like to surf the 'Net?

Then chalk out an hour each morning (and again in the afternoon if you can justify the time expenditure) and do NOTHING but surf the 'Net.

Turn the phone off. Close the door. And take notes.

Don't surf like a zombie…

… instead, surf DEEP.

Take the full hour to follow up a single thread -- finding other relevant sites, seeing what blogs are saying about the subject, exhausting every virtual avenue of research available.

This will hurt your brain at first, if you've been aimlessly surfing like everyone else.

Because it's the difference between a passive behavior…

… and an active one. The kind that gets stuff done.

Most people read newspapers, watch TV, and scan Web sites passively. If you tested them right after, they would score abysmally low on retention.

Same with talking to someone on the phone.

Academic studies show that the simple act of writing down a note during a conversation, or a lecture, or while reading or watching something...

... increases retention of input by, like, a thousand percent.

The reason: Forcing yourself to cognitively recognize something as worthy of writing down...

... and then processing that thought so it can be written...

... requires gearing up more of your brain.

It requires concentration.

Right now, though, I'll bet your powers of concentration suck.

For most Americans today, trying to concentrate on anything is like asking a monkey to do math. One plus one is a challenge.

And yet, you KNOW that the human brain is capable of amazing feats of memory, creativity, and data processing.

It's just not automatic.

You must discipline your brain to go deep.

And it's hard.

But it's also a requirement, if you want to make the Big Bucks.

You can still be a slacker, and you can still indulge in aimless surfing, gaming, gossiping and whatever other worthless endeavors the shallow part of your soul craves.

Just SCHEDULE that aimless stuff OUTSIDE of your "get it done" business life.

For most entrepreneurs, just the act of scheduling a SINGLE hour of dedicated writing time… and a SINGLE hour of concentrated Web research… and a SINGLE hour of managing goals…

… will revolutionize your entire life.

For three lousy hours each day, don't mingle your input.

When you write, that's all you do.

When you business-surf, that's all you do.

When you think the Big Thoughts, that's ALL you do.

You will stun your brain with what you can get done, minus distractions.

That's not new advice -- I'm sure you've heard it before (I know I've suggested it before).

But have you DONE it?

You KNOW it'll work. You KNOW it will increase your productivity, move you to the next level of deeper living, do all kinds of wonderful things.

So why aren't you already doing it?

You know why.

You're distracted.

It's simple to break out of the ADD rut you're in, though. Turn off the phone and the music, let your monitor go blank, shut the door…

… and just sit with your bad self for half an hour.

It's harder than you think it'll be. Your brain will squirm like a three-year-old getting ready for bed, and resist all efforts at discipline.

Just remember this: You lose this small battle, and you aren't going much of anywhere in your life.

The paths that MATTER are long and dangerous and fun. But you gotta pay attention.

Distraction is a parking lot on that path. Where you will sit until your ticket is punched.

You'll have lots of company while you devolve and melt into goo… but the people you'll meet if you get your mind back in disciplined shape are MUCH more interesting.

And guess what?

This same discipline can make the non-business parts of life more interesting, too.

If you like music… try scheduling an hour for nothing BUT listening to music.

Close your eyes, get comfy (but not so comfy that you'll snooze), settle into the most expensive headphones you can find…

… and listen.

I'll bet you haven't done that in a while.

Look -- I know I'm a geezer, and I know it's irritating when guys my age start talking about how it was in the old days. Boomers can be VERY annoying, in fact. Even to other Boomers.

But the thing is… you gotta operate on the same 80/20 principle when you encounter advice-givers, just like everything else in life.

Eighty percent of the input you get from other people is gonna be nonsense.

And you may have to work a bit to find the twenty percent that has substance.

What's more… eighty percent of that twenty percent will still be lightweight.
So, when you're after the really good stuff, you're looking at twenty percent of twenty percent.

In other words, you gotta dig through a HUGE damn pile of crap to find the hidden treasures.

This is true of ideas, and of people.

So, yeah -- most Boomers are sleep-walking zombie morons, unworthy of listening to.

But then, so are most people in every generation.

This is why I've always enjoyed having friends of all ages. The input is more nuanced, and you don't fall into the many traps of moronic thinking that can happen when you only hang out with your age peer group.

And when your friends are among the smart, wide-awake minority, even the finger-wagging advice can be right on.

So cut me some slack when I bring up the "old days". I'm not gonna tell you it was better back then, because it's not true.

Life is great at EVERY turn, when you're living deep. It also can break your heart, or be boring, or dangerous, or fill-in-the-blank.

That's what makes it such a friggin' adventure.

And the adventure never has to end...

... though most people seem eager to nest-up and ossify.

And you just cannot allow that to happen to you.

You're on the other path.

The one going somewhere.

That's why, as an entrepreneur, you gotta stay frosty. Alert to what's happening to you, and around you. And remain completely and utterly open to good advice, even if it's annoying to your slacker tendencies.

Okay?

Okay.

So, that said, I'm gonna risk being a boring Boomer here for a second.

C'mon, lighten up. It'll be good for you.

Here's the tale: I've been blessed by a pretty good long-term memory. I remember a lot of stuff from my childhood and formative teen years… but two particular memories stand out.

There had always been music in our home. Mom had a succession of table radios in the kitchen that -- if we'd kept them -- would be a stunning collection of mid-century post-modern design.

The sound wasn't so hot, by today's standards… but then, we had no reference point for sound quality. And most music was produced to be played on single-speaker radios anyway.

Mono.

Anyway, 1964 was a strange year. Kennedy was shot near the end of '63, and the Beatles arrived in January.

And I had just turned thirteen, suffering from the rude onset of puberty.

I don't remember the day, but I remember the situation. Up until this one specific moment, I had been a casual listener of music. Doo-wop, folk, Sinatra, Patsy Cline, whatever.

The only songs that had caught my attention to that point had been the novelty tunes now heard on Dr. Demento's oldies show: Purple People Eater, Alley Oop, anything by Alvin and the Chipmunks, that sort of crap.

And then, in a matter of seconds, something snapped deep inside me.

Someone was talking to me, but, like a special effect, my existence zoomed away from Planet Earth, and all senses except hearing music were suddenly frozen.

It was the Kinks, blasting out from that small table radio: "Girl, you really got me goin'… you got me so I don't know what I'm doin'… ah yeah…"

Bam, as abrupt as getting slugged with a hammer.

Entire sections of my cerebral cortex shifted like tectonic plates, and I was done with every other distraction in life. Rock and roll had arrived like invading berserkers, taking over my brain.

That night, I huddled under the covers with the single ear-plug from my beat-up transistor radio connected to me like an umbilical cord. There were precious few local stations on all night long, and none played rock and roll… but Wolfman Jack was manning the controls down in Tijuana at the "X".

50,000 watts of pure rockin' power, coming in clear as a bell through a radio that fit in the palm of my hand.

That was my first experience with deep, consuming concentration.

I barely breathed, for fear of missing a note.

I'd never felt so alive before.

So… awake.

It's a cliché image, I know.

But it really happened.

Much later in life, I discovered many other Boomers who had that same breathtaking moment of discovery, hiding under the covers with a transistor radio.

It's as close as many of us ever came to a real rite of passage. Discovering Ken Nordine at three in the morning, sandwiched in between The Who and Muddy Waters… and with no respectable advertisers believing prospects could possibly be listening, it was forty-minute runs of pure, uninterrupted music.

Wow.

I get chills just remembering.

Flash forward a few decades…

… and I've got a gazillion dollars worth of primo audio gear. The kind of stuff that lets you hear the intake of breath on early Beach Boy recordings, or a dropped pick on the reissue of Forever Changes.

And I'm not listening very closely to anything. It's become almost painful to sit through a five-minute tune by anyone. I have to be doing something else at the same time.

Can't sit still.

Then, one evening last week… intervention.

The power goes out.

Michele and I gather up flashlights and candles, get the fireplace going, and haul out some heavy blankets.

And, while in the garage looking for the little propane heater, I stumble across an old transistor radio. And, for the first time in decades, I am forced to not be distracted while listening to music.

The computer is dead, the phone silent, the TV blank. Outside, passing gaps in the cloud cover bathe us in moon beams, while the streetlights snore.

It wasn't exactly going back to living in a cave, but it was primitive, compared to the tech-heavy lifestyle we'd become accustomed to.

I found a jazz station I didn't know was out there…

… and allowed the music to enter my awareness undisturbed for the first time after a long, long exile.

Be-bop era Miles. A little Brubeck. Lionel on the bones.

Tiny speaker. Mono. Faint amber glow from the dial.

And it was heaven.

The next night -- with the power back on -- I sat down with a great book and just read for a couple of hours, in rapt silence.

I'd almost forgotten how the simple nuances of good storytelling can send your mind soaring.

God, it was delicious.

Again, I'm not saying that Boomers "had it better" than kids today. No way.

I've talked at length with people of all ages (many of them now long gone)…

… and one thing I know for sure: Your youth is special because you're young, and you are just beginning to engage the world on your own terms.

The gadgetry is irrelevant.

And if modern generations are somehow being distracted from the truly good stuff, then it is a shame of cosmic proportions.

If Boomers had any advantage, it was simply a lack of overwhelming high-tech stimuli to distract us. For a few precious years, anyway.

For anyone with the courage to gobble up huge chunks of life, what matters are the visceral experiences: Consuming passion, the thrill of independent thought, friendship.

Love.

Nintendo doesn't have a game to replace that stuff. Microsoft hasn't developed software yet that can thrill your senses as much as a single heady whiff of good Chianti.

And there isn't a chat room out there that will let you look deep into her eyes while your hearts tumble in synch.

Compared to all of that… Web 2.0 is just a duck fart in the distance.

I'm telling you -- cut off the power once in a while.

And take a radio under the covers with you.

Department of De-Zombie-ization

To finish up this subject, allow me to share with you my notes for chucking the zombie lifestyle, and waking up a bit. And kicking your ability to concentrate up several notches.

My recommendation is for a daily 10-minute "sensory wash".

Find a place where you won't be interrupted for ten crummy minutes -- go out and sit in your car in the garage if you must -- and get comfy.

Close your eyes, because you're getting too much visual stimulation anyway.

Then, go slowly through each of your other senses.

Taste the inside of your mouth. Take a breath to fire up your buds, and experience your tongue for a moment.

No matter how long ago you ate, there are still remnants of bitter, sweet, salty and other surprises in there.

We ignore our mouths and tongue all day long, assaulting it with gum, spicy food, coffee, all sorts of treats and horrors…

… and we rarely experience ANY of it.

I like cultures that appreciate things like great coffee, and make a ritual out of drinking it. (Go get a hand grinder and a French press, and put a little attention and effort into your next cup of joe. Experiment with savoring the brewing process.)

Keep moving, one by one, through your senses. What do you hear? Even in the quietest room, there are ticking clocks, the creak of beams, the distant howl of a dog or rumble of cars on the highway.

Pick each sound out. When the weather is nice, do this sensory wash outside… and be prepared to hear a symphony that's been rumbling under your radar.

Cramming all incoming sounds into a ball of "white noise" isolates you from nature.

I'm not gonna get all romantic on you here…

… but hey, that flock of Canuck geese soaring overhead and crapping on your car is truly a wondrous thing to behold, if you will just experience it.

You can clean your windshield later.

During your mini-meditation on senses, however, you're more interested in honing your listening skills.

It will blow your mind.

Pick out, with your eyes closed, each different quack of each bird. This instruction sounds insane to the average modern man... because most of nature is just a blur, and an irrelevant blur at that.

How, for God's sake, could it possibly be important to pick out the different quacks of different birds flying overhead?

Well, it IS important...

... if you want to move beyond a slumbering zombie state. So don't just tell yourself during this sensory wash, "Okay, I hear some birds off to my left."

Instead, acknowledge the aural input and start delineating it. Four different birds, about two blocks away to the northeast. A dog barking, across the main road... being answered by another pooch a half-mile farther north.

Notice the smaller sounds, too -- of the wind whispering past your ears.

Of your own heartbeat inside your head.

Eventually, you'll be able to pick up subtle sounds that never entered your consciousness before. Even cats won't be able to sneak up on you.

Next: Tactile sensations. The pressure of your butt against your chair, your arms against your stomach, the slight weight of your shirt on your shoulders.

The feel of the breeze against your cheek.

Then, smell the world, deeply. Everything around you has an odor -- even glass and plastic.

Wood is especially pleasant, man-made fibers less so.

Just continue to differentiate each piece of incoming data.

Start with ten minutes, and if you enjoy this process, bump it up to half an hour, twice a day.

For sure it won't kill you.

But the potential upside is, for most folks, a small tentative step toward becoming **fully awake**.

The world is your stage, and you have the power to write most of the script.

It's also your choice entirely whether you blunder through your life's play half-asleep, unprepared and deadened to the world (and unproductive as hell)…

… or alive, alert, and feasting on the sensory motherload of wonders that surround you.

Okay, sorry. I did get a little romantic there for a minute.

The lure of zoning out and becoming a zombie is always there, always looking for an opportunity to take over control.

If you want more from life, you've got to take full responsibility for doing it.

And, while this awakening process can be annoying and hard at first, the payoff is fantastic.

Stay with it.

And stay frosty.

Comments and rude asides: Lots of new (and free) blog entries at www.john-carlton.com, and you are personally invited to partake of the fray in the comments section (where I frequently hang out myself).

<u>Chapter Seven:</u>

Your Big Bad "Reality Check" System

A sweet, fast little shortcut around the deluded demons populating your brain, so you can stop operating in Fantasy Land and return to the real world, where all the serious fun, happiness, and profit is...

Oh, waiter? Can I get my reality check, please?

Actually, that would be very cool... having someone come by each day and deliver a cold, uncensored, soul-searched dose of reality. Maybe a DVD from some angelic being who's been studying you, and offers a free prime-time report on how you're doing.

I, for one, would welcome such an examination.

But I also realize that most people would freak out.

So... in the interest *of* freaking you out (which I consider one of my primary jobs)...

... I'm gonna share with you my private technique of performing **vicious reality checks on your own bad self.**

Scary stuff.

Coming to terms with reality is something you -- as a human being hard-wired with denial and a thick protective wall of self-delusion -- have to cultivate. It doesn't happen naturally.

The desire to strip yourself bare and invite a critique of your vulnerabilities just doesn't sound like a good time for most folks.

But if you want to *grow*… really move beyond where you're at right now, and test the air in the upper levels of existence…

… you gotta develop a taste for self-examination.

Who was it… Socrates or Aristotle or Jung or whoever who said: "The unexamined life is not worth living"?

Okay, I looked it up. Socrates, facing the judges in his trial for heresy in 366 BC Athens, essentially told them to shove it.

Of *course* he had challenged religious and political orthodoxy… that's what a thinking man *does*.

He then offed himself with poison, rather than shut up and be a good little zombie citizen. Became a martyred pitch-man for reality.

And yet here we are, 21 centuries later, most of us still pretty much deadened to self-reflection and avoiding reality with all our might.

When I went solo as a freelancer, I made a couple of vows that I suspected were necessary if I was gonna succeed.

The first was "**business before pleasure**"… an old-school rule that brutally chafed my party-boy slackness. But I stuck with it, refusing to engage in ANY social niceties until all my work for the current project was done.

Turned out to be a very *useful* rule, too. I quickly noticed that the unsuccessful people around me were loathe to put off immediate gratification, and allowed themselves to be easily distracted from goals.

Taking the easy road all the time won't cut it, though, if you strive for a full life. It's like learning to play guitar -- before you get up on stage to wow the crowd, you need to log a lot of lonely, painful hours attending to the "business" of honing your skills.

It separates the wannabe's from the real performers.

The *second* vow I made was to never shy away from being honest with myself.

This was kind of risky... because you have to separate "honesty" from that dour, cynical voice in your head that insists you're just a total loser who should quit and go die.

Most of us have that disapproving voice -- Freud called it the "super-ego", and likened it to an internalized version of a stern parent.

In cartoons, it's the devil on your left shoulder calling you a wimp for not doing whatever juicy vice you're contemplating, coupled with the angel on your right shoulder scolding you for thinking about sex too much.

If you're gonna climb on the fast track to success, you gotta haul BOTH that devil and that angel off to a distant cell in your mind, and lock 'em up.

You need to look *clearly* at reality... not through the crusted lens of guilt or perfectionism.

I couldn't afford real therapy at the time, so I indulged in self-help books. I read at least one for every biz book... and when Og Mandino, for example, told me to recite a little pep talk every day and visualize my goals, I did it. (His book was "The Greatest Salesman In The World", and yeah, I can recommend it if you're strapped for good vibes.)

The notion that I could have *any* influence at all over how my life played out was alien to me. I'd spent thirty years as a piece of driftwood buffeted by the waves of destiny...

... and discovering the concept of setting goals -- and then going *after* them -- was like turning on a light in a dark room.

Wow.

But you gotta be careful when courting reality. I kept journals back then (there are ten banker's boxes of them in the garage) and, perusing them now, I see there was a disturbing tendency to beat myself up for sins real and imagined.

That's not reality. That's wallowing in shame and remorse.

Just another version of sleep-walking.

No. Getting access to the *reality* of any given situation requires you to hone your chops for stepping back and looking *dispassionately* at yourself.

No name-calling, no judgments, no excuses.

In fact, to properly look at reality, you can't assign any "good" or "bad" stickers to any of it. At least while you're gathering the raw data.

You gotta look at your life as it IS... not as you wish it was, or hoped it had turned out, or think it should be.

This self-reflection, it turns out, is hard to do.

Go pick up a rock. Go on. Walk outside and pick up the first rock you come across.

Ask yourself: What is the *reality* of this rock?

It's neither pretty nor ugly. Neither useful nor useless. Neither heavy nor light.

Those are "values" you may assign to it as you *judge* the rock. What a pretty little thing you are, all smooth and rippled with color and texture… good and solid, yet amazingly easy to heft…

Nope. In the universe, it's just a rock.

Well, not "just" a rock. It's *your* rock, now.

To do a proper self-reality check, you gotta examine your entire life with the *same* detached observation.

It's not "I'm angry." It's "I'm in full anger mode at Joe for missing his deadline…"

And "My anger is manifest as rising blood pressure, furrowed brow, a little heat in my belly from adrenaline, and a primal murderous urge to throttle Joe's neck…"

And…

"This anger is familiar to me. I've felt it often…"

And so on.

Your anger is neither bad nor good while you're examining it. You save your judgments for later.

For now… while you're reacquainting yourself with yourself… you're looking at your own actions and thoughts and emotions *as if they were animals in the zoo.*

(**Side note:** This examination often works as a *mood modifier*, too. When you break down something like anger into physical components of adrenaline, tense muscles and a tweaked brain stem lit up with ancient survival options... the actual anger *dissolves*. Just goes away. Many of the moods you thought were controlling you are actually so flimsy that they cannot withstand even cursory examination.)

(Anger, especially, is something that comes on like a beast and can vanish like a ghost. I knew a shrink who ran anger management groups... and while he admitted that many people are too addicted to their rage to be helped, the ones who regained control did so by *observing* their feelings and behavior and thought processes. In other words -- they broke their anger down into rock-sized components, small enough to deal with, and realized they were NOT helpless slaves to it.)

(But this worked ONLY for folks willing to disengage from the joy -- and it *is* a perverse form of joy for the primitive part of our brain -- of indulging in passionate rage. The ones addicted to the hormonal "high" of being flooded with the chemistry of anger refused to let go.)
(Can work for headaches, too, by the way... though Excedrin's faster. This kind of **defining-and-observing** tactic is how people with chronic pain *manage* it organically.)

This "watching the funny animals in the zoo" approach to self-examination works just as well when you look at everything *else* happening in your life right now, too.

Business problems, spats with the little lady, car trouble, stubbed toes... everything.

I'm not suggesting you attempt to turn yourself into an emotionless robot. Far from it.

Instead, the act of stepping back and observing allows you to actually learn to *appreciate* all the things that make you human.

The feelings, the memories, the regrets, the anticipations, the love and the hate…

… all of it becomes *more* real and *more* alive when you examine it.

After a good reality check, you are actually a **better human being**.

Why? Because you're no longer operating at the mercy of hormone dumps, fear triggers, reflexes, or learned behavior.

You're in *control…* probably for the first time in your life.

Not in control of things you *can't* control, like going back in time and not walking under that falling safe.

But you CAN control how past traumas affect you *now…* how you regard safes today, for example, and how you react to emergencies, or even how your body functions under stress.

For me, discovering self-examination was like unexpectedly finding the key to paradise in my pocket. It helped me get past my dreamlike tendency for wishful thinking and regrets over past failure.

I stopped, almost immediately, being a piece of driftwood tossed about on the tides…

… and instead became a real ship, with plenty of sail and a compass and a good strong rudder, heading somewhere I wanted to go.

Wow.

Not everyone shares my enthusiasm for reflection, of course.

I remember someone close to me explaining why he threw away a self-help book he was reading. He felt it was describing his life and problems just a little too clearly for comfort.

He didn't *like* facing up to reality.

Brrr. No thanks.

He's not alone. In fact, he's in the *majority* of people out there.

But I'll tell you this: In my non-scientific study of *successful* colleagues… every single one of the movers and shakers who are living full lives… are gourmet-level reality fans.

It's like a big valley cleaving through the ranks of professional people.

There are business owners out there who take refunds, for example, as *personal* attacks. That's not reality -- that's allowing your inner child to rule the roost.

There are freelancers out there who are oblivious to the ways they alienate potential clients. They've got some weird unresolved rebellion thing with authority that gets played out with every job. (I had a rather virulent form of this myself when I worked for The Man.)

And there are lots and lots of people out there headed for the Jerry Springer Show because their brain has been hijacked by hormones and delusion and behaviors they can't even clearly identify (let alone begin to change).

The reality is: **Most people live *outside* the Reality Zip Code.** Sometimes *waaaaay* the heck out in the boondocks, beyond easy redemption.

As an entrepreneur or small business owner, you simply cannot set up camp too far away from reality, if you want to succeed.

You gotta live the examined life.

And here is my super-simple tactic for getting started:

**John's Big Bad
Reality Check System**

This will be simple and amazingly pain-free.

Nevertheless, it is NOT something the "control center" of your brain will delight in doing.

And to begin, you must suffer through a brief explanation of the *disconnect* between "you" and that part of your brain you deal with in your normal awake state.

You see, your brain *likes* the status quo, no matter what it is.

If you're miserable, it likes being miserable.

If you're stressed out, it likes being stressed out.

If you're lonely, it likes being lonely.

Why?

Because your brain (the part of your mind that runs things) doesn't place *values* on any particular state.

There's this huge bell-curve of acceptable conditions that aren't always logical or in your best interest.

If you've seen serious addiction close up -- either in a friend, or in yourself -- then you've witnessed this in action.

People have been trying to figure out this seemingly self-destructive part of our nature since the dawn of civilization…

… and while we're not gonna solve the riddle here, it IS important that you understand it's *there* and cooking in your life.

On one end of this bell curve is a non-responsive, catatonic state. No reality exists there at all.

On the other end is the out-of-body transcendent state that most Americans can barely imagine… where you become "one" with the universe.

Or something like that.

In between is everything else. Depression, manic elation, murderous rage, sociopathic ambition, creative glee, lust, love and looniness.

And your "control center" brain is fine with *all* of it.

Everyone has done something they knew or suspected was wrong… knowing the consequences would bring swift and terrible retribution down on their heads… felt guilty even considering the act…

… and then *done it anyway.*

And suffered.

And felt crushing shame.

And swore to never, ever do it again.

And then… after a short burst of redemptive behavior… *did it AGAIN.*

I'm not even talking about addicts here.

Just watch a kid around a cookie jar when he thinks he isn't subject to immediate adult intervention… and you are also watching the same basic brain activity of a compromised CEO contemplating embezzlement.

I'm not saying we're all hopelessly bad, and the world is doomed.

For most folks, the transgressions of their own moral code are relatively minor (or at least manageable, in terms of consequences).

Frankly, I'm just gonna assume you've lived as good a life as you've been capable of living to this point. I know I have, and all of the people close to me have, too.

We struggle with doing the right thing sometimes… but mostly we keep the lid on harmful, selfish behavior. (Most of the time.)

There's even some anthropological studies coming out that explain our tendency to cooperate with each other in rather reasonable terms (as an evolutionary tactic for survival of the tribe).

Anthropologists love to find reasonable explanations for things. It helps keep them sane. Just like second-year medical students start fearing they suffer from every disease they read about, so do grad-school anthropologists suffer from the nagging suspicion that society is a barely-contained riot of rape, pillage and murder just waiting to spill into the streets.

And, yes, I'm way off on a tangent here, but it all comes back to *reality*.

From the moment, as kids, we start to craft arguments in our head over whether or not to do something -- steal cookies, bash Jimmy in the face and eat his cupcake, torture the cat, scream bloody murder just to watch the reaction of adults -- those arguments get more and more sophisticated.

It's easy to see how they can get TOO sophisticated, especially when we observe other people. The neighbors are clearly insane, your ex was a cruel, conniving witch, and the other driver is shamefully inadequate to the task of staying within the rules of the road.

It's *obvious* to everyone, right?

Except *none* of these people agree with your assessment. The neighbors think *you're* the nutcase, your ex is absolutely positive (beyond a shadow of doubt) that *you're* the worst person on earth, and the other driver is clearly the *only* guy behind the wheel today who knows how to maneuver in traffic.

This is why laws exist. To *force* consequences and redemptive behavior on people who refuse to believe they're responsible for anything that happened.

No one loses a lawsuit and admits, honestly, they were actually wrong.

There are no truly guilty people in our jails.

And every asshole who ever got booed by the audience on Jerry Springer is *astonished* the boos were for him.

Inconceivable!

Okay, sure, there are people who admit to being wrong, who accept their punishment with grace, who do their best to make amends when they've screwed up.

But they are clearly in the minority. Because to be able to see how you might be at fault, you need to be awake and see reality clearly.

And, if you've been reading my stuff for any length of time, you know that top marketers all share the same secret: They never doubt for a moment that most people, in most markets, are *sleep-walking zombies* desperate to hook up with someone who will tell them what to do.

And I'm NOT being cynical here.

Because I also know -- from painful personal experience -- that it's possible to *wake up* from your zombie state, whenever you decide it's time to do so.

You can begin thinking for yourself, being independent, and living your own life the way you want to... free of the shackles of emotional tyranny and thought-control... simply by ceasing to see the world as you wish it were, or believe it should be.

And start seeing it *as it IS.*

Reality.

What a concept.

But, again, your brain will *resist* attempts to see reality clearly.

It likes the status quo... whether it's being a couch potato, or constantly taunting death with adrenaline-fueled adventures, or living a double-life of secret behaviors that would get you arrested, divorced, or impeached if discovered.

As an adult, you've come a long way from the days of trying to rationalize your abject NEED to rob the cookie jar (and make Mommy upset).

The little angels and devils on your shoulders have gone to law school and majored in debate.

The arguments going on in your head have gotten very clever, devious and convincing.

And often, the loser in these inner arguments is *reality*.

If you're ready to face reality, you need to develop *new* skills... because your brain has been busy since birth stacking the odds against you.

Thus -- the Reality Check.

Here's how it works: When you're experiencing discomfort with your life -- and it's not disease-related -- the problem is probably *resistance* to reality.

It's the main culprit behind stress, the inability to act decisively, and making bad moves that seem to fly in the face of self-survival.

And what makes it complicated is that you aren't just resisting reality... you're resisting *several versions* of "reality" that have been crafted by warring departments in your brain's control room.

It's exhausting and disorienting when you're not sure what's going on. Like trying to fight multiple attackers in a dark room.

Sleep walkers are under the delusion there is just *one* "you" in there at the controls...

... when, in fact, there's a small *crowd* in your brain vying for dominance, and each entity generally despises all the others.

You don't need to earn a PhD in psychology to get the gist here. I'll never be invited to lecture at Harvard on this, but I think I can help you understand why there's *conflict* in your brain.

Now, you may have more characters than these basic types... **but you don't have** *fewer.*

Once you start paying attention, you'll begin to recognize who's gained control of your brain by the way they argue their version of reality to you.

Here are the usual suspects:

Your **Inner Brat**... who has clung to the trauma of vulnerability and the humiliation of childhood dependence all this time. He will nurse a grudge forever, and use immature stubbornness to get his way. (I was astonished the first time I dealt with a surly client who insisted we do things his way "because I say so"... but by the second or third time, I realized I was dealing with someone who had ceded control to his childish compulsions.)

Your **Inner Perfectionist Bastard**... who sternly believes that any behavior that isn't *perfect*, is despicable. And cowardly. And deserves to be punished. This inner voice is quick to cruelly judge everyone around you, and even judges *you* harshly when you're not meeting expectations. (Idealists, partisan politicos, and sociopathic scamsters have all allowed the drill sergeant in their heads to dominate.)

Your **Inner Wimp**... who is all too eager to admit failure, long before failure is a certainty. He loves to inject doubt and feelings of worthlessness into every endeavor. (After decades of dealing with bodybuilding clients and self-defense experts, I can tell you the main motivation behind most of their dedication is an attempt to shut up the *wimp* inside their head.)

Your **Inner Caveman**... who hates the notion of deferred gratification, doesn't see the point of manners or political compromise, and craves a permanently sated condition, with all immediate needs met *regardless of consequences*. He's the one who wants to shoot the motorist who cuts you off in traffic.

And, finally... there's **YOU**. We'll get to him in a minute.

Once you realize there's a mob scene in the control room of your brain, you can begin to appreciate the need to acquire the skills of seeing reality clearly.

You can, if you like, spend a fortune in therapy sorting the mess out.

Or, you can at least try this much *simpler* method, for free.

Here's what you do: First, set aside at least an hour where you will not be disturbed. No phones, no one knocking at the door, no distractions whatsoever.

You need this "mind space" so you can *concentrate* -- what a concept -- and also because you do NOT, under any circumstances, want anyone to see what you are about to write down.

In fact, I recommend that -- until you find a way to keep this material *absolutely* private (very hard to do, even with hidden safes) -- you give yourself the option of *shredding* all or *deleting* all documents at the end of the hour.

Just keep the option available. You may decide to file everything intact, and that's fine… as long as you understand the possible consequences and are cool with them.

Now, sit down at your keyboard, or with a short stack of paper and a pen, and get busy.

The key here is to write *as fast as you can*, without editing and without stopping to think about what you're putting down.

You want to *bypass* your inner editor… and you *especially* want to rush past your brain's control room, where all those warring characters are desperate to interfere with any attempt at a reality check.

No one else is gonna read what you write. (When you get good at this tactic, you REALLY don't want anyone reading what you write.)

You absolutely must feel confident -- beyond a shadow of doubt -- that you can lay out the **uncensored truth** here. No niceties, no consideration of other people's feelings, no "being fair" or being a gentleman.

You want to tap the rawest possible examination of your current state...

... *without* getting emotional or judgmental about it.

You don't have to be in a bad period of your life to do this reality check, either. Though, when you're feeling good about things there's not much motivation to deconstruct your happiness.

I do a reality check whenever I feel overwhelmed, or whenever I sense I'm acting from a defensive position. Or especially when I'm *resisting* something.

That sense of resistance can be pretty subtle and hard to identify at first. But it's a sure sign there's unrest in your control room.

Write out, to get started, the answer to this simple question: **"What's going on with me *right now*?"**

Write fast. It can be a list of grievances and problems, or a big laundry list of the tasks you're expected to complete in the near future.

Don't dwell on anything -- just write out the basics. Work, relationships, commitments, life, death, and existential despair.

The last time I did this exercise, I was feeling crushed by deadlines and requests for my time by friends and family. I knew I was ripe for a reality check, because my dreams were getting vivid -- I was being chased by monsters in haunted houses, and showing up in high school classes without pants.

High anxiety alerts.

So I wrote down the facts of the situation -- there were deadlines coming up, other commitments were clogging the calendar, and I was feeling inadequate to the tasks.

There are no exact rules to how you proceed with this writing -- just try to dispassionately lay out the situation as you see it.

And be *honest* about the **emotions** accompanying each item.

You may be mad at someone, scared of someone else, freaked out by your bank balance, or depressed about the paperwork needing attention for tax filings.

My last list filled two pages, just getting the bare details down on what my situation was. Those two pages took only a few minutes to type up, however -- it came out in a gush.

When you get good at this, there is a definite sense of relief just in facing up to the list of obligations and problems on your plate.

But you're not just after relief.

You're after *reality*.

So, next, go back and start writing down (as fast as you can) every emotion you have about each item.

The rule is simple: **There is NEVER just one emotion involved.**

When you're angry, you're also often scared. Two sides of the same coin.

When you're disappointed, you're also maybe feeling out of control.

When you're depressed, you're also feeling robbed and cheated.

Or whatever. Maybe your coin has different flip sides. Doesn't matter -- the idea is to start realizing the ingredients of your discomfort.

Now, here's the big trick: Force yourself to consider *alternative emotions* on every point.

Engage in a quick debate with yourself, using the great eye-opening tactic of all debate education: *Seeing the other side.*

I was turned onto this concept as a freshman in college. I took a debate course with a teacher who forbade any of us from arguing positions we already believed in.

She forced us to take, whenever she could, the *opposite* stance of whatever we thought we considered the "real truth".

For me, an idealistic young man, this was very troubling at first. The crowd I hung out with would be *horrified* to learn I was even *acknowledging* that another point of view existed.

Let alone that I was creating an argument in *support* of "the enemy".

And yet... that tactic was probably the single greatest tool I learned in my entire college education.

You have to erase the word "but" from your inner dialog to do this. You can't say "Well, sure, you have a point there, BUT..."

Nope. To argue persuasively for the other side, you have to adopt their beliefs in one whole gulp.

No fudging.

That pretty much took care of my partisan hippie politics, overnight. I've been an independent ever since, unable to swallow any more one-sided propaganda from either liberals or conservatives.

When dealing with *yourself*, at first it will be hard to understand that there are, indeed, at least two sides to whatever's troubling you.

So after you write down your "what's going on" rant…

… go back and write quickly how you *feel* about each item.

Then *challenge* that feeling… and write out quickly how you might be actually having the opposite (or near-opposite) emotion instead.

You're already way deep into the self-examination process at this point.

Then… the biggie: Answer the question "*Why* **do I feel this way?**"

For most folks, the answer to "Why are you mad?" is "Because I'm *mad*, that's why."

Not good enough.

What IS it about the situation, or the person, that incites anger?

Challenge *everything* you believe about your insight. Don't accuse yourself of sins (that's your Inner Wimp interfering), and don't compare yourself to any ideals (that's your Inner Perfectionist).

Try, as dispassionately as you can, to observe what you're feeling as if you were watching monkeys frolic in a zoo cage.

Do NOT make any *decisions* during this emotional download. This isn't about decision-making. It's about getting a good view of the *reality* of the situation, minus all the sugar-coating and the gloom-and-doom hand wringing.

Most people get hung up on interpersonal relationships during attempts to see reality. There may not be (and often aren't) any easy ways to consider complex situations involving lovers, partners and foes. You can't control other people…

… but you *can* control how you *react* to them, and to the situations they affect.

Just keep after the bottom-line truth.

Business stuff is easier, usually. The reality of any situation is probably somewhere between your imagined disaster and your wish-fulfillment fantasies of world domination.

I've confided many times about suffering from self-doubt during deadline crunches. The reality is, of course, that I have many successes behind me that seem to imply I actually know what I'm doing.

Still, past success is no guarantee of future results. So the reality is… yeah, I have the chops to do this project. My Inner Brat wants to whine anyway, and my Inner Caveman wants to go outside and play in the sunshine.

And I'm *resisting* everything. I don't want to do the work, I don't want to fail, I don't want to feel bad, I don't want to throw my career away, I don't, I don't, I don't... lots of "don't"s in there.

Here's where the magic happens: Just by writing everything down, you relieve your brain from having to continually *conduct* the ongoing argument over your situation.

The repetition is for memory's sake... and, written down, memory is satisfied.

So the internal dialog can calm down.

That, alone, lets the air out of most emotions. There may be wolves at the door... but if you're safe for the moment, you can let go of the panic and consider options coolly.

The "you" you're after in all this...

... is the guy who isn't under the influence of the demons and angels populating your brain.

He's the guy who, with Zen calm, can pause in the middle of the action and *observe* "I'm feeling angry" or lonely or stressed or whatever. And, not unconsciously controlled by any emotion, he can *adjust* his emotional thermostat so things get done.

It's tricky, but like all skills, once you do it a few times, it gets easy.

Reality is actually a very nice place to hang out. Really.

<u>Chapter Eight:</u>

Making An Ass Out Of You And Me

How to position yourself for maximum connection with your audience... why freaking folks out with naughty language may actually be your best possible plan... and how to use sneaky revenge tactics correctly...

Several years back, there was a risk-taking (and low-rated) comedy show on cable that occasionally used Gilbert Gottfried as an on-the-spot reporter. Funny man.

You may remember him from Saturday Night Live, where he was a featured player for a while. Small, squirrelly guy with a scrunched-up face and a cartoonish voice. (In fact, most of his roles these days involve *just* his voice, in animated films.)

Anyway, Gilbert would never be described as a "hunk". He's this generation's version of Casper Milquetoast -- the meek Everyman who never seems to get a fair break.

I only remember one segment from that cable comedy show.

In it, Gilbert was interviewing two very beefed-up and attractive young men about picking up women. They were sitting in a hot tub (Gilbert was fully dressed, I seem to recall, and in the middle).

It was just after a commercial break... and the two studs were about to reveal their "big damn secret" on meeting hot ladies in crowded bars.

Both of them agreed on the tactic, too.

"Here's what you do," they said. "The trick is, *never* talk to the girls right away."

"Never talk to them right away," repeated Gilbert, taking notes. "Okay, got it."

"That's right. Just ignore them when they first come up to you..."

"Just ignore them..." says Gilbert. "Hey, *wait* a minute."

"Yeah, the first ones who come up to you will be less desirable than the ones who beg for your attention later..."

"Hey!" says Gilbert. "I've never had a woman come up to me and start talking in my life! *It doesn't happen!*"

The two studs looked genuinely stunned and taken aback. "Really?"

"*Yeah*, really. This advice won't work for me. What have you got for a geeky, unattractive guy?"

And the studs just shook their heads sadly.

Anyway, that's the way I recall the segment. I was rolling on the floor, laughing.

Lately, though, I get reminded of that scene when I'm critiquing sales pitches during consultations.

See... way too often, rookie writers make *awful assumptions* about their readers.

Or, worse, they have something within the pitch that will ultimately *eliminate* most of their readers from the offer...

... and they try to hide it. Or ignore it.

This is all about what people do with incoming data, and how they process it. In Gilbert's case, he was riveted and super-eager to learn the "secret" to scoring with the ladies that these two studs possessed.

And, when he discovered they were making a ridiculous assumption -- that *all* guys held the same attraction power they did -- he was overcome with the *"Oh yuck!"* reaction.

His hopes were cruelly dashed.

Don't make *any* assumptions about your prospect at all. (The common saying is "When you *assume…* you make an *ass* out of you and me" Ass+u+me. Get it? Of course you do. But knowing the saying, and USING it effectively in your marketing remain two very different things.)

How does this play out in real-life marketing?

First Assumption-Murdering Tactic: Don't use insider slang, or abbreviations, or references, without *explaining* them… unless you would bet your life that every single one of your readers understands it all.

I just critiqued an ad from a guy selling a product that would help you sell your own house without using a real estate agent. And it was rife with "insider" real estate terms and buzz words that would go right over the head of the average reader.

It was, essentially, a foreign language to the average prospect he was after.

This is a common blunder. You live with your product every day, and you breathe, eat, and sleep the language and concepts.

But your reader is an *outsider*, in most cases. He often hasn't given a single thought to what you offer before encountering your sales pitch. You may be introducing him to the entire concept.

So, you don't want to *lose* him by *confusing* him.

When I'm writing copy that must include highly technical terms, I *explain* them the way I would face-to-face with someone I'd just met.

Often, I'll use parenthetical remarks like this: (That's just a fancy way of saying [insert non-fancy explanation here].)

Or: (In plain English, that simply means...)

Second Assumption-Murdering Tactic: You cannot be too careful about "letting your reader in on" what you're talking about.

That's why I construct my sales pitches with lots of "here's what to do next", and "here's what that means for you" type paragraphs.

I literally imagine I'm leading the reader through a dark room.

I know the path, *but he doesn't.*

And I don't want him to knock his knees a single time on any hidden obstacles.

Third Assumption-Murdering Tactic: There's yet another angle here. If, like the hot tub studs, your product requires special skills or assumes the reader already has certain attributes...

... don't wait until the last minute to spring these tidbits on your audience.

At its simplest, this is the reason so many good pitches start out with some version of the "If/Then" proposition: "If you're finally ready to do [whatever]... then this will be the most important message you ever read."

This is also the mindset you want to use even when the pre-requisites for your offer are much stiffer and more complex. Say, if you're selling yachts, or a super-expensive seminar, or something aimed at a very specific market niche (like aeronautic engineers or French cooks).

Decide how you're *positioning* yourself first. If you're deep into the niche yourself, and you're offering *truly* advanced secrets... say, for example, you are a stud, and you have some juicy secrets for other studs (which would never work for lesser men)...

… then *use* that as part of your pitch.

It's called "exclusivity".

Don't waste time or copy trying to *lessen* the "insider-ness" of your offer, or water it down.

Instead, *embrace* your advanced nature, and don't worry about readers who do not fit your "perfect prospect" profile.

On the flip side of that... if you're positioning yourself as the "outsider", ***then don't hide it.***

Gilbert himself could actually float a product on being successful with the ladies.

He would sell a ton more than the studs ever could, too, because his potential audience is nearly *unlimited*. (Of course, he still needs some kind of *success* to tout in the first place. Don't think he'd sell much of a product titled "How To Be A Total Loser With Women".)

I helped one client sell a mountain-range of teaching videos to the golf market using this very tactic…

… because most golfers are older, out-of-shape, and haven't seen their toes for years as their bellies took on the shape of a basketball. Plus, *ouch*, the arthritis and creaky joints mean they can't come remotely close to the gorgeous, loose, athletic windmill swings of the young pro's who dominate the golf magazines.

So, we found older, battered and less-fit teachers who were just like most golfers…

… except they were actually GOOD at golf. And the sales just keep flooding in. (I am, in fact, still collecting royalties on ads I wrote 20 years ago for that client. Because the appeal never changes. Those ads have gone from direct mail letters, to magazine ads, to video sales letters online… with almost zero editing.)

Bonus Section

While we're on the topic of communicating with audiences…

… let's just address the big question so many ask me about the title of this book.

"Why," I am often asked, "do you insist on using words like 'shit' in your book titles?"

It's a fair question. I even had several colleagues BEG me not to use the title "*The Entrepreneur's Guide To Getting Your Shit Together*", because they thought I would alienate too many potential buyers.

And yes, I figure (from the occasional bad review I get on Amazon) I've offended a few folks here and there across the globe.

But here's the thing: I would have eventually offended those folks *anyway*, no matter how bland the title of the book was.

Because my writing style is very aggressive, and very much the way I speak around my closest pals and clients. Getting past the title of my books isn't your only opportunity to be offended.

When I write copy for a *client*, of course, I use the language appropriate for their audience (and you should, too). And I've successfully penned ads for nearly every market out there (including such "conservative" markets as global finance, Christian health experts, survivalists, gold bugs, and farm maintenance)…

… never uttering a single controversial or offensive word.

However, when I write as a *teacher*… in my newsletters, blog posts, social media rants, books, and seminar speeches…

… I *respect* my audience by writing or speaking to them the *same way* I do for my friends, colleagues, fans and clients.

And I let 'er rip.

I feel I *owe* it to you to treat your ears – and your mind – the way I treat the folks who pay me for advice.

And I *do* occasionally catch hell for it. (In fact, I've had folks insist I'm GOING TO HELL, simply for using the hard-edged language I use.)

So allow me to share a couple of thoughts on this very critical matter:

First thought: The latest offended guy to write to me called himself a "marketing professional". And he thought he'd just do me a little favor, by pointing out what a *horrendous* blunder I was committing.

In his eyes, I was turning off a *huge* segment of my potential customer base by writing "too rough".

And, as a marketer, *wasn't my main job to reach as many people as possible?*

I usually ignore these "white mail" complaint letters. But this time, I dunno, I just sort of snapped. And I wrote an email back to this guy.

What I told him -- and it's the truth -- is that while he may indeed be a "fellow marketer"...

... he is also the guy everyone else hopes will leave the room soon. So they can get down to *real* business. Without having to stop every two minutes to apologize for using real language.

Look -- I've spent half a lifetime hanging out with movers and shakers. And nearly *all* of them swear like drunken sailors when they're among friends.

Part of it is just the pure enjoyment of being around like-minded people, and relaxing.

And another part of it is about *bonding.* Since most of us *do* watch our language in "polite" company, letting go with the blue stuff while hanging with our pals gives us the feeling we're in a special club of insiders.

Which, in this case, we *are.* A club of business insiders. Marketing homeboys, if you will.

It's the old "wink, wink, nudge, nudge" school of tribalism.

You know, people used to come up to me during seminars and ask what Gary Halbert and I were whispering about on stage. They imagined we were sharing some amazing insight or advertising secret, or floating concepts and ideas.

Nope. Usually, we were trying like hell to crack each other up, and make the other one lose his composure.

You know -- like third graders acting up in class. To cut the tension, keep stress low.

One time in Key West, in the midst of an intense Hot Seat session with someone who had paid outrageous money for our advice...

... Gary leaned over and said "Hey, John -- look at the woman on the far end of the second row. You can see up her dress!"

I almost spit up a mouthful of coffee. And these things were being recorded from start to finish.

He got me.

Brutal, childish comedy. It's the best.

There's a kind of "M*A*S*H" sick humor at the far edges of the business world.

For the combat surgeons, you either laughed at the impossible carnage you were expected to fix, or went insane.

For businessmen, you either learn to appreciate the ironic and unintentionally-hilarious parts of corporate life...

... or *burn out* from the seriousness of it all.

Nearly every single one of the top copywriters or marketers I've ever met have *excellent* senses of humor. They love to laugh (even the many criminally-shy introverts). (And no, don't try to hit me with your latest pun or joke -- I'm talking about *real* humor here. Spontaneous wit and savage repartee. It's rare.)

And what makes us laugh most of all...

... is the English language.

I have a serious tome here called "Maledicta 1981". (Latin for "bad words", if you must know.) It's a doctorate-level examination of -- you guessed it -- insults and swearing. (One of my favorites is the medieval insult, where you show the back of your upturned hand, with the middle finger pulled down -- like this: **0o00**. It's called the "negative bird", and it means "*I hope you die a virgin!*")

Okay. Where was I?

Oh, yeah. Swearing.

My other favorite book here is the American Slang Dictionary (2nd Edition).

When I was in high school, more than once I spent an entire study period combing the big damn 200-pound Webster's dictionary in the library for naughty Anglo-Saxon words.

As a writer, I am fascinated by language in *all* its forms. None of it scares me.

You've probably noticed that I use a lot of slang and misspellings in my writing (such as: *ain't... gonna... didja... naw... wannabe*). Along with enough blatantly incorrect grammar to choke an English teacher.

And I do it on purpose.

In school, I learned how to write painfully well.

In advertising, *I learned how to write like people talk.* Who cares if I sound like a hick fresh off the hay wagon sometimes?

As I've said before, the best salesman is often <u>not</u> the suave, debonair gentleman in the tailored suit...

... but rather the schleppy little mutt who looks like he slept in his clothes.

The guy you can *really talk to* and identify with.

I'm a communicator. More specifically, I'm a word-gunslinger. And the language is my weapon.

BANG!

Back to my first thought on the whiner: I wrote back to that "marketing professional", saying (a) hadn't he *noticed* that people were waiting for him to leave in meetings, and...

... (b) had he even *glanced* at a television set or magazine lately?

He was stuck in a mental state where Gilligan's Island was as risqué as it got, while the rest of us had moved on to The Sopranos. He was watching black-and-white network TV, while everyone else was riveted to HBO.

I immediately remembered why I have a rule against answering white mail when he wrote *back* to me. Suddenly we were pen pals, I guess.

He just couldn't let it go. He insisted the world *had* been a better place when the strongest word you'd hear on TV was "golly gee" or something like that. And we *never* got to see Barbara Eden's belly button on I Dream Of Jeanie. (I'm still pissed over that, by the way.)

Hmmm, I thought. Those references would be from the mid-sixties – civil rights riots, the Vietnam war, Mutually-Assured-Destruction nuclear brinksmanship with the Russians, Jim Crow segregation laws, commie witch hunts, presidential assassinations...

... oh yeah, those were *highly moral times*, all right.

Because people with super-sensitive ears never, ever, *ever* heard a disparaging word.

Bullshit! Free speech... our most basic right, and the *foundation* of a free society... isn't there to protect you from hearing what you don't wanna hear. It's cemented into the Constitution to protect the *least*-popular voices.

People get confused about this. Conformity is the *death* of freedom (and a stake to the heart of your marketing).

If what I say makes you uncomfortable, well, too bad. No one's holding a gun to your head and forcing you to read it.

Are you catching on that this stuff drives me nuts? That's why I gotta stop replying to these Puritans. It's not like I'm gonna change their minds about anything.

Second thought: Okay, let's *skip past* my outrage at someone bristling at the way I write. I'm thin-skinned about that subject, I suppose.

But let's take the *second* part of the Puritan's argument -- that, as a marketer, *I should be tailoring my writing to appeal to the greatest number of potential prospects as possible.*

Do you believe that?

This gets back to the very heart of great copywriting. The vast majority of people who create advertising want to appeal to the *wrong* targets. Madison Avenue hot-shots weave incoherent "insider" jokes into their television commercials all the time.

They aren't trying to reach *anybody at all* with *any* sort of sales pitch.

Naw. They're either trying to win an award or make their ad agency peers think they're cool.

And I think that's criminal. They're *wasting the client's money.*

But even smarter marketers make the mistake of not *zeroing in* on their "real" audience.

To go further with the golf story from earlier…

… the golf magazines (before my stuff arrived and shook everything up) used to be crammed with ads that tried like hell to appeal to every golfer who opened the publication...

… without offending any of them.

Every ad essentially said the same thing: "We're the best product out there."

Yawn. It was very much like most of the bad advertising out there -- redundant bragging at best, baffling irrelevancy at worst. Not a good sales pitch in the lot.

So, when my first ad arrived ("*The Amazing Secret Discovered By A One-Legged Golfer...*") I'd have to say the majority of the readership probably recoiled in horror.

But a huge number of them read it anyway.

And *bought*.

So... no, I *don't* try to appeal to the largest audience possible with my copy.

Instead, I zero in on that small segment of the audience out there...

Who Will *Buy!*

What do I care if Tiger Woods turns his nose up at my golf ads? He isn't a potential customer, anyway.

And what do I care if all the buff, limber, cocky young golfers with low handicaps snicker and mock? I ain't after *them*, either.

Instead, I want the guy who is *suspicious* of all the "fat cat" manufacturers out there, who he's pretty sure are ripping him off.

The guy who hasn't been in decent physical shape since high school, who's nursing a pot belly, a bald spot and arthritis in every joint.

The guy, in short, *who's ripe for a sales pitch that talks to him like a real person, with something of real value to offer.*

An ad, at long last, from a regular guy he can *trust*.

And how do we establish that kind of trust?

By writing "real" copy. By connecting on a deeper level than every other shallow ad he's ever seen.

By being the *one thing he reads today* that gets his blood moving.

By, essentially, sitting him down and sharing some really juicy stuff that will change his life.

That's why I call my style of writing: **"Just You And Me Talkin'."**
It's *not* a mistake to ignore that part of your "potential" audience who probably won't buy anyway. Remember -- the Puritans who write in to scold me are NEVER customers. They aren't writing because they want the secrets I offer.

Naw. They're writing because they feel it's their duty to police the world for petty offenses. They are stuffed to bursting with self-righteousness.

Don't fall into the trap of thinking you *have* to appeal to "everyone".

You'll get a lot of people wringing their hands when you run a *truly exciting ad.*

Heck, your own spouse may cringe at what people will say. (This alone has murdered many a great ad campaign.)

Look -- I don't write the way I write because of any other reason than... *that's what works the best.*

If writing lame, mushy copy that never rubbed anyone the wrong way *worked...*

… then I'd *do* that.

But it *doesn't* work.

Last thought: Let's be crystal clear here, however. I do NOT recommend you "swear" or be insulting in your advertising.

If you scour my ads, you will notice the "voice" is not anywhere near as rough as the one I use in my teaching materials. It's *close*...

... but it's softer.

There's a reason for this. In these coaching materials, I want to give you an honest peek into how insiders work and think.

Not all of us are as outrageous or in-your-face as I tend to be. But *most* of us are. At least when we're around other insiders.

And sure -- there have been times when I've purposely reined my personality in around certain clients. I worked with Mormons for years in Utah, for example. Doesn't take much to titillate them. (Halbert once dropped his pants at a seminar in Provo, though, just to wake everyone up. They're *still* talking about that gig.)

But I gotta tell you -- the clients I'm *most* comfortable with (and stay with the longest) are those with a wicked sense of humor, and not a trace of self-righteousness.

And those are the guys who get the *best* from me. Because I'm not always watching my mouth around them.

Ain't the world a tough enough place to get anything done in, without pretending adult life should be like junior high?

See y'all in Hell.

Oh, and about the sales of *"The Entrepreneur's Guide To Getting Your Shit Together"*...

It was a scorching-hot best-seller on Amazon (and still occasionally pops into the Top Ten sections of "starting a business" and "entrepreneurs"), while generating a TON of great publicity all around the globe.

And, I'd have to guess it's done a great job of keeping the Nervous Nellies away, too, which makes my life enormously easier.

Another Bonus Section

Ah, what the hell.

Let's just squeeze a few more advanced and super-edgy tactics into this chapter, while we're on a roll.

I've long since misplaced it, but I once owned perhaps the sneakiest and nastiest "how-to" book I'd ever seen.

It was all about getting revenge. Safely and without consequence.

I shudder to think that book is still in print somewhere. Lord knows we already have enough psychopaths out there nursing grudges.

Most of the tactics involved non-lethal methods that would only wreck someone's marriage or get them fired. You know, planting phony love letters where your opponent's wife would find them, or having disgustingly-raunchy magazine subscriptions sent to your rival's office in his name. That sort of thing.

I've never used any of these dirty tricks...

… but I'm glad I'm *aware* of them.

Because a new wave of this type of terrorism is upon us.

A close friend just recently had some twerp send him threatening emails under a stolen identity. This is where knowledge is power. What could have been a truly confusing and nasty situation was defused, because my friend was hip to this possibility, and had a geek track the real culprit down, following the cyber-trail of the email.

The perpetrator was flabbergasted at being caught. And the guy whose identity had been stolen never knew the drama was even taking place.

So there's a *practical* side to having an otherwise unhealthy interest in dirty tricks.

Which I do. (There once was a show on cable that featured hidden video people took of their roommates and friends and spouses and such... and it can rock your world-view seeing what otherwise normal people do when they think no one else is watching.) (Yes, they *do* look through your stuff... and worse.)

Anyway... one of the least obnoxious dirty tricks I read about in that "revenge" book was to give someone a $500 gift certificate...

... toward a brand-new Cadillac.

If you do this to the right kind of guy, you can ruin his life from that point forward. Because some people will see that Cadillac as "almost" theirs (at least the first $500 of it)...

... and bankrupt themselves trying to come up with the other $62,500.

That's *sneaky*.

It's also a great marketing tactic. In fact, here are 3 variations based on it:

First Variation: *"I've just put $50 in your account here."* I've used this as a headline in ads to house lists. Instead of discounting the product by $50, or half off, or whatever...

… I just convince the client to open a special account for current customers.

And into this account, put a $50 (or whatever) credit. Which can *only* be used for products the client sells. It's also perfectly legitimate to make the "money" good only for the product you're trying to sell at the time.

Put a time limit on it. The "money" is only in the account for the next 11 days, say. Then, it's gone. If you act fast, you get $50 off your order.

And if you dawdle... *you lose it.*

Now, that's an All Star interest-getting tactic. It's also a prime example of the "take-away" angle that all great salesmen use.

Here's another version...

Second Variation: *"I have one set aside here in my office, with your name on it."* If you can, put the prospect's actual name on the box or the product.

It's earmarked for ya, Bucko. Got your name on it. Sitting here. Waiting.

But there is such a limited quantity that, if you don't call in and claim it (and pay for it) within, say, 11 days, well, we'll have to take your name *off* it...

… and give it to the *next guy* down the list.

Imagine a friend calling you and saying he's just put a steak on the barbeque for you... and it's yours, everybody there knows it's yours... but there are 15 other people at the party and not enough meat to go around.

So, if you aren't there in 11 minutes, he'll be forced to give your nice, juicy, succulent, mouth-watering steak to *someone else.* That's dirty pool.

And *great* marketing.

Third Variation: *"There's just one small catch to this offer..."*

I give the great Jay Abraham credit for this one. At one time, he never let a letter leave his office without a paragraph near the end starting out with this exact copy. Sometimes, when he was feeling frisky, he would use the word "caveat" instead of "catch". Didn't matter.

What he was doing was giving a small, reasonable, and non-onerous "condition" to the offer. Which served to make it all the more *believable.*

See, when non-world-class marketers create an offer, they often go *too far.* They remove all risk, make the price as low as they can, and guarantee everything under the sun.

Which, when read by a skeptical prospect, can sound **"too good to be true"**.

Jay's genius was in taking the promise *down* a notch. So it, very suddenly, *wasn't* too good to be true.

His "catch" or "caveat" was usually a version of the take-away. "There's just one small catch to this offer. It's a small matter, and very reasonable. But it may affect your decision. You see, this deal is *not for everyone.* If you are afraid to..."

And then he would list all the reasons many people would, logically, not be "right" for the offer. Scaredy-cats, cheap bastards, cynics, and looky-loos, for example. (Though Jay would always use much fancier language.) (Such a silver tongue he has. He's the Shakespeare of advertising.)

It's still the classic "take-away". Very effective at riveting the reader's attention.

"Hey," you want him to say to himself. "If I don't get on this, like, right friggin' now, *he's gonna give it to someone else!"*

Can't have that, can we.

And that, my friend, is an entire short course in effective direct response psychological theater, in three short sections.

Chapter Nine:

Guts And Gurus

Why your cultivated, well-thought-out notions are often dead wrong, while your knee-jerk instincts turn out correct... and how to turn your other hidden psychic powers into ridiculously-massive success...

I whacked myself in the testicles the other evening with a tennis racquet.

Hard as I could, full-out. *Wham!*

God, that hurts.

Sure, go ahead and laugh. My opponent nearly bust a gut howling at me.

He had just returned my serve with a cruelly high lob shot that hovered up in the vapor lights for, oh, maybe twenty or thirty minutes before falling back toward my end of the court.

I had time to check my watch, tie my shoes, and develop a new thesis on quantum physics while waiting for the ball to drop.

If you've ever played the game, you know exactly what happened next. *I just had too much time to dwell on my options.*

If he had fired a low shot back at me, I would have reacted without thinking, letting my instincts and talent (I use the word loosely here) do their thang. And leave my brain out of it.

But no. While that ball lazily drifted in the early spring sky above me, my gray matter just had to muscle my instincts aside and screw everything up.

Suddenly I was considering and rejecting and reconsidering from new angles a *dozen* different return shots -- overhead blast to the far corner, sneaky drop shot just over the net, forehand right back at his chin, spinning head kick resolving into a *pas de deux* from Swan Lake, four-iron into the lake...

My mind was all over the place, like a terrier stumbling on a herd of wild rabbits that suddenly run off in every direction.

So, by the time the ball decided to return to earth, I was *overwhelmed with choices.* Couldn't make up my mind.

At the last possible second, I decided, *yeah, I'll drill a shot deep, blast it like a howitzer canon...*

And then thought *mmm, howitzer canon.* Funny name. What does a howitzer *look* like, anyway? And hey, look, there's a flock of geese chugging our way...

Oops. Ball inches from my face. Must... swing... hard... *now!*

Result: Flail futilely, dump ball into net, crush family jewels, fall to knees in stunned disbelief.

Marvel at the ability of nerve centers to register and share pain with every other part of the body so quickly.

And, finally... *endure ill-natured mockery from opponent.* (Must remember to get him back, soon.)

I'm only glad there were no cameras running. I would have been the heavy-rotation Play o' the Day on ESPN.

And yet, there was a *good thing* to come of this debacle.

Yep. **There's a marketing lesson here for all of us.**

I call it the "**Guts and Gurus**" lecture.
Here's how it goes: There's a book out titled "The Paradox of Choice".

The author takes a disciplined, scientific look at how humans process **choice**.

And what he discovered fits nicely with what most "classic" salesmen already know: That, while we *think* we want as many options as possible…

… in truth, unlimited choices can cause our little heads to explode.

There are two basic styles of handling too much choice:

(1) Running every option through an internal "happiness" meter, and trying to guess what will please us the most (evidently most people *suck* at gauging future happiness)… and…

(2) Settling on something that is "good enough".

I've always been a "good enough" kinda guy. Whether it was building sand castles as a kid, or putting together song-lists for fledgling bands just before the gig, or deciding when an ad was "ready" for showtime…

… I always said "*it's a go*" long before any of the perfectionists around me were anywhere near their own comfort zone.

This often horrified them, of course.

But then, perfectionists seldom feel "ready" to even *begin* any project, let alone finish it. With humans being such a decidedly imperfect lot, perfectionists are sort of screwed right out of the box.

Even so, not all "good enough" types are the best man for the job.

We all have this internal "satisfaction alarm". When it goes off, we're happy with what we've done, or what we've decided on. Some people are satisfied with garbage. You want to avoid them.

Others, like me, have developed a decent "gut" sense about what truly is good enough.

Often, this is through **experience**.

My first sand castle, first gig, and first ad were occasions for stomach-wrenching anxiety and endless doubt. Fortunately, by the time that anxiety bubbled up to the surface, it was just too late to turn back.

So I was rewarded with an extremely valuable experience. Good, bad, it didn't matter in the long run. I had *input*. **I had something to measure future efforts against.**

I suspect I also have a high tolerance for humiliation and pain. How else could I have survived those disastrous early attempts to play music in front of crowds of kids my own age? Or allowed some of those lame rookie ads to be seen by a client?

Heck, that first huge sand castle nearly buried us all alive. (Not understanding the peculiar architectural guidelines necessary for building with beach sand, I'd gone for a dungeon below the moat. Bad idea, especially at high tide.)

Anyway… my gut now groans in horror or gurgles with bliss before my brain can even finish synthesizing incoming data.

As someone describes an idea or project to me, I get a *feeling* about it, based on my experience. And how my gut *processes* that feeling affects my judgment.

I don't always go with my gut, of course.

Often, it twists up in revulsion at the first glimpse of a difficult job. Work? Ugh.

My gut is very, very lazy.

Or, it may start dancing and saying "yes, yes, *yes*" to a proposal because of some specific part of the promised reward. Money? Fame? Yeah, baby.

My gut is also very, very *greedy*.

These initial reactions are not always the right ones to follow. So I stay mum, and wait for my brain to put in its two cents of **reason and logic**.

If Mr. Brainiac agrees with Mr. Gut, we're in business. If they quarrel, I've got a choice to make.

Now, over the long course of my career, my gut has been right an astonishing percentage of the time.

My brain has a decent enough average… but when it's gut vs. gray matter, *I most often follow the feeling over the reasoning.*

Again, this is based on my *experience*, over a very long time period. Other guys -- who are equally good at what they do -- don't trust their gut instincts so much, and prefer brain power.

You gotta work it out for yourself, over time. Pay attention. Keep score.

Because one or the other may have mitigating factors that affect your ability to *make a good decision.*

Which is the foundation of a successful career in business. (Or anything else.)

The mitigating factors can be crucial.

For example: Some folks who grew up in the Depression developed an *aversion to risk* -- so their gut recoils whenever risk is involved, no matter how reasonable the actual gamble is. (My folks were like this. They just wanted a nice, quiet life after the double whammy of the Depression and World War II.)

Some unfortunate men are saddled with a cockeyed belief system that won't allow them to, for example, work with women. (My Significant Other comes up against this kind of miscreant thinking all the time in her job, since she works with construction contractors. They refuse to recognize her abilities, and will even *sabotage their own success* to keep her from being "right".)

(The other side to this, of course, is that the ones who admit she's got what it takes are *rewarded* by having a powerful ally in their corner.)

So, once again, you must respect Socrates' number one rule: **Know thyself.**

If you've got demons in your gut or head, get rid of them…

… or learn how to recognize when they're *skewing the equation.*

And take your quirks into account. You can work around anything, *once you know what you're dealing with.*

It took me forever to know my own thinking system. These days, I always listen to my gut first -- by asking "**How do I *feel* about this?**"

I long ago gave myself absolute permission to say "no" to any proposal... and walk away, without even needing to give a good reason why... whenever my gut insisted.

When something doesn't "feel right", back off. Give your brain room to mull it over. This is tough to do when you're a teenager, and what the crowd thinks matters to you.

But you're all grown up now, aren't you? It's time to stop making decisions based on how you processed input when you were sixteen.

The only time I pause is when my head and feelings don't agree.

Occasionally, I'll *think* myself back into the idea -- but only if there is a blisteringly good argument for doing so. Most of the time, I find my gut is pretty right on.

And this brings me to the "guru" part of the marketing lesson.

You see, even though I earned the respect of my colleagues years and years ago...

... I never felt qualified to *give* advice to anyone else until I worked out this battle between my head and my feelings.

Once I did that, my advice became potent. I found I could look at *any* copy, ad, letter, or project proposal...

... and almost instantly see and *feel* the mistakes, the brilliance, the pitfalls, the potential, and the clearest path to success.

It's not because I'm smarter than anyone else.

Naw… it's simply because I've logged so much time in the front-line trenches of advertising that I've seen most situations run their course. I've logged years and years of working through problems… learning from mistakes… breaking the code on difficult projects…

… and all the insight that comes from surviving a long career at or near the top of the pile.

I can now *trust* the symbiotic interaction between my gut and my head.

Plus, I started out when *analog* still ruled the roost… so I can put the domination of digital into perspective. So to speak.

My first ads were pounded out on a beat-up typewriter, back in the days of cold type, Xacto blades and tee squares. So I have no illusion that this gigabyte brute of a computer I'm writing on now has anything to do with writing, other than recording what I put into it.

I straddle the Old and New worlds of advertising… **and this perspective has given me a perch from which I can accurately pass judgment on other people's work.**

So I threw my hat into the "guru" ring. It's a crowded ring, as you already know.

And most of the other "experts" in it pretty much embarrass those of us who know what we're doing. I honestly felt I *had* to start sharing this stuff, just to finally bring some ground-level veteran experience into the mix.

Does that sound arrogant?

I'm sorry. Those who know me expect a little brashness now and again… but they also know I'll watch your back, if we ever do business together, while delivering the goods.

And that brings us to the segue that will tie all this blathering together for you.

The point I'm about to make has *enormous* impact for you and your business, no matter what market you're in.

<u>First,</u> you must learn to gauge your gut against your brain.

Over the long term, this is merely a matter of keeping track, keeping score.

Over the *short* term, it will pay off enormously to give very close attention to the *interaction* of your consideration processes. So you can learn how your own system works.

Your Inner Salesman is in there somewhere, wandering around aimlessly right now. You want him, awake and slathering for the sale, **near the intersection of your feelings and your rational mind.** This will give your sales pitch *passion* as well as *logic*.

And that is how *magic* happens in crafting killer sales messages for ads, email, and webpages.

<u>Second</u>… once you prove to yourself you can trust your consideration of any idea (and it doesn't matter if you are gut-heavy or brain-heavy)… you can finally step forward with complete confidence and announce to your market…

**"I'm the one who can take you
where you want to go."**

This kind of confidence, when supported by the chops to back it up, will take you to the top.

If there is a lack of leadership in your market, you can assume the guru position.

Or, just become the *best option* out of many, no matter how expensive you are.

In the car market, for example, BMW has near-absolute respect. When they tout themselves as the best (and charge appropriate prices), they get *no direct argument* from the likes of Ford or Chevy. When a General Motors company puffs up its chest and brags, it rings hollow -- they've got a long history of inferior product that turns their bluster into mush.

That's why I always urge clients to err on the side of *quality*.

Put your heart and all your resources into your product, and make it the *best damn thing available.* That way, you can go balls to the wall with your advertising, without blushing or feeling like a pretender.

And when that happens… **people will <u>flock</u> to you.**

Here's why: As I said, humans are *horrible* predictors of happiness. They don't know what they want. They often *hate* what they thought they wanted when they get it. (This is what generates buyer's remorse.)

So how do people eventually handle this culture of too much choice? Just to stay sane, most develop variations of **brand loyalty**.

This is the one and *only* time you will ever hear me talk about branding. Most folks misunderstand the concept -- they think they have to design a cool logo, write a spiffy slogan, and "get their image polished". You know, like Coke.

That's not the kind of branding I'm talking about. Nope.

What I'm talking about… is the reason people stick with a brand: **Trust**.

Let's say you're a movie nut. Especially the old films from the "classic" era of Hollywood in the thirties and forties.

Up until recently, choice wasn't an issue. Every blue moon, a golden oldie would show on late night television, or pop up at the local art movie house. You took what you could get.

But suddenly, with joints like Netflix, Amazon, and 70 different movie channels on cable, a fan can get lethally overwhelmed. You no longer have to wait for a movie to appear. You can find it streaming online in minutes … or download it in seconds. And that includes almost every movie ever made.

It's the same now with a lot of things. Information. Books. Career choices. Travel options. There aren't any decent *limits* anymore. You can jet over to Europe roundtrip for $130. Become a doctor, detective or ditch digger, and get excellent tutoring the entire way. Find books that have been out of print for centuries. Get *any* morsel of information you desire, whenever you want it.

To someone without choice, all that sounds just dandy.

But to anyone faced with having to make a decision… it can be *paralyzing*.

So what do you do?

To feed my movie jones, I learned to trust Turner Classic Movies. Sure, I could find any movie I want on my own, and watch it anytime I want. But that would require some serious decision-making… and how do I know I'll like what I ordered when it arrives? (Back in the day, I was notorious for renting six videos on Thursday and returning them all on Tuesday unwatched.)

So I let TCM decide *for* **me.** Over the years, they've been a consistent source of quality choices. They pick movies with care and thought, and often have mini-festivals around a theme, actor or studio. We are simpatico.

As devoted as I am to film, they're *more* so. It makes my life easier. At least once a week, I can count on TCM to run a flick that feeds my soul.

On the other hand, the *other* "old movie" channel on cable, American Movie Classics, has let me down so painfully -- by interrupting the flow of each flick with bad commercials -- that I won't watch it even if a rare treat is playing.

They actually insist that focus groups told them people *wanted* commercials.

They're like the disc jockey who talks over the music -- just *clueless* about their core audience. I can't trust them not to befoul the mood.

I'll bet the market you inhabit is just as crowded as the movie market, or any other major market you can name. In most cases, people can choose to deal with you, or any of a large mob of *other* guys.

You're just one of many options.

Therefore… *be* **that marketer people can** *trust*. If you've got the chops, uncork the confidence. Take a stand, and don't be shy about advertising yourself as a filter to help people decide.

Brand yourself as a "go-to guy" by going the extra mile in your production, your guarantees, your customer service, and your whole attitude.

Don't just say it. Do it.

People are walking around in a daze, confused and bamboozled by too much incoming data, and *too many damn choices*. If they could only find someone, or some company, they could trust to make decisions *for* them, they will happily follow.

Result: You build a solid customer base *eager* to hear from you... quick to forgive your occasional lapse or mistake... and ready to *give you money* whenever you hit their sweet spot.

That's what real branding is all about. It's a jungle out there. And you gotta be the grizzled, veteran guide who's seen it all, knows the secrets, and has a tender spot for helping people... even when you're young.

You have to earn trust, of course. But it isn't hard, when you focus on quality.

Be that guy.

Big Side Benefit: The most common question I get asked is "How much should I charge for my services or product?"

And the answer is: Simply become that guy your customer can trust to bust through all the agonizing choice out there, *and give him what he wants.*

Especially if he needs help deciding what it is he really *does* want.

Do that, and satisfy him completely and utterly... and guess what.

You can charge anything you want.

Quick bonus story about learning to gauge my own gut: My first assignment with Gary Halbert was nearly my *last*. I liked the guy, and even did a little jockeying after meeting him to angle my way into a job at his office on Sunset Blvd.

But the first gig was a *nightmare* waiting to happen.

You see, Gary's mind works in peculiar ways. He can write a world-class ad using a pencil stub and a bar napkin in a crowded airport -- somehow, he's able to concentrate like a sculptor even in the midst of total pandemonium.

I don't work that way.

I have my own rituals and habits and requirements for writing well. Quiet and uninterrupted periods of concentration are absolutely necessary. And I never considered this unreasonable until I met Gary.

For my first job, he led me into an empty office. Just a lonely metal desk and plastic chair. He tossed me a legal pad, a pen, and a faded copy of an old letter he'd written…

… and told me to craft a brilliant winner for a new client, using the opening tactic in that old letter.

Then he left and shut the door.

I looked at the yellow paper and the pen lying there, and despaired.

I write by *typing* -- my mind flows through my fingers. With a gun to my head, I can write using a pen, but my handwriting is awful, and my fingers cramp easily. I can't think *slow* enough for handwriting. I need to whiz along, ripping at the keyboard.

That's how I'd written all my ads that had caught Halbert's eye in the first place.

Still, this was the hand I was dealt. I sat at the desk, put my mind into the task, and started scribbling away…

… and, two minutes later, Gary waltzed in again and told me we were taking a ride.

I got up, followed him into the parking lot, jumped in the Mustang he was leasing… and played road dog while driving him around Hollywood for the next three hours, talking about advertising and clients and money and sex. (He liked to talk about sex.)

I learned to treasure these little road trips. I learned a lot, and got to experience the process he went through coming up with grand schemes and plans and ideas and even copy.

However, this *first* trip was a little discombobulating. We finally returned to the office, and I went back to my cold desk, sat down, wrote a sentence or two…

… and then Gary burst in again.

And asked if I'd finished the ad yet.

I'd just spent the entire afternoon with him. He *knew* where I was. I'd had all of ten minutes to work so far…

… and he wanted the ad?

He wasn't joking, either. It wasn't that *he* could have come up with copy in that short of time, and was disappointed that I hadn't. That wasn't it at all.

Nope. Gary just didn't always operate in the same time/space continuum everyone else does. It's not his job to keep track of your efforts. **He just wants results.** And wants you to not be such a wimp about getting them.

Now, at this point my gut kicked in. I knew I would never get any good writing done in that office. Wasn't gonna happen.

I needed to take this project back to my home office, where I had control over the environment. I could work late, in my sweats, take naps when necessary to let copy gel, not be disturbed, and mind-meld with my trusted keyboard.

I knew, in my gut, I *needed* to go home to work.

I also knew I was risking a lot by insisting on doing so. Gary was suspicious when I told him what I intended to do the next day. I could sense he figured I would just goof off at home.

He had hired me -- at a good wage -- to write for him, and he wanted me in the office *doing* that. Not lollygagging or goldbricking back at my crib.

My gamble: I had to write such a *killer* pitch that he would forget what I needed to do to get it done.

Took me three days. Each day brought me closer to the burning core of Gary's outrage…

… but I broke the code on the project, and wrote a piece that mailed for two years and earned *millions*.

The first few paragraphs were all Gary -- it was a typical penny letter. (A penny was glued to the top of the page in lieu of a headline, and the copy began: "As you can see, I have attached a shiny new penny to the top of this page. Why have I done this? Simple – what I have to share with you involves money (*lots* of money)… and I thought using a penny as an "eye catcher" was a great way to get into the story. Here's what's up…")

But after explaining why there was a penny attached, it was all me. I buried myself in research, mapped out a dozen special reports, and nailed the passionate sweet spot of the intended audience.

I could have *never* done that job with a pen and legal pad. My mind races too fast, and I would have lost half the ideas before getting them written down. I needed to stay up until dawn, and not worry about being on the sixth floor of a strange office building. I needed snacks, comfort, familiar furniture, everything that made concentration easy.

But most of all…

… I needed a gut instinct that *overcame* the fear of risk in my brain.

Even a year earlier, I wouldn't have had the nerve to stay home to write. But at that point, with the extra experience I had (and the extra confidence), I sized up the situation, and *insisted* on doing what I thought best without hesitation.

Without hesitation. *With* confidence.

Even so, there was never any guarantee that what I wrote would be a winner. You can't expect guarantees in this biz. You can only put all the odds in your favor…

… and then *go for it.*

Even Roger Clemens loses a game now and again. But you still want him on the mound during crunch time.

The Pro Copywriter's Bag O' Tricks

An alert fan wrote in with a *very* interesting question recently. I've been asked this same thing a lot, and I suppose it's high time to share what I've told people privately.

Here's the question, in a nutshell: "What do I do to expand my vocabulary of expressive ('power') words… so I can stop being such a *boring* writer?"

The answer is both simple, and convoluted.

Different copywriters have taken different paths to get to the same place -- a palpable *clarity of writing* that gets the pitch across in a way that demands the reader's full attention.

It's serious salesmanship, combined with world-class story-telling.

But the foundation is always the **love of language.** An appreciation for the wicked turn of a phrase. A thrill when the perfect power word fuels a thought directly into your heart. The pure bliss of penning a sentence that sings…

… and also advances the sales pitch.

Top copywriters are a mongrel lot. Some of us were born with an ear for language…

… and others had to *earn* it. (Some manage to get by with a tin ear, but that's a hard way to make a living as a writer.)

In my case, it was a little of both. There weren't a lot of books in the house I grew up in… but there were enough to get me *started.* Big damn encyclopedia, good dictionary, a raft of textbooks, and a healthy shelf of hard-cover novels. We were working class, and while curiosity was rampant, intellectual skills were less valued than physical skills.

More or less, at least. While my father rejoiced in teaching me how to hammer, nail, saw, and not bail out on an inside fast ball...

... he also never objected to my pleas for yet another trip to the book store.

By the end of high school, most of the books in the house had been hauled in by me. I still have boxes crammed full of the first used paperbacks I ever bought. The written word has always been precious.

So my first -- and most urgent -- piece of advice, if you want to hone your "ear" for language, **is to *read better stuff*.**

Today's best selling novels *suck*, as far as writing craft. Make the effort to immerse yourself in *expert* writing.

Get Jack Kerouac's "On The Road" and "Dharma Bums". Read Hunter Thompson's earlier stuff (while he was still sane: "Hell's Angels", "Fear and Loathing in Las Vegas"). Kurt Vonnegut. Henry Miller's "Tropic of Cancer" and "Tropic of Capricorn." Thomas Pynchon's "Gravity's Rainbow", if you're up for a challenge. Robert Stone's "Dogs of War."

Pay attention (if you buy these on Amazon) to the suggestions of other titles people also bought. There is an entire *world* of breathtakingly good reads that has been half buried in our Attention Deficit culture.

Notice, too, that these are all *American* writers -- stay inside your culture.

Get hip to the way Americans talk now, and how we spoke in previous generations. (Just the evolution of the word "cool" will take you across the culture wars of the last hundred years.)

Even better, find collections of the respected and notorious **newspaper columnists** we've been blessed with. Herb Caen was THE best -- wrote for the San Francisco Chronicle for most of the last half of the twentieth century, and perfected the "three-dot thought" style that had been introduced in the thirties.

VERY expressive writer. Cared deeply about language and often nailed the *exact* right phrase (including the double and triple entendre, layer upon layer of meaning and reference, *like a complete story in six words*).

There are several books out there about Herb, but try to find the collections of his actual writing. They're out there. Get transcripts of Walter Cronkite's broadcasts, if possible. He's writing a column nationally these days, but he's not as facile as he used to be.

The "old" guys all knew how to turn a phrase. They were just **filthy-good wordsmiths** -- proving with every column that the pen was mightier than the sword. Reading a few pages of Red Smith, the notorious sports writer, will change your life. Mark Twain, one of the best. H.L. Mencken is a must.

Also the "classic" noir writers: Raymond Chandler, Dashiell Hammett, and all those other hard-boiled authors from the 20s, 30s, and 40s who knew how to craft a page-turner.

If any of these names bring up blanks in your memory files, blame your stripped-down education, get over it… and then get *with* it.

It's never too late to start.

Civilization is impossible without language. Most people can sleep-walk their way through life with a vocabulary like a chimp's…

… but to *lead*, to *persuade*, and to *succeed* requires a complete and obsessive knowledge of the language you're working with.

You know I love slang, and often intentionally use bad grammar. That's because I aim to *communicate…* not please an English teacher.

Great salesmanship is communication at the *far edges of language*. You must learn to talk a pretty game outside the restrictions of rules.

Insider tip: Get the lyric sheets for the more erudite bands. Mick Jagger really knows how to cram amazing imagery into a few lines. John Lennon was also a master at it. Tom Waits. Bob Dylan (at least the early stuff).

Get the lyric sheets for Ry Cooder's albums (it's not all his original stuff, but he has a knack for picking cool songs to cover). Don't ignore the very old country tunes -- just *reading* Hank Williams' song titles can give you a thrill. Google your way to them.

The key is to develop a feel for the integral beauty of a metaphor. Most people use boring metaphors, or the same pet phrases over and over. Great writers are *never* predictable, and are careful not to overuse anything.

I *never*, for example, want to see the same verb or noun twice in a paragraph.

Sometimes you have to work for hours to find a way around repetition.

It's like a puzzle, or a maze -- you have to backtrack, erase your steps, start over, try again, maneuver this way and that, looking for the perfect path through the thought in your head.

Lazy or rookie writers are usually so astonished they actually put a thought down on paper, that they are too exhausted to finesse it by exploring *other* verbs or power words.

The example I use most often: Just take a regular sentence, and see how it can be tweaked into a storyline. *He walked down the street. He glided over the sidewalk in a trance. He bolted headlong through the crowd, toppling little old ladies and upsetting tables of wine and cheese.*

Or:

Her perfume was strong. She smelled like a 13 year-old who'd just shoplifted half of Macy's cosmetics department. She reeked like a truckload of Giorgio that jackknifed on the Interstate. Et cetera.

What a good writer does is play with word combinations… especially the unexpected or "perfect" word or phrase. Strunk and White explore this in "**Elements of Style**", also required reading.

Often, to keep the flow going, your best choice will end up being the simpler "He walked down the street."

But you don't want to *accept* that without checking out other options.

Great copy is like great songwriting. Think of how the lyricist must twist and reach to find words that rhyme, yet still fit the thought...

… and also elicit groans of bliss from attentive listeners, when he hits a coy phrase. Jagger: "*Gold coast slave ship bound for cotton fields... sold in a market down in New Orleans... scarred old slaver knows he's doing all right... hear him whip the women, just around midnight.*"

Now, you may cringe at the associations and cruelty of the image, but the pure poetry of the *delivery* is undeniable. The words sing.

It's a horror story, to a great beat.

These are two- and three- and four-word phrases slammed together in a story, minus any hemming and hawing.

Not a single word can be removed without changing the meaning of the line or making it incoherent. This is totally stripped-down, lean and mean, *fire-breathing* writing.

And that, my friend, is your bonus copywriting lesson for today.

Chapter Ten:

Pissing Off Women

And paying the price for it, one long day at a time...

Hey, let's see if we can't piss somebody off this month. I feel like living on thin ice.

How about... *women?*

Okay. Let's do it.

Here goes: Doc (long-time client and friend) calls me yesterday in a near-panic.

Says, "I am more confused than ever! I don't see how *anybody* can sell *anything* to *women* at all. All they want is to do is wander around in an emotional fog, *feeling* things. It's scary!"

Ah, Doc, I reply soothingly, it ain't that bad. Go ask your wife...

"No way! She's one of 'em! Probably downstairs in the television room this very minute, sharing *feelings* with Oprah and her evil cabal..."

Eventually he calmed down, and I didn't have to dial 911. He was even laughing about it -- a little -- by the time we hung up. Shaken, but not so frightened anymore.

What had caused this reaction?

Simple.

Doc is a rabid marketer with a brilliant mind, always sniffing around new opportunities for his direct marketing business. *Very* successful in several ventures into male-dominated markets (sports stuff)...

... and very eager to tap into the larger female markets out there. Bombed with his first weight-loss product, but knew the numbers were there for other marketers, and was frustrated that he couldn't seem to "crack the code" on selling to women.

So I gave him a homework assignment.

Told him to hustle down to the local magazine rack and pick up every major women's magazine there: Oprah (you can't miss it -- she's *always* on the cover), Cosmo, Redbook, Mademoiselle, Self, Glamour, Vogue... geez, there's a lot of 'em... Marie Claire, Us, Martha Stewart Living...

"Then what?" he wants to know.

Read 'em. Every one.

Pay close attention to how the stories are "sold" with cover blurbs (written by some of the best writers in the biz, by the way)... and what the stories focus on.

More importantly, pay very close attention to the *ads*. What hot buttons they aim for, how they craft their sales pitch, price points... and, especially, which ads are running over and over again.

That required a quick trip to the library, to thumb through back issues.

Now, for the male readers of this book: Is there any question in your mind *why* I had Doc do this homework?

Good. It should be obvious.

And guess what? Unless you have an extra "X" chromosome yourself, you need to do the *same* assignment. Right away.

Because most men simply do not understand women. Yes, even big successful studs like you. Almost no real clue at all. (Female readers here will be nodding in agreement. Men can be SO dense.)

Doc, for example, had been married to a perfectly wonderful woman for 15 years (and had a pretty impressive bachelorhood before that). Seemed to be able to communicate with women well enough. Just *assumed* he "understood" them.

Clueless.

And you desperately need to GET a clue, just like Doc.

Why? Well, for starters, women control 90% of the wealth in this country.

The hubby may have written the check, but *she* most likely chose the house. The furniture. The car. The family summer vacation to Disney World.

Even his ties and underwear.

But there's more to it than that.

Learning how to understand women is the first step toward learning how to *sell* to them effectively.

It will be, for most men, one of the hardest things you ever do.

Also, one of the most *rewarding*.

Your personal life will get better overnight (whether you're married, single, or considering the priesthood). And, financially, your business bank account will swell to obscene proportions.

If you learn to sell to women, you will never want for anything the rest of your days.

Women-primary markets dominate direct sales (QVC, diets, "make your kid a genius" products), retail (check out your local mall), food (besides big damn hamburgers and beer, what other food group is being sold to men?), even cars and politics (SUV-driving soccer moms can swing any election).

And yet most marketers are guys.

Not the kind of guys who were considered hotties in high school, either. Most of the entrepreneurs I know can weave a pretty sad tale of woe about their social lives (at least up to the point they started making some bucks).

Not too many student body prez/quarterback/homecoming king/honor roll/most- likely-to-succeeds among us.

Hey, if you have trouble getting a date because you can't figure out what women want, you're gonna run into some very nasty obstacles trying to sell the ladies *anything at all.*

Thus, the homework assignment.

And what did we learn, Doc?

"Feelings, just like I thought! Oceans of feelings! Good grief, they're like *alien creatures from another planet!* But… but at least I'm starting to get a handle on it now… it doesn't seem too scary anymore… *"*

Now, I'm not gonna present myself as some kind of know-it-all regarding the ladies. I learned what I know through grueling years of trial, error (mostly error)...

... and *unfair inside help.*

Through my pal Gary Halbert (himself an admitted ovary-challenged human), I met a shrink who shared a couple of **critical classified secrets** that were nothing short of a complete *revelation* in the gender wars.

After that, I had a toe-hold in the female psyche and could start navigating that wild world with a modicum of confidence.

I love women, I really do. I have always sought out close women friends, and I *never* reject their point of view casually. No matter how insane and irrational it might seem at first. (It's the same process I do with guys, who are just as insane and irrational most of the time.)

More importantly, I've championed female copywriters my entire career, pushing for clients to hire them, and pushing for more women to consider the gig.

Freelancing, in particular, is an awesome gig for women – once you reach the professional level with your ability to write sales messages *no one can tell what gender you are.*

No glass ceiling.

The ad world needs more female writers and entrepreneurs. The guys tend to get a little fusty with no feminine input.

Still, it took me *years* to learn how to consistently craft compelling sales pitches to the ladies.

Most clueless guys attempt to sell to women as though they were "men with breasts".

In other words, men assume the thought process going on *her* head is similar to the one going on in *his*. Or should be.

And it *isn't*. Not even close. If you could take a woman's thought process and transplant it into a typical man's brain, his head would explode. (And vice versa.)

The big difference... is, yes, *emotions*. Feelings, as Doc said.

If it helps to think about this stuff in simplistic terms: Women *feel*. Men *think*.

Yes, that kind of statement can get you into trouble in civilian circles, where folks don't have to craft ads that actually bring in results.

Copywriters have no such luxury. We have to exist in the real world, where politically correct attitudes can murder a campaign in a hurry.

This fundamental difference in thinking is why I don't even need to know the gender of the rookie writers I critique ads for. Cuz it becomes so obvious in the first paragraph:

Men tend to overdo the *features* of any product -- they want to bowl you over with the force of size, performance statistics, heft and expense.

In other words, the "quantity" of the thing.

Women, though, get lost in the *benefits*.

They go off on tangents about how it *feels* to experience the thing -- how the softness soothes, how the delicacy satisfies deep needs. The "quality" of it.

Now, all copywriters learn early on that you must attach benefits to features for effective selling.

But rookie lady writers often forget to mention any features at all. (The boys forget to attach clear benefits.)

Sometimes, you can't figure out what the heck the product actually *is*.

The shrink explained much about how women think... and perhaps I'll share more of the juicier details with you in a future tome.

It's pretty damn interesting, I gotta say. (Maybe I'll call it a "short-cut sex ed class for clueless guys".)

But what he told me about *emotions* is more relevant here (for *both* men and women entrepreneurs). It has stuck with me all these years, and I use the knowledge often when I know there are women in the audience I'm pitching.

You see, there have been many studies concerning how men and women *translate emotions in their brains*.

I don't have the exact figures handy... but researchers found that men can identify only a *handful* of emotional states (and they often incorrectly classify "being hungry" or "being sleepy" as emotions) (or "being really, *really* horny, man").

Let's say most men have nine operational emotions. Which is being generous.

Women, however, have something like *200 operational emotions*.

Feeling "cherished" carries very much different emotional weight than feeling "loved", or "adored", or even "worshipped".

And they can explain these states in *detail*. Just mapping out the landscape of "envy" versus "jealousy" could take a lifetime.

Women also *multi-task* feelings with ease – a woman with low self-esteem can coexist quite happily with the sense she is a reincarnated princesses worthy of ruling the world. Or, in another case, high self-esteem can sit right next to feelings of utter worthlessness.

And they are capable of hating your guts, wanting to have your baby, mentally listing 14 super-detailed ways you should change immediately, and wishing you'd just step up and take control of the damn situation without being a jerk about it...

... all in the same nano-second that you're saying "Huh?" (They're also wondering what's good to eat in the fridge, and how the couch would look better over *there*.)

Men tend to be narrowly focused on single things. Which may explain their love/hate relationship with good grooming habits.

Trust me on this. Right now, if you're an average Joe, you have *no frigging clue what women want.*

So get hip. Read a couple of romance novels. (*That* will open your eyes. Especially when you consider that many upper-class, upper-*income* women devour these things to the tune of three or four a *week*. They are shoveling romance into the bottomless pit-of-yearning in their hearts.)

Pay close attention to ads that run month after month, year after year, in the women's magazines. HOW are they pushing female buttons?

Open your mind to possibilities the omnipresent horoscopes offer. (Just remember that until the FTC cracked down recently, psychic hotlines dominated late-night advertising... to the tune of *billions* of dollars in income. Primarily from women.)

And copy out, in longhand, the blurbs on the magazine covers. **It's one of the best ongoing educations on *power writing* you'll ever get.**

Plus... you know those words and phrases have already been "field tested" on the ladies. You'll see certain verbs and word-clusters appear again and again. The word "sex" is there a lot, for example.

But don't be shallow -- pay attention to how the writers quickly *tie* the word "sex" to an unrelated subject. (And don't pout when you discover -- as you will -- that the actual articles have little or nothing to do with sex as men understand it.)

Make this exercise an essential part of your continuing education and research into world-class marketing.

And please -- *don't be afraid, guys.* The opposite sex is still the same sweet, loveable, mysterious, nurturing and exciting half of the species they always were.

You're just going to lift the veil on the "mysterious" part a little, and educate yourself on the details as they pertain to marketing.

The girls won't hurt you.

Unless you piss them off, of course.

Tales From The Vice Squad

Do you think I honestly angered any of the many women readers with the above rant?

I don't. You know why?

Because most of the women I know in this business have something a surprising number of the guys do not: **A sense of humor**.

And a good sense of "if it's right, it's right, so don't have a fit about it."

That, of course, is *not* the case outside of the business world.

And it's something I truly love about direct response advertising: All cries of unfair "good old boy" advantages, glass ceilings, and gender victim-hood are completely irrelevant.

As I said, no one can *see* you when you write a letter or ad. Prospects don't know what color, sex, nationality or age you are, unless you choose to tell them.

Nope. You must *earn* the sale by providing credibility on the strength of your mojo, your expertise, and your ability to craft a convincing sales pitch.

Written ads, websites and video-sales-letters are the most "blind" kind of salesmanship there is. You could be a trans-sexual, trans-species Siamese twin whose visage frightens little kids on the street. Doesn't matter.

In direct response, *it's what you can deliver in terms of useable information and useful product that counts.*

Pure equality in action.

I've even taught special seminars directed *only* at women -- revealing the amazing opportunities for independence and fabulous incomes and compete control over your future inherent in forming your own direct response business.

You want better child care, flexible hours, a workplace free of harassment? Then *create* one, with your own business. No one's stopping you.

There are no glass ceilings in the entrepreneur biz – especially online.

Women business owners have little patience with anyone who complains about "the boys playing too rough". They just play rougher, if they have to... or create the atmosphere they *want* in their own workplace.

Again: **No one is stopping you.** That's kinda scary to most people -- it's much easier to blame your lack of success on outside factors.

If your "movie" isn't progressing as excitingly or romantically as you'd like... *change the script*. It's up to you. Unless you're literally exiled to some deserted island, *nothing* is holding you back but your own inner nonsense.

You know, you don't hear much complaining from street-wise hustlers, either. They don't expect life to cut them any slack, and they have learned long ago that they must *take* what they want, cuz nobody's gonna give it to them.

I didn't grow up on city streets. My childhood was spent running unfettered around the endless orchards and deserted foothills and small-town streets of Cucamonga, in Southern California.

And maybe it wasn't as dangerous as the ghetto neighborhoods of Compton or Brooklyn, but there were plenty of opportunities to get your head kicked in.

There was class warfare among the street racers -- you were either a committed "Ricky Racer" or a serious lowrider or you had no business being in either's company.

There were some nasty race conflicts, too -- my closest friend was Hispanic, but that didn't mean I could waltz through the local barrio safely.

For every good vibe available cruising around on a Friday night chasing girls, there was a nasty *surprise* just as easy to run into on the wrong street.

If you were scared, you had to stay home.

The only rule was: You were responsible for your own safety. It was understood that you would make mistakes...

... but you were expected to *learn* from them quickly.

It's the same with the business world, though few people realize it. There are no guarantees when you get involved...

... and there are plenty of unsavory types out there who will happily eat your lunch and steal your bike.

I was thinking about this when I saw the movie "Snatch" the other night. Great flick, if you haven't caught it. Brad Pitt as a gypsy bare-knuckle fighter in a riveting plot full of thieves, killers, cops, diamond merchants with no ethics... and wannabe thugs.

It's entertaining as a movie... but if you look at it as a metaphor for *business*, it just sings.

In a nutshell, here is the lesson: Rookies get eaten alive. Lucky men run out of luck.

And only the ego-less, cool-thinking pro survives.

Lots of self-centered pros get their clocks cleaned through hubris. They get cocky, or self-righteous, or just forget there's *no rule against them losing.*

Rookies are shocked when they lose, but they aren't necessarily surprised. The look on a pro's face when the unthinkable happens can quickly cure you of any silly feelings about your own invincibility.

In whatever market you're in, you really should understand *all* aspects of it with as much detail as an ego-less, cool-thinking pro about to enter a dark alley in a crime-soaked part of town... who wants to make damn sure he comes out alive.

You don't go in unprepared. You don't figure on God watching your back. (He's too busy these days.)

And you don't go in with *fairy tale ideas* of how the world works.

You won't "magically" succeed in business just because you try. It's not like Hollywood movies at all. Not one little bit.

Screw waiting around for something magical to happen. The savvy businessman just takes control right off the bat. And learns *all* about his market...

... so that he knows every detail, and knows it *better than anyone else.*

I can't tell you how often clients send me ads to critique... where it's obvious the writer has *no clue whatsoever* what motivates the prospect he's after.

It's insane.

In fact, it's exactly like taking a bus to the worst part of town, and walking into an alley without the slightest notion of what to do when confronted by a hard-ass thug. Or two.

Or three.

Okay, so maybe your market isn't full of thieves and street fighters. The point still holds. If your market is strictly little old ladies in need of knitting supplies, **you still have to understand them at their deepest level.**

Because even a little old lady will blow off your ads with the scorn of a Mafia boss, if you don't immediately hit her sweet spot with your pitch. And the competition will rejoice in your failures, and hasten them with glee.

Salesmanship 101

Experienced marketers nod in agreement when I talk about hitting the "**passionate sweet spot**" of your prospect. They know that cold, lifeless, boring ad copy seldom gets read, and almost *never* gets acted on.

So I tell would-be writers, over and over, to put more *passion* into their copy. (See how we're coming back around to feelings?)

But there's a catch: Once you've effectively tapped into your own passion for your product... you must then put a *lid* on it.

Confusing?

Naw.

Let me explain: What you want to be is like the super-focused, super-calm salesman... who has a glint in his eye...

... and seems barely able to contain his glee and wonder at the benefits of this product.

But he *does* contain it. You *sense* the passion... but he's not bowling you over with it.

Too many writers think that tapping into your own passionate sweet spot is akin to getting all riled up and insanely persuasive.

In print, the effect is like a three-year-old kid pestering you for attention. It's damned annoying in kids, and a huge turn-off in adults. Don't grab my lapels and scream in my face, no matter how blissed-out you are about your product.

Passion makes your copy powerful not because people respond to wild-eyed true believers...

... but because passion attached to a *reasoned and focused sales message* zeroes in on the human element in the process.

Imagine a guy asking his beloved to marry him. Jumping up and down and hollering may show that his passion runs deep... but she'll think he flipped his lid, and will certainly think twice about hooking up with a nutcase who can't control himself.

On the other hand, popping the question in a cold and casual way won't exactly melt her heart, either.

No.

You must find that *delicate middle ground...* where your passion shows as a gleeful glint, something powerful that is yet under your control.

True salesmen know that effective passion is something the prospect *senses*, and senses clearly. It is a tool to help the pitch.

Unfocused passion is not a *replacement* for the pitch.

Examples: "I have just discovered something so exciting that I feel I'll *burst* if I don't share it with you..."

"Right now, it's past midnight here at the office and I should be home and in bed. But I can't sleep. There's something *urgent* I have to share with you, and it just can't wait..."

"Something incredible has just happened here... and the first person I thought of to tell this amazing story to was *you*."

Get it?

It's not: "HEY! Look at *this*!!!"

It's: "If you have just two minutes, I have an *amazing* story to share that will shock and delight you..."

Great salesmen know that, to make the sale, you must be in *total control*.

If there are choices to make, you must guide the prospect to *make* them during the pitch.

If there are problems or objections, they must be addressed and *solved* during the pitch. The role of passion is to keep the prospect riveted to the story, so these things can be reasonably taken care of... and the sale closed.

Effective passion -- just like laughing -- is contagious. You can (and should) infect your prospect with it, straight from your heart, but through your *brain*.

Think of it as "passionate reason". You're not a professor in a lab coat explaining a cold equation... instead, you're a regular dude (just like your reader) *letting him in* on something truly fabulous and worthwhile.

Do it with an urgent gleam in your eye, and barely-contained excitement he can clearly sense.

How-To Department

Before my good friend, Stan Dahl, became my partner in our marketing biz… he was a bit of a legend in something called "information systems".

He talks about the "architecture" of data, and has worked with such massive collectors of information and data as NATO, Starbucks, and AM/PM Mini-marts. These organizations brought him in when the mountains of data threatened to crush the system. (You don't wanna know how disorganized NATO's Belgium headquarters were. Scary.)

Anyway, I've known Stan for twenty years or so, and it's taken about that long for him to explain what he does to me in a way I can understand.

It's not that the architecture of data is all that hard to explain, or that I'm that dense… okay, maybe I *am* that dense, but that's not the story here.

It's sort of like a major league pitcher trying to explain the mechanics of a true knuckleball to someone who's never played baseball… or a musician trying to explain music theory to someone who's never touched an instrument.

However, once I "got" it, I realized I'd been practicing my own form of "data architecture" ever since I created my first ad.

And -- just to show you how all things in this universe eventually intersect -- my own style of managing massive amounts of information are almost identical to what Stan tried to teach the brainiacs in charge of missile silos.

Namely -- he has a tactic he calls "**Find 3 Rules That Work**".

Briefly, he teaches the info wranglers to stop trying to embrace the *totality* of any one project -- which usually creates more confusion and logjams of data -- and to simply find 3 basic categories or rules or activities that accomplish something, and to build from there.

It's like creating a foundation that you know is viable, before going on to the layers that must stand on that foundation.

Well, guess what?

When I'm confronted with a fresh copywriting project (especially with a new client), the first thing that often lands on my desk is a Federal Express box (never a slim envelope, mind you) crammed with paperwork and videos and notes and transcripts and manuscripts.

This is everything the client can find explaining the product, showcasing other marketing efforts made, other ads run, studies done, and committees convened.

In short... it's a big honking pile of data that must be wrangled.

And my job is to take that honking pile, digest it... and come up with a slim, snappy sales pitch that *condenses* all that information into plain English.

And I have to do it in my head.

Now, those of you who have studied my ads and letters (and shame on those of you who haven't yet) will notice that often, my headlines are structured with three benefits.

Sometimes less, sometimes more... but most often, it's three.

Three is a very important number. It's the least number of legs needed to support a stool. Most huge literary efforts are in trilogies. Most religions have some version of the "father, son and holy ghost". It's a prime number. It's the number of fingers on Mickey's hand.

And so on.

At first, I created this "3 Benefits" thing unconsciously. It just seemed right. Had a bit of poetry and rhythm to it. Da da *da*.

And I suppose, were I to corral a smart guy like Stan and grill him extensively, I might discover that I'm using a kind of information system to distill all that data.

But it doesn't really matter. At this stage in my career, I can simply look back and see what worked (and still does work).

And using three benefits for your Unique Selling Position, or your headline, or your basic sales pitch, simply makes sense.

Because it *works*.

Look at your own pile of data. If you're working for clients, you're faced with a bunch of new stuff. If you're writing for your own product or service, you're up to your neck in details about it.

Hard to see the forest for the trees.

So begin by breaking it all down to *three simple benefits* that you can easily explain, and back up. Even the most complex product or service can be knocked down to size -- and should be, anyway.

I don't care if you're launching satellites into space, starting a local bakery, or selling yachts to rich folk.

What you offer, whether in product or service, can be broken down to three basic benefits. You can have more benefits, of course. But those come up later in your pitch, as you're turning up the heat (under the category of "but wait, there's more"). That's how I load up my bullets.

But when you're crafting your all-important USP... which is the basis of all great headlines, by the way... you need to get down, dirty, and direct. (See, there's three benefits right there.)

Here are a few examples:

1. **Fast, cheap, and good.** (One of my favorite ways to start the process is to see how the job meets these criteria. At least half the time, if you can justify to your reader that what you have is of high quality... a bargain... and brings results quickly... you're off to the races.)

2. **Simple, easy, and lucrative.** (Combined with fast, cheap, and good, these pretty much take care of the entire consumer landscape.)

3. **Get good, get connected, and get paid**. (This is the basis of my "how to be a high paid freelancer" course, but it applies to other ventures as well. It means "become an expert, become a functioning part of your market, and demand you are paid what you're worth.)

4. **Consistent, accurate distance**. (Very elegant phrase I've used a lot in my golf pieces. Covers the three primary concerns of most golfers.)

5. **Buy your dream home, sell your old house fast, and get a great mortgage rate even with lousy credit**. (An example of how this might work in a real estate ad.)

I could go on... but I won't. You get the picture, and that's all I wanted to convey.

Mostly, to be honest, I just wanted to impress you with my savvy in ultra-modern techno-babble. Or, at least, my ability to lay out a good line of persuasive copy. (Copywriters can be a little defensive about our "geek" credentials.)

But the power of "**Find 3 Benefits That Work**" stands. Once you distill all the available info you have down to three compelling benefits, the rest of your headline and copy practically writes itself.

Coaches Corner

I often teach newbies to research infamous persuasion wizards (like P.T. Barnum) because good guys *need* to know a few dirty tricks.

I feel pretty strongly about this subject. Too many people live in a black and white world, where everything is either good or evil, and there's no gray area.

And that's just nonsense.

Some of the most fascinating people I've met are street-level hustlers. Jumpy, excitable guys always looking for a way to make an easy buck. They're fun to share stories with over a drink, but you don't want them to know where you live.

And nearly all of the most *boring* people I've met aren't excited about anything.

They're sleep-walking through life, afraid to take a risk, terrified of a little pain, scared of confrontation. They can put you to sleep in a two-minute conversation, but you'd trust them to water your plants while you were away.

There *is* a middle ground. I'm living proof. I grew up around vandals and risk-takers and ballsy hustlers who were just as frightened of the dangers of life as the boring guys... but who just went ahead and *did* the risky stuff anyway. Cuz that's the *only* way you got anything worthwhile done.

It was also a total blast.

So, yeah, I've fallen out of trees, been chased by cops, knocked senseless in an alley, and stayed up all night long for no good reason at all. I wouldn't have it any other way. It's kept me edgy, interested and interesting. (How I avoided being arrested and hauled off to the hoosegow during my wayward youth remains a mystery.)

You don't have to leave your family and start sleeping in gutters, either, to shake off the dust.

Just start showing a little honest enthusiasm for being alive.

Give your senses brief and intense "field trips" a couple of times each day: Look at things in terms of the opportunity they might represent... keep an ear to the ground so you know what's happening around you (both personally and in business)... feel the pulse of your neighborhood and market.

Learn to love and appreciate short bursts of super-focused, disciplined work. Hone your convictions and develop a friggin' opinion once in a while.

Don't be afraid to be wrong, either -- just admit it quickly when you are, and adjust your mindset appropriately.

And always do the right thing. Don't dither. Show some leadership, take more responsibility, and follow through on *everything* you attach your reputation to.

Are these "dirty tricks"?

In a way, yes.

Because if you follow my advice, many people who heretofore had no opinion whatsoever about you... will start to *hate* you.

I've said that the best salesmen know to take command of the situation, steer the prospect where he should be going...

... and *push to close the deal* by solving problems and meeting objections right away.

That's not exactly playing fair, according to most folks. They dither away their time, avoid decisions, and put off duties.

You force them to *want* something so bad they feel compelled to take out their money and hand it over...

... and you've taken them *waaaay* out of their comfort zone.

This will often make them a little mad at you, even if you also make their lives better. This is the reason for "buyer's remorse".

So you use another "dirty trick"... and *confront* that remorse right away, before it even surfaces.

You never allow the customer to find a "way out" of the sale -- because you keep him happy, continue to meet his needs, and solve every little dilemma that comes up.

Money will be an issue, so you explain the *value* in a way that makes price irrelevant.

After-sale service will be an issue, so you make him feel completely secure he'll be taken care of.

He will be anxious about what his spouse, friends and colleagues think, so you provide simple reasons he can repeat on why he got a *bargain*.

These are all "dirty tricks", in the way you must trick your puppy to become house-trained, or trick your child to eat spinach, or trick your girlfriend into believing you're worthy of her love and affection. (You bad boy, you.)

The biggest "dirty trick" of all is to take control of your life.

Step up the plate and take your hacks.

Never threaten or cajole -- just get things done, and don't waste time on the small shit. Get negative people out of your life, fast and without apology. Make sure your actions are proactive, not reactive.

Be a big man, and ignore what you can endure. Never listen to any critic who's never had to meet a payroll. (This, too, is a dirty trick, because all critics demand attention as their birthright -- it's just *mean* to withhold it.)

Learn to trust your own judgment. No ideology allowed. True believers need to constantly twist facts and reality to fit their pre-determined view of the world.

Don't fall into that trap. When you sign on to be a world-class marketer, you *must* agree to let the blinders fall from your eyes. And you may have to let some old friends go their own way, and build a new group of confidants.

You *can* be an "ethical hustler" -- someone who learns to spot and embrace opportunity, is at home with ambition and a little healthy greed, and isn't afraid of a little risk. Or afraid of doing the right thing.

The meek may indeed inherit the earth at some point... but only *after* the bold are through with it.

Chapter Eleven:

Greed

And jealousy, and needing to feel superior, and more greed…

Here's something you don't hear every day: For most folks, you gotta be *selfish* in life…

… before you can enjoy the luxury of being *unselfish*.

And *greedy* about attaining your long- and short-term goals…

… before you can afford to be *generous*.

Let me explain.

First, "greed" is *not* a bad word in the marketing world.

It is, rather, simply an *identified emotional state* of the human brain – essentially a step stronger than the milder "desire".

It's that *overpowering need to possess* that marketers count on when selling their wares.

When creating a sizzling sales message, top copywriters know to tickle the greedy parts of the prospect's mind…

… without thinking less of anyone for desperately wanting something. (Especially when the writer is responsible for creating that want.)

Gary Halbert used to speak of the best markets as consisting of a "starving crowd" – essentially a mob of folks whose eyes light up and their Pavlovian response kicks in when they see what you offer. (Google "Pavolov's dog" if you forget what that's all about.)

And admen going back over a century have spoken fondly of "greed and fear" being the primary motivators for turning prospects into customers.

Greed simply isn't the bad word you're used to thinking of, when you're taking your product to the world and trying to sell it.

No, it's just shorthand for that *upset emotional state* your Perfect Prospect will attain when he reads your awesome ad copy…

… a riled-up internal mess that won't calm down until he whips out his wallet and gives you money. In a fair exchange of goods or services for coin.

Okay, I can tell you need more explanation.

So here's a story about greed, and why it's so necessary for you to succeed, in three parts:

Part One: Wake Up

Gizzled veteran salesmen understand that looking into the things that truly motivate people isn't always a pretty sight.

Humans construct fancy fantasies around their own actions -- and the actions of people they admire -- *that make them look good.*

We're all heroes, in our own eyes. No matter what foul or stupid or riot-starting deed we've just blundered through.

The truth behind most behavior, however, is much more brutal…

… and also much more *interesting.*

Here, for the rookies, is the primary list of motivations behind most buying decisions… in *any* market, for *any* transaction:

1. Greed.
2. Greed.
3. Jealousy.
4. Greed.
5. The need to feel superior.
6. Fear.
7. Greed.
8. And greed.

This is roughly why free offers and "How To" headlines involving credibly-easy ways to amass moolah work so well.

And why the "take away" will forever be the most *potent* salesmanship tactic in your bag of tricks.

It's also why people are reluctant to respond to even good, decent and easy offers that will make their life better…

… if it isn't *also* a big damn secret few others know about.

You'll notice that "curiosity" didn't make the short list.

That's because it's *waaaaaaay* down the line… and the only kind of curiosity headline or copy angle that works, anyway, has to arrive in the prospect's mind arm-in-arm *with* a big ol' dose of greed.

Curiosity, standing all naked and alone in your headline, won't hook the reader anywhere near as effectively as curiosity aimed directly at the *greedy little dark heart* of your reader's most urgent and desperate desires.

So it's not "Why Some People Get Rich."

Rather, it's "Why Your In-Laws Are Getting Filthy Rich Behind Your Back (And Why They Will *Never Share* These Amazing Secrets With You)".

A very savvy salesman once told me his biggest "knock 'em off the fence" line -- when confronted with reluctant prospects who were *this close* to buying but backing away…

… was to bring in the idea that, with this product, they could finally *show up* their jerk-off brother-in-law.

Being able to quit his day job, tell the boss to go die, work at home and earn six figures right away…

… none of that made much of a dent.

Too vague in the prospect's mind.

Too full of *"but what if I screw up, as usual"* possibilities.

Install that crystal-clear image of being able to lord his success over his arrogant family nemesis, though…

… and he can't get his wallet out fast enough.

This won't work all the time, of course.

Still, once you understand the power of finding the most *relevant* motivation in your reader…

… you're off to the races, dude. It's all about getting hip to the way great salesmen channel psychology, sociology, and biology.

That translates to understanding the *nasty little dreams* your prospect is harboring: How he sees himself, and (more importantly) *wants* to see himself, in the hierarchy of his peers…

… and what *you* can do to trigger an adrenaline rush in him, combined with raw jungle-level ape-brain *greed*.

Don't get scared.

The task isn't really all that daunting… once you shake yourself (and your Inner Salesman) awake.

All you really need to do…

… is get wise to the forgotten fundamentals of classic salesmanship.

It won't kill you to read a few of the great books (like the salesman's bible "How To Win Friends and Influence People" by Dale Carnegie, for starters). And pay attention when guys like Gary Halbert, Dan Kennedy, and me tell you what's what.

Most people live dull lives because they're *half-asleep.*

Numbed by television, X-box, social media and the rest of our dumbed-down culture. (Not to mention those snarling fears deep in their soul.)

You will know that *you*, too, are still stumbling around half-asleep…

… when you hear things like I'm telling you now, and your natural impulse is to *disagree*.

"No, no, no, John. People are really nice and loving most of the time. And I've *never* had a greedy twinge in my life."

You're asleep.

So, first step: Allow good information -- even when it offends your long-held fairy-tale belief systems -- to come aboard *without argument.*

Just let it simmer in your noggin for a spell.

I'm not making this "greed" stuff up, you know.

It may seem outrageous at first…

… but as you observe how people really act (and *not* how you *wish* they'd act, or *believed* they were acting before you woke up) you'll understand.

And it really is all about observation.

I have never been bored observing people. Including myself.

The key is to have a Zen attitude -- to be able to step back and stop trying to twist reality to fit your nervous psychological needs.

When you realize you're trying to sell hot dogs to a crowd that only wants hamburgers… *stop.*

Don't get mad, don't argue with people, don't look for reasons why you're really right and everyone else is wrong.

Just observe, acknowledge, learn the lesson… *and move on.*

This is a vital part of Operation MoneySuck…

… and something that people violate regularly. Because, as humans, we just tend to get too tied up in our own drama.

We don't WANT reality to be the way it is, sometimes.

We REALLY don't want it to do what it's doing when it makes us uncomfortable.

And we get dazed.

And even wander *away* from what's working, what's making us happy… and what's good for us (and our businesses, and our love lives, and our lifestyle, and everything else).

So don't do that. Allow reality to dominate your perception of the world and all the funny people accompanying you on this wild adventure of modern life.

Part Two: Stop Hitting Yourself With The Hammer

Not so long ago, I actually had my life in a very nice semblance of working order.

I was logging maybe twenty hours a week… earning stupid amounts of money from clever royalty deals… and taking off obscene blocks of time.

For several years, I routinely took the phone off the hook and split for three-to-six-*months*-long adventures.

And because I had arranged things the right way… everything just clicked back in like clockwork when I returned.

What I was doing, essentially…

… **was being selfish**. Very, very, *very* selfish.

I didn't understand it at the time, but this was the first stage of a *process* I was going through.

Unconsciously, I was getting somewhere important, by traveling through "Selfish Land" first.

The best way to explain it is the order you're given on airplanes about the oxygen masks that may drop from the ceiling (in the event of a drop in cabin pressure).

First, you put on your own mask.

Then, you attend to the people who are dependent on you.

Do you know why they take the time to explain this program?

It's because most people are not well-versed in taking care of business while under pressure.

So they see to the needs of everyone *around* them first, and respond in what *seems* like the right way. Heroic, even.

But it's wrong.

Animals will always save themselves first. The rats scurrying off the sinking ship never stop to alert the passengers. (Okay, man's best friend can be trained to ignore personal peril to save stranded skiers and drowning kids... but that's *serious* training.)

However, humans have all this extra hardware in our brains, and sometimes it gets in the way. And that's a good thing, when it's your job (or duty) to save others, even when it puts you at heightened risk.

But it can get in your way when what you really need to do is: **Tend your own garden first.**

You won't be much help to *anyone* on the plane if you pass out, trying to be "that dude who never thinks of himself first".

You've got to remember: *You're* the one strong enough to drag your dependents out and handle emergencies, should it come to that.

They *need* you to be alert, not in crisis, and calmly attending to what's important…

… in the correct order.

It's your JOB to make sure you're *in shape* to handle things.

In business -- specifically, employing Operation MoneySuck -- *if you're the guy who's bringing in the dough, then that's what you need to be doing.*

It doesn't matter that you know how to fix the copier, or that your negotiation skills will shortcut the problem with the landlord, or that (metaphorically) someone let the dogs out and there's panic in the hallways.

If you're the guy who takes care of the bottom line, *you* need to get it done.

Cut the deal, meet the deadline, whatever it takes to bring in the moolah.

This requires selfishness. This requires shutting the door, not returning non-essential calls, even being rude about protecting your trances when you're writing.

We don't like being rude, do we.

If you're basically a nice person, it rubs you the wrong way.

Get over it.

You're not going to blow past the roadblocks in your life until you understand that one man's rudeness… is another man's way of *getting it done.*

Step Three:

One of the MAIN things I teach is that success *cannot* be measured by piles of cash alone.

This was made manifest to me in a lesson I call "The 29th Auto Supply Store". I'm sure you've heard me talk about it.

Years ago, after a grueling seminar down in Miami Beach, I was relaxing with colleagues on the boardwalk, winding down. One of the attendees weaseled his way into a chair, and immediately tried to grill me for extra marketing advice.

This was one of those great lessons that became clear as it happened.

This guy owned 28 auto supply stores. He worked all the time, was 100 pounds overweight, had a wife who despised him and kids he barely knew…

… and while we sat on Ocean Boulevard, basking in the glow of sunset, watching a parade of gorgeous women walk by in bikinis, a gentle breeze off the waves rustling the palms…

… *all* this guy could talk about was opening up his 29th auto supply store.

Something seriously wrong there.

And what did he need another store for? How much more money would be "enough"?

Of course, for a guy like that -- glued to the job like a Siamese twin -- there will never be a point where he's amassed "enough" money.

Because money isn't going to make him happy.

He was already rich. He couldn't spend what he had. He, in fact, had no idea how much he was worth... beyond being "rich enough to buy this hotel with a check".

Man, I couldn't get away from that unhappy pest fast enough. I only hoped that whatever was festering in his soul wasn't *contagious*.

The only truly successful person is rich in ALL the areas a good life offers.

Friends, family, freedom, fun... and all the other "f" words that come to mind. (Don't be rude -- I was thinking of French fries, furry animals, and Fender guitars.)

All this ranting about greed, and about waking up, has lead to *this* primary realization: Greed may be a hot motivating factor while you're asleep...

... but once you wake up, the selfishness of basic human greed is only good as a *means to a better end.*

Namely... your new ability to indulge in all the wonderful things that are difficult to indulge in while you're dirt poor.

Like... oh... being *unselfish*. Sharing, and helping others without holding back. Being ridiculously generous with time and money and advice.

That's real freedom.

That's a kind of fun, too, that most people never get to experience.

Being greedy about attaining that level of mojo is how you get there.

Make sense?

Firing up your initial greed and selfishness is simply a way to stay focused and disciplined on what needs to get done, so your natural sweetness and generosity can come out later…

… fortified with the fruits of success your greedy little hands have created.

Be selfish about your time and energy, while going after the Big Bucks.

And be greedy about attaining your goals, whether it's a thriving business or the safety of your loved ones or a better lifestyle.

This is how stuff gets done in the real world.

Chapter Twelve:

The Two Keys To Getting Everything You Want From Business And Life

And how to start scaring the bejesus out of your competition…

It's, like, nineteen degrees outside right now.

That's unusual for Reno, nestled as we are in the protected high desert bosom of the Sierras…

… but up on the pass, another couple of thousand feet higher, this would be considered downright toasty.

Truckee, shivering at the pinnacle of Interstate 80, is frequently the coldest town in the country. Even occasionally beats out Montana and North Dakota cold spots (but only when they're having slow days -- hard to compete when they're posting minus-thirty degrees).

Every time we drive over the Sierras into California, we pass the notorious Donner Lake just after Truckee -- where a bunch of clueless pioneers tried to slog covered wagons through the snow, got stuck in the worst winter of the nineteenth century, and wound up with each other on the dinner menu -- and count our blessings for having the sense to be born in a time when cars are equipped with seat warmers.

I think about stuff like this often. Maybe because I have morbid tendencies (I was raised on horror movies and pulp science fiction)…

… but more because, in my job as a teacher, I field so many complaints about how "hard" it is in the nasty, brutal world of modern business.

Please.

Let's all get a grip.

My father got up every damn day before dawn and worked outside -- rain or shine -- as a construction foreman for nearly half a century.

He worked hard, too… literally forcing steel and wood and brick to do things they don't naturally want to do.

I am no more amazed at the Pharaoh's pyramids than I am at the massive structures in downtown Los Angeles Pop can point to as having helped build.

He got so good at what he did, he began teaching rookies how to do it, during night school at the union hall. (Only he called them "apprentices".) Never quit his day job, mind you. Just put in a solid eight hours, and then traded his hard hat for a teacher's thinking cap.

I had two major revelations from observing my father engage in his trade:

1. I knew I had to find another way to make a living for myself. Just getting up that early every day made my brain curdle. And I

suspected -- rightly -- that my entire soul would chafe under the yoke of hard physical labor.

2. And yet... there was something about the way Pop could figure out how to build or fix just about *anything* in our environment that appealed to me greatly.

This yearning to avoid "work" -- which was defined, in my working class mind, as getting up early and breaking your back all day -- made me feel like a goldbricking traitor.

An outsider... unworthy and shiftless.

And I became very, very confused throughout my "formative" years about *where I could possibly fit* in the world.

It took a while to realize, for example, that I *did* crave hard work -- just not the physical kind.

If you've had the opportunity (as most of my generation has) to compare working outdoors with working inside your head, you know both are just as taxing on your system.

Except that, instead of tired muscles, "head work" leaves you with an exhausted cerebral cortex.

Still, it was a huge jump in finding my *right* "job" to discover that there *was* a kind of hard work that would excite and nourish me.

And -- big bonus -- I could do the gig during odd hours, and sleep until noon, as long as I met my deadlines.

The "job" I found, of course, was freelance copywriting (with a little marketing consulting on the side).

Now, after a couple of eventful decades in the front-line trenches of marketing and advertising, I actually feel qualified to teach rookies how to make the career work. (Just like Pop.)

And -- in a big ironic twist -- after teaching for a few years, the importance of the *second* revelation, above, has started to become more evident.

To succeed, you gotta have the urge to want to *fix* things… and to *figure out* how things work.

The necessity of this "curiosity tool" can slip by you… so I consider it worthy of an entire chapter.

As a business owner, you must apply the full force of your curiosity and your "drive to conquer" to what you do.

As a freelancer, you *really* gotta amp it up…

… because you'll be dealing with many different businesses, and many different marketing situations.

You gotta be like the guys on "Myth Busters", in short. (Fabulous show on the Discovery Channel.) They never look at anything as a mystery…

… just a bunch of working parts or physics principles waiting to be disassembled, probed, and figured out.

Calling anything a mystery is just an excuse to avoid dealing with it.

You gotta roll up your sleeves and dig in.

This kind of curiosity is second nature to me. I can't remember the last time I looked at an ad without immediately tearing it apart. Or the last time I watched a television show without trying to predict the plot points or next line of dialogue.

Heck, when I see the latest Ford or Volvo or Beemer racing past, I go into a brief trance, wondering what the designers were thinking -- especially with the recent design lurches toward huge spoilers on four-bangers and the super-boring "blunt object" look of luxury SUVs. (I'm mostly disappointed in automotive design these days. And I either laugh or shudder at the endless commercials that flash the profile of the latest sedan like it was a centerfold. Be still, my heart.)

(Early in my career, I got to meet the guy who designed the original '55 Thunderbird for Ford. Now *that* was a car. Submarine windows, removable hardtop, shark gills, torpedo headlights… the works. Back then, cars really *were* like centerfolds, and unveiling the '57 Bel Air or the '59 El Dorado or the -- *gasp* -- '64 Mustang really DID make your heart flutter. Somewhere along the line the automobile gods have gone to sleep.)

As a kid, this urge to figure things out manifested in breaking stuff, examining road kill, and crawling through underground pipes to see where they went.

That's a *passive* way of looking at the world.

Even the later stage of blowing stuff up (instead of just breaking it), and (regrettably, for the few pre-teen years when my parents accidentally gave me a BB rifle) shooting birds and lizards (and, on occasion, each other) wasn't getting to the bottom of how things *worked*.

My first brush with actually having an "*a-ha!*" experience came from drawing. While my friends all devoured comic books, I found myself wanting to *create* them. And that required figuring out how to start with pencil and paper and idea, and get 'er done.

My first efforts were crude, but I kept at it. I drew World War One bi-planes over and over and over, from scratch, until I actually got fairly good at it. Pop later stopped by my desk one day while I was attempting to draw a pirate ship. He thought about it for a moment...

... and then drew the outline of a rudimentary galleon, complete with foredeck, poop deck, rudder and single-sail mast.

That confirmed, for me, a **rudimentary concept of comic art**: First, just get the iconic "oh, that's a pirate ship" image down. Later, you can add fancy details, and make it your own. (I still occasionally put those ships into my doodles.)

After that, I was off to the races. I started drawing graphic novels thirty pages long -- this, as a fourth grader, mind you -- filled with my own designs for spaceships, aliens, castles, medieval weaponry, and lots of lots of monsters. Plus, of course, the surrounding landscapes of hills, trees, clouds, birds, and celestial bodies.

There's a darn good business point to all of this, so hang with me.

See, I do NOT have anything you'd dare call "natural talent".

I didn't pick up a pencil and start knocking out perfect circles (as it's said Michelangelo did), or see twenty different colors in a small cloud (as Vermeer did).

In fact, I was (and still am) red-green color blind. I see three or four bands in a rainbow -- nowhere near the full spectrum. True story -- which illustrates the point that I didn't have *any* "official" support for my efforts: In kindergarten, before I could read the names of the crayons, I once colored Little Boy Blue purple, the grass red, and the trees gray.

The teacher -- who obviously was in the wrong profession -- *ridiculed* me for this obscenity, in front of everyone. (No one discovered my lack of color perception until I was in junior high. The same year I also discovered I was severely near-sighted and needed glasses. I remember walking outside after picking up my first pair of horn-rims, and being *dumbstruck* while looking clearly at the rising moon for the first time in my life. The whole world changed for me that evening.)

(I also, for the first time, realized why I was not half-bad at shortstop, but a complete failure in the outfield -- where, standing out there isolated, there was just a chaotic blur of action far, far away… and every now and then a baseball would appear from nowhere and land nearby.)

So, no, I didn't have any head start on any of the other kids. I simply wanted to create my own comic books…

… and, like Pop, I just started *figuring it out.*

It was hard, and there was no relief from failure at first -- every attempt sucked -- but I could feel myself slowly starting to "get it".

Each new drawing was just a tiny, tiny bit better than the one before.

And I enjoyed the process, because eventually I started creating enough recognizable figures to populate a real storyline.

When other kids expressed amazement, I just shook my head. *Anyone* could draw -- I knew this for a fact. No big deal.

And when they said "Well, it's easy for *you*", I told them they were idiots. It *wasn't* easy for me. I couldn't draw a dinosaur or a horse or a good hand yet… and, in fact, my stuff was still a far cry from the quality I was aiming at.

"You can do this, too," I said, over and over. To deaf ears.

That's been my rallying song in business, too. Writing good ad copy isn't brain surgery. *Anyone* can learn how…

… but it doesn't happen just by wishing. (Even if you wish really, really, *really* hard.)

No… *you still gotta apply yourself.*

The thing that most frosts my ass is how *fast* you can learn, once you're shown a few shortcuts. I'm a big fan of shortcuts, because I never enjoyed them myself.

For me, literally a few minutes of insight from my father -- who was not an artist, but who was fearless about figuring things out -- was all I had… and yet it was a huge leap in discovery.

Still, if I had met a real comic artist at some point who could have shown me a few tips… well, who knows.

As it was, I learned slowly and painfully. My journalism teacher spotted my doodles one day, and without asking assigned me as staff cartoonist for the high school newspaper. I'd never worked with ink before, and suddenly I was fiddling with nibs, bottles of India ink, and no way to erase my mistakes.

And I had to fill a strip four columns wide and three inches deep, due in two days. Without resorting to the juvenile humor that made my friends crack up. (I literally had to get my material past an *English teacher*.)

This was my first introduction to the tyranny of deadlines, and the terror of dealing with unreasonable censorship. (Years later, I again had a cartoon strip in my college newspaper… minus the oversight committee, and armed with better equipment and the advantage that underground comix provided -- I no longer needed to be funny, or even make sense, as long as I drew trippy stuff.)

I just figured it out.

And failed a lot doing it.

Failure never scared me much. I grew up thinking I was already a complete loser, because I measured myself against what I *couldn't* do...

... and never gave myself any credit for what I *could* do.

Because, as I knew from all my struggles, anyone *else* could do it, too.

Just figure it out. It's not a big deal, once you adopt this simple tactic.

This has all come home to roost, now that I've become a teacher. I hang with genius all the time -- many of my colleagues and former mentors are off-the-chart smart -- but I'm never cowed by any display of talent.

Because *anything* that *anyone* does...

... can be figured out.

Sure, for some projects (like going to Mars) you may have to log twenty years of advanced education, with access to NASA-level equipment and resources funded by the government...

... but with the right mindset you could, eventually, figure much of it out. (Witness what Elon Musk has done, with zero government help, in getting his SpaceX project to Mars so far along. Brass cojones, that guy.)

And if you can't -- if you just don't have the aptitude for math, or electronics, or dissection, or whatever -- then it's hardly a big loss for you.

Because there are lots and lots of *other* things in this world that DO fit your innate desires.

Figure it out. Understand what you're good at, what thrills you, what floats your boat...

... and figure out a way to make that your livelihood.

It ain't rocket science.

Here, in the cruel world of business and marketing and advertising, it's even *simpler*.

It's all about salesmanship, and figuring out what your prospect wants and how to give it to him.

And yet, it's not so simple that my job as teacher isn't safe for a while longer.

This was made clear to me when my colleague Rich Schefren called in for help with his USP.

Graciously, Rich has agreed to let me use him as an example for a VERY important lesson.

Let's call it...

Figuring Out Your Damn USP

Forgive the invective -- but sometimes I just want to reach through the phone lines and throttle people...

… because they refuse to let the simple elegance of a great USP break into their clouded consciousness. (I'll explain the meaning of USP in a minute.)

Rich is a great example. Brilliant marketer, who's made gazillions. Understands the Web, and offline retail, in ways that make even hard-core geeks stutter and back away in his presence.

And yet… *he still has trouble figuring out what he actually does to bring in the money.*

He can't figure out his own USP.

I'm being overly critical, of course, because Rich is a friend, and thus has earned the right to be ridiculed by me. (It's a much-sought-after privilege.)

His difficulty with his USP, however, is illustrative of what so many other people go through. I've explained, in excruciating detail, how to construct a killer USP many times before.

It should be sinking in by now.

But maybe it's like drawing a horse -- no matter what else you draw well, *this* particular aspect of the gig is just more difficult.

So let's figure it out.

This is gonna be good.

The road to *everything* you desire in business lies through your USP.

You can write an okay headline without knowing your USP… but it will never be a *killer* headline. You can make a lot of money without knowing your USP, too…

… but for every dollar you earn, you're probably leaving *ten* on the table.

As you'll see, even the *name of your company* gets better when you have your USP down pat.

It truly is the foundation of everything else you do.

Rosser Reeves, one of the great admen of the last century, originally coined the term USP. He talked at length about the dire necessity for having a "**U**nique **S**elling **P**roposition" -- a simple way of informing your prospect base that what you had was *one-of-a-kind*.

The impact of this insight has never ceased to be an essential part of professional advertising. I just Googled the term, and there are 1,660,000 entries… including ads for 7-day seminars in Australia teaching you how to create a USP, a couple of multi-CD courses on the secrets, and several guys who will consult with you personally on the subject (for a price).

Yikes.

It's important…

… but it ain't *that* tough to understand.

I can't even imagine what the heck you'd teach in the second *hour* of a 7-day seminar on USPs.

The mystery, I believe, comes from the term itself. So, in my clearly egomaniacal new career as a teacher, I have *re-defined* the acronym this way:

Unique Sales *Position*.

I'm not the first guy to re-define the term. But I've never, ever heard anyone else explain it the way I do.

My explanation came about after years of figuring USPs out for businesses as a freelancer... because there wasn't time to wait for the client to do it with deadlines looming... and because -- as I said -- everything else flowed from understanding the USP.

If I tried to write copy without an *intimate* knowledge of my client's USP, I was setting myself up for a painful job, full of tortured logic and dead-end tangents.

It's like trying to cross a busy town blindfolded.

Here is how I ask clients to define what they do:

How do you *Position* yourself in your market...

... *Uniquely* among your competitors...

... in order to *Sell?*

And, yeah, I know that arrangement of words makes the acronym "PUS"... but I don't think I can sell a concept that brings to mind oozing infections. So I stick with USP.

Think about the question I've posed here.

Each part matters, *hugely*.

You'd think that positioning yourself in your market would be a no-brainer... but it isn't. A common example is any of the many restaurants that opened, and then closed, for business in your town over the last year. It's a cliché, but it's not one that lends itself to clueing in those who don't *get* it.

You cannot just decide you're gonna "open a restaurant". That's too general.

What *part* of the "restaurant" market are you gonna be in? The fast food part… the family dining part… the steak house part… the sea food part?

Even Denny's doesn't try to be all things to all people. They have carefully carved out a niche in the entire "eating out" world, and they know who they are. You can get a salad, a burger or spaghetti or roast pork, a beer and desert there.

It won't be the best meal you've ever eaten, but it'll do in a pinch. They don't pretend to be otherwise.

When I use the restaurant analogy, most people nod in agreement. They "get it" about restaurants.

But they don't see what it has to do with THEIR business.

So let's get this straight right now: I don't care if you're online, off-line, in retail or in direct response, selling nails and widgets or the *secrets* of nails and widgets…

… you're in a market.

And that market is defined by your *competitors*. (If you think you don't *have* any competitors, you very soon will be right. You'll be out of business.)

So: **How YOU compare with your competition is your "position" in the market.**

There are people charging more than you do… less than you do… and in different ways than you do.

They package their product differently -- maybe you have a twelve-CD course plus a tele-conference… while others do actual seminars, or have a book, or go door-to-door.

If your business were a person, who would he be? The smart-mouthed high-priced expert, or the calm genius? The girl next door, or the va-va-*voom* seductress? The guy driving a Ford Taurus, or the smooth operator in a Ferrari Spyder?

This *matters*. Think about single guys in a nightclub, angling to meet and woo women. If you're driving the Ferrari, and that's a big part of "who you are", then you'd be foolish not to *position* yourself as that guy.

On the other hand, if you're in the rusted Jeep with the torn canvas roof, you would have to *position yourself differently* to succeed.

And both of those characters *can* succeed.

But not with the same positioning.

In the marketing world, you're essentially in a police line-up. Especially online -- where your typical prospect knows there are dozens more just like you on the Web…

… and they're all reachable with the click of a mouse.

Thus, the need to be *unique*.

Back to the bar: If there are six other guys driving hundred-thousand-dollar cars there… and you were counting on that advantage to make you stand out… you're out of luck, aren't you.

It's the same in business. You can position yourself in what *should* be the right spot: lowest price on the best quality with the best service…

… and still not stand out. Because everyone else is promising the same thing.

Uh oh.

Hey, good for you if all your competition refuses to offer a long guarantee, or makes people wait two weeks for delivery, or offers shoddy service.

All you need to do to stand out is offer what they're too dumb to provide.

However, most modern marketers are getting way too hip to be caught without the basics of good salesmanship -- namely, risk-reversal guarantees, high perceived value, and great customer service.

You can't just shout it louder.

You gotta find your own *separate* mojo. I don't have a general one-size-fits-all rule…

… except for the theme of this chapter: *Figure it out.*

Jack In The Box has used creativity and a deep war-chest of advertising dollars to differentiate themselves from Burger King and the others. Taco Bell and Del Taco fight over miniscule price differences. Chili's is Denny's with a real bar attached.

Tough market, the fast food jungle. Your own market may be easier, or harder. Real estate agents are never alone in a town. Information marketers are now a seething mob online.

Do you have the secret for creating Websites that make money? Last Google count on that term was a shade over 161 million.

The truth is, you may have to face the fact that the broad appeal of what you offer is NOT unique.

In my years of freelancing, that has been the case more often than not.

And yet, there are still ways to stand out. If your competition does what you do to a "T", but doesn't advertise it... blitz them on that. Like Claude Hopkins did with Schlitz -- he made a big deal over the careful brewing process, the selected hops and barely and malt, the way the vats were scrubbed down so often...

... things that every brewer did, *but never talked about.*

I know a real estate broker who had a standing offer to buy *back* any house he sold within six months, no questions asked. He seldom *told* anyone about his guarantee, but he was damn proud of it, because no one else did it.

So it *didn't* help him stand out.

Probably, there are details to what you offer, or the way you offer it, that would make you unique among most of your competitors...

... if only you TOLD people about it.

And that brings us to the last part of the USP: *Selling*.

You want to position yourself, uniquely among everyone else...

... in order to *sell*.

Positioning yourself in order to be thought of as a really nice guy doesn't cut it. Even being the coolest guy in the pack won't pay your rent.

The way you stand out, within your market niche, must begin the *sales* process.

This brings us back to my friend Rich.

He asked me for help with his USP, because he was having trouble creating a name for his business. This, of course, underlines the fact that everything depends on the USP.

He was smart to sweat over the name. Now, normally, I don't believe the name of your business is all that critical...

... as long as it's not misleading, or so clever it's stupid. (I used to keep a log of all the restaurants I saw in my travels with names that had nothing to do with being a restaurant. It's okay to call your establishment "Bubba's", if you immediately put "Bar-B-Q" underneath it. It is not, however, okay to have "*Gendarme*" emblazoned in neon on a blacked-out window, with no other identification.) (Hair salons are even worse offenders, always coming up with too-clever-to-live names that *obscure* the actual business... like "Lox R Us".)

If you plan to sell your business at some point, you *don't* want your personal name to be an integral part of what it's called. A nearby example: Gary Halbert could never sell The Gary Halbert Letter (not that he ever wanted to)... but Dan Kennedy could easily unload his No B.S. Marketing Newsletter.

On the other hand, these names often become subservient to the personalities behind them -- nearly every time I hear someone reference those fine publications, they say "Halbert's newsletter" or "Kennedy's newsletter".

So, no matter how carefully you design the name of your biz, it can mutate.

(**Side note:** *Personality*, of course, can be your ace-in-the-hole when creating your USP. It's something entirely unique to you and no one else... and it cannot be easily ripped off. I rejoice when I have a client who both *has* a real personality... and will let me *use* it as the "voice" of the copy. Doc O'Leary, the semi-insane golf nut, is my favorite example... his emails get devoured, because his list just can't wait to "see what that nutball is up to now".)

Nevertheless, when naming your business, it won't hurt to make it a **mini-headline**.

Rich's biz was coaching -- he discovered he had a knack for taking groups of distraught marketers, quickly helping them identify their hottest profit potential...

... and then getting it all down in a *system* that ran like clockwork.

His first efforts at naming the enterprise included "IBProcess" (short for Internet Business Process)... and BGF-Process (or Business Growth And Freedom Process). Bulky, and too close to "BFD" for his liking. (Big Friggin' Deal, if you're having trouble deciphering that last acronym.)

So I asked him to write a list of all the words he actually USES in his program.

You know: The words that come out of his mouth while he's coaching people.

This exercise is important... because too often, we get too *close* to our business, and start thinking about it in high-handed terms that are never really part of the idiom. (Like saying "Mature Bovine Tissue Accumulation" instead of "hamburger".)

This problem gets nasty when you end up calling your company something like "Advanced Business Solutions." Generic, boring, essentially meaningless.

Words matter. When creating the name of my first business --
Marketing Rebel -- I used "marketing" rather than "advertising" or
"business" because it was more targeted to who my prospect was.
The word "advertising" was too narrow, "business" too broad.

And I chose "rebel" over "outlaw" after careful deliberation of the
way the words could be misunderstood.

Early in my career, the book "In Search Of Excellence" hit the
best-seller lists, and suddenly every headline was sporting the
term… as if the word itself possessed magical powers to bestow
real excellence (whatever that means) on anyone using it.

And the word became meaningless.

Same with the word "solutions". I *hate* that word… because,
during my last get-up-early-and-wear-a-tie job before I went
freelance, the marketing vice prez forced me to use it as a one-
word headline.
Again, he was convinced the *word* possessed so much awe-
inspiring draw that merely printing it in 72-point Helvetica would
crush us with new customers. Idiot.

Words matter… but only because boring words can drag your
marketing down a black hole. **You want to find words that *do the
job.***
In Rich's case, the most important part of what he offered was
coaching. So, that word should probably appear in the name.
Other words that kept coming up were "growth", "system", and
"profits". Not bad words…

… but not self-explanatory, either.

When I lecture about Power Words, I start with the word
"humiliate". It's one of the best examples of words that carry
innate emotional content -- people will actually flinch when they

hear or read it. Everyone's been humiliated, and it left a stinging scar. (Of course, as more and more people listen to me, the words I use as examples may also start to lose their *oomph*.)

Words matter. Looking over all the verbiage Rich used in his day to day hands-on servicing of customers, I found tons of generic, yawn-inducing words. But also interesting Power Words that created semi-fascinating combinations… like Wealth Coach, or The Coaching Profit System.

Yet, every time I found a new combination with some bite, it came up short. *Because he still didn't have his USP down pat.*

He had what I call a "starter" USP: "Enabling business owners to unleash the hidden potential in their profit model to maximize growth, profits and freedom."

Quite a mouthful. It's good to get all those words down on paper, so you can see how generic and useless they look. But the *essence* is there.

The key phrases and words he was struggling with were the ones that had the *least* mojo. He needed to find something that *better* explained the concepts of "enable", "maximize", and "growth".

The way he was describing his company made it sound like a bad MBA program.

So I had him meditate on key words.

Like headlines, the best USPs often have some versions of *faster, cheaper, easier,* and *simpler* in them. Also *newer, unique, proven, urgent* and *limited.*

It's a rare treat when you can fit all those concepts in… but it's a good exercise to try, regardless.

This is what I came up with… without knowing anything about his business other than the few vague USP efforts he mentioned: "A proven system that allows smart-but-overwhelmed business owners to quickly identify your hottest profit generators, eliminate wasted effort, and put the *best possible version* of your business on autopilot. So you rake in more money, spend less time in the office (and more time on vacation)…

… while everything runs with amazing professional efficiency."

That was written in about two minutes, off the cuff. It's still not exactly right, but it takes all the things Rich does, and puts them together in a coherent couple of sentences.

Like a good bullet, actually. A real explanation… using the word "you" (which few companies do), avoiding twenty-five cent "big words" that lack specific meaning, and *humanizing* the copy with terms like "rake in".

Think about your USP as a "tag line" you use right after you introduce yourself to a stranger.

Here's the company name, and the USP phrasing he finally came up with: "Hi, I'm Rich with Strategic Profit Systems. We specialize in something called 'Profit Coaching', which immediately increases your bottom line, while decreasing your time in the office… since putting your biz into a good system means putting the money-machine on *autopilot*. More money, more business, more time off."

That's good.

That's *really* good.

I like tag lines that rattle off things in three's like this: The word "more" repeated three times, with critical noun/adverb explanations that cover the essence of what you do.

In my experience, a killer company name isn't going to win you any business… and a bad name on a hot company won't hold it back much.

Still, just like a few good key words can get your Website noticed in searches (and a great combination of power words can get your AdWords campaign rocking)… your USP and your company name are both wicked good ways to *start your sales process.*

Think about that conversation you'd have, face to face with someone, explaining who you are and what you offer.

Imagine their eyes rolling back into their head as you try to wow them with boring, generic terms…

… and, instead, figure out a slick turn-of-phrase that, instead, makes their eyes *light up* with a little honest excitement.

"Hey," you want them to say, "I *want* that."

The sweetest words in business.

Chapter Thirteen:

Advanced Life Lessons

Bludgeoning passing opportunities and deconstructing Salesmanship 101…

T here are a couple of keys to learning the advanced lessons in life and biz.

Lesson One is to be relentlessly open to following every whisper of opportunity that comes your way.

Most folks need to be bludgeoned over the skull to realize they have an opportunity trying to get their attention…

… and even then they shrug it off, thinking there will be more, and easier, chances down the line.

Which doesn't happen. The great opportunities *never* announce themselves…

… but rather arrive so quietly and inauspiciously that you *miss* them if you haven't got your radar on full-alert all the time.

The reason some entrepreneurs seem to be living an adventure-filled movie script, is that they seek out and *pursue* opportunities others miss. Sometimes you make a mistake, and have to backtrack…

… but it is NEVER an error to see what's afoot when new choices, and new paths, open up for you.

You take risks, you never treat failure as the final word in anything you do, and you pay close attention to the advantages *as well as* the disadvantages of what happens.

As an entrepreneur, you will constantly be gearing up to head down some fresh road that no one else around you has even noticed yet.

The second lesson is tied into the first: You must learn to look at your life, your successes, your failures, and your efforts in a very critical way.

This means you are constantly *deconstructing* what's going on, what happened, why it turned out the way it did, and (especially) *how you can do better next time.*

This deconstruction of experience is where your best new lessons will come from.

And because you're learning your lessons, it *doesn't matter* if your early experiences are good or bad, successes or dismal failures.

You break *everything* down, like a good detective figuring out a crime scene...

... and you ask the hard questions, while seeking the hidden truths and sometimes uncomfortable answers.

For me, this deconstruction process was kick-started early on, before I became a freelancer. I was hungry to learn everything I could about salesmanship... and I knew that the good stuff wouldn't be found in books.

So I engaged in some real-life hunting for clues in what I call...

<u>Salesmanship 101.</u>

When I finally got serious about becoming an expert in business, I vowed to shut up and *listen* whenever I was around people with experience.

That was a *huge* decision for an arrogant young man to make, and it's paid off in spades over the years. I stopped pretending I knew anything at all about life, and starting soaking up wisdom whenever I got close to it.

In fact, I've been soaking up wisdom and advice for so long, I've actually *forgotten* about some of the early mentors I had.

So… it's time to pay some dues.

I want to tell you about Milt -- the first "real" salesman I ever learned from. And the first man I'd ever met who had figured out how to make life *work*.

Here's the story: In the months just before I began my adventures in freelancing, I took a "transition" job to pay the rent.

I was a one-man art department for a small company, with total control of all advertising. I wrote the copy, designed and pasted-up the ads, and dealt with the media the ads ran in.

Plus -- a *big* plus, too – all the tie-wearing 9-to-5 drudgery and lack of freedom in that office finally impressed upon me the horrible fact that I was working like a dog to make someone *else* rich. That short hitch was my last "real" job.

However, there was one *other* benefit.

Milt.

I'm not gonna sugar-coat this story. There are elements here that may appear quasi-psychotic, and certainly Machiavellian ("*the ends justify the means*")... and I neither agree with Milt on everything, nor encourage you to change your style to mimic his.

Still... coming face-to-face with a guy who had life by the balls was a genuine wake-up call for me.

He was a walking novel.

Milt joined the company the same day I did, as head of the sales department. As I was setting up my little office, he strode in, shook hands enthusiastically, laid a smile as big as the horizon on me, and announced that he was *damn* happy – just overjoyed -- we were gonna be working together.

Now, after spending many years in corporate backwaters (and getting fired a lot) I'd come to distrust elegantly-dressed older guys who glad-handed their way around.
This time, however, I decided to wait and see what happened.

I'm glad I did. Not only did Milt show us all a *deep* bag of salesmanship tricks... and he sold the bejesus out of every product the company offered (blowing away objections like a man puffing at dust and turning skeptical prospects into rabid customers in droves)...

... but he also revealed lessons about *life* (during the after-hours cocktail meetings he insisted upon each day) that held the captive attention of an entire table of "been there, done that" arrogant young men.

The Milt I knew was rubbing up against the far edge of his prime. Not out of it yet, but clearly adjusting his game plan. He was turning sixty, I recall. His current wife was slightly younger.

And, she was also a former Miss America contestant (from Brazil), just like his previous several wives. There are some things Milt would never compromise on.

Like not letting his wife cramp his style. He set her up in a lavish home in San Diego -- over an hour away -- and set himself up near the office in a bachelor pad that would've done Hugh Hefner proud. (One of his nods to getting older was to enjoy well-heeled nightclubs that attracted a slightly more "mature" crowd, and avoid the trashy younger singles bars the rest of us haunted.)

Ol' Milt got around, yes he did.

He never told me what his salary was… but my drinking buddies in accounting let on that he'd negotiated a breathtakingly generous package. It was rumored he took home *more* than the CEO.

He was, apparently, worth it.

In a matter of days, he created a sales team out of thin air… stealing top salesmen from other places he'd worked. They quit their old job while still on the phone with Milt, and raced over to be part of his new venture. The man had mojo.

My first impression of him was vague, but soon solidified. I attended the little "educational" meetings he had with his salesmen, and was blown away by the world-class tactics he taught. It was a very sophisticated blend of street psychology, with classic salesmanship techniques…

… and just a dash of "so good, it should be illegal", slightly-hypnotic mind control. (It should be noted that this was *before* NLP –Neural Linguistic Programming – was popular. Milt had invented his very own brand of persuasion, unique in every respect.)

He was the first true *expert* I'd ever met. He had mastered his chosen field utterly.

Milt was also clearly an Alpha male (despite his slender, non-threatening build)… with perfect posture, a wardrobe like James Bond's, brand new company-leased Cadillac, and a fearless gaze that made you trust your life with him, instantly.

The selling tactics were cool…

… but I was more interested in the back story.

What, exactly, *propelled* a man like this? A man who so confidently strolled through life, brazen in his passions and so completely in charge it was as if he'd scripted each day.

How had he arranged to be the hero of his own movie?

I don't think Milt particularly liked me much. I was the opposite of him in so many ways (being miserably out-of-place in the world, lost and desperately seeking clues without knowing what those clues even looked like)…

… *but he enjoyed my attentive grilling.* (Good side lesson there for anyone looking to get ahead by studying experts.)

Like most geezers, with their glory days fading, I think he was also just happy to tell his tales one more time to an eager audience.

Here's how he became who he was: First -- as in all good adventures -- there must be **motivation**. Something has to happen to stir the passions, to get things moving.

For Milt, it happened in an afternoon when he was barely past puberty. He had sex with the babysitter -- an "older" woman in her twenties.

Today, we'd call it child abuse on her part… but for a guy like Milt, it was a galvanizing moment. He liked it, and wanted more.

Not just with the babysitter, either, and not with the gum-snapping teeny-boppers around him.

It was a teasingly brief taste of the grand feast that life offered... but refused to dole out easily. So he set his sights "Miss America" high, despite all the obstacles in front of him.

While his peers quaked in fear of the challenges ahead, Milt started *planning* how to get what he wanted, in step-by-step fashion.

Now, I was raised without a hint on how to tackle life -- and this was the first time I'd ever heard anyone talk about "**breaking it down**".

You start with the *end result* you desire... and work *backward*, figuring out what skills, tools, resources and experience you need to get there.

Hearing Milt talk about planning his life made me realize how rudderless I was, and I've used that concept of "breaking it down" ever since. (It is, in fact, the *foundation* of my entire "Hot Seat" consulting model.)

He had his work cut out for him, too. He was a poor kid, in a hick town in the middle of some landlocked state without a major city nearby.

So, after getting motivated (and sex truly was a great motivator for him)...

... he mapped out his journey *backwards* from his desired goal.

And got busy with **goal-directed behavior**.

This meant finding a way to earn lots of money without family connections or inherited wealth. It meant learning to blend in with well-heeled people, and making his lower-class telltale habits disappear.

It also meant creating opportunity where none existed, and where no easy handouts were likely to be offered.

For a clueless guy like me, this was fascinating stuff. Maybe you grew up with a world-wise uncle giving you good advice, or maybe mentors stepped out of the crowd to single you out and lead you to the promised land.

If so, good for you.

But, for most entrepreneurs I know, that never happened. I describe myself, at seminars, as being like the pig that broke into the farmhouse kitchen…

… and just sat there gazing at the fridge, knowing it held a feast, but not having a clue how to get it open.

For me, learning about goal setting and motivation and focused energy was the equivalent of acquiring opposable thumbs for a pig -- suddenly, *you can get the fridge open.*

Milt's goal-directed behavior was a fairly straight path -- he quickly figured out that becoming a salesman on commission was a way to earn money far beyond a fixed salary. So he sought out mentors when possible, and read books like a demon to get his salesmanship skills honed.

He did the same to "fix" the gaps in his manners, his posture, and the way he dressed and carried himself.

The idea was *transformation.*

He cared not a whit what his peers thought. The other kids went about their adolescence in ways that pretty much guaranteed they would end up in the same position as their parents -- never leaving town, working for The Man, cursing dreams of glory as unattainable nonsense.

As for opportunity... there was *none* in the town Milt lived in. So, he left, as soon as possible. Worked hard at the best sales jobs around, saved his money (but never scrimped on looking good), studied the world as best he could...

... and split, as prepared as a kid from nowhere could be.

Not for Hollywood or New York, either. *Europe* was his destination.

I'm short on details here, but Milt had figured there were several ways to break into the feast from the "outside". He decided not to do the officer-in-the-military route (which has helped many men get into politics and the upper class). And he had no time to waste *working* his way up any ladder in a corporation.

This guy understood, even at an age when other young men believe they will live forever...

... **that he needed to sit at the feast as soon as possible**, so he could enjoy it for as *long* as possible in a too-short life.

Most people -- me, included, before I got hip to waking up -- tend to look at life as some endless stretch ahead of them. Plenty of time to pursue those dreams. No need to knock yourself out. Go ahead and crack another beer, watch some more TV.

It's nonsense, but it's the way most of the slumbering masses get through their days.

If they were meant to be at the feast, they'd just somehow get *invited* or something, is the common thinking.

Milt knew there was no invitation coming, and any adventure would need be his to initiate. So he went to Austria, and learned to ski. Learned very well. And earned a spot on the Austrian Ski Team.

I saw his jacket. Just showing the emblem to anyone in Europe, at that time, was a ticket into *any* party or closed event. It was like being one of the Beatles. It triggered invitations.

And when I suggested he must have been some kind of "natural" athlete, he scoffed. He figured out, before he even tried, which sport he could both excel at *and* get the most benefit from. And then he went about excelling, and benefiting.

He told me that when the team performed, he could single out any woman in the crowd as he skied past and "have" her that evening.

When I protested that married women surely were immune, he scoffed some more. Believe what you must, he said. No one was safe from the charms of ski team members.

This hint of sociopathy turned me off a bit. Milt was an extremely likeable guy, but I sensed he was using bonding *tricks* to bring out those feelings in us.

He never committed to anything, including friendship, that would compromise his style. There was definitely a dark side to his on-going quest for what he had targeted as the "best" seat at life's feast.

Still, I continued to learn from him. One day, he *ordered* me to ask him out to lunch. I said "What? Just you and me?"

Yes, that's *exactly* what he meant.

Turns out, every other man in the department had already asked for, and received, a big raise.

They did it by asking Milt out to lunch, and having a man-to-man talk about their worth and value… after which, Milt went back to the CEO and negotiated more money.

He was concerned that I was simply unaware of this "rite of passage" in a corporate setting… and he was right. I had never considered raises as something you negotiated -- they just *happened*, if you were "good", somehow.

God, was I dumb.

During this concocted lunch, he insisted on going through the motions as if I had initiated things. It was a severe reality check, my first major one. This was a great example of *how things worked* at a level far above anything I'd ever experienced before.

Milt was *forcing* me to grow. I don't know why. Like I said, I don't think he even liked me particularly -- my slacker/hippie past offended him, as did all types of cluelessness and aggressive stupidity. Maybe I was a challenge.

Later, he gave me an explosive lesson in *rewards*. I had accidentally found a prospect for the company's wares, and handed that prospect over to one of the salesmen to close. I never considered myself a salesman -- I was the "ad guy".

However, when that account came on board, Milt invited me over to his apartment… and gave me his nearly-new stereo equipment. I'm talking about *beaucoup* bucks worth of nice stuff.

It was, he said, my *commission* for the sale. He was *forcing* me to see the potential of salesmanship.

That episode rocked my brain. It started a rumble that became the avalanche of my freelance career…

… and I was one of the first freelancers, years later, to jump on the royalty paradigm when it was created, getting a piece of the action my copy generated, way beyond just the initial fee.

Milt had lifted the curtain ever so slightly, and given me a glimpse of the possibilities far outside my cramped little world.

Just a wee peek.

He didn't single me out for anything. He did things like this -- offering intense little lessons in life -- for *everyone* in his department. Maybe because it bonded us to him like dogs. (It was soon clear why the salesmen had left other jobs to come work with him again. They would have followed him anywhere.)

That "break it down" process he started as a kid preparing his life's trajectory never ended. He took every detail of life, and broke it down.

If he didn't understand something, he would soon *figure it out.* At an expert level.

If a door was closed to him, he soon had it open. And knew what to do, once he got in, to be instantly accepted. Because he figured it out, and prepared.

This small-town kid had grown up to become a modern Renaissance man, comfortable with luxury, hip to the good life, knowledgeable, wise, fearless…

… and *experienced.*

He saw the world as it was… not as he *wished* it was, and not as he felt it *should* be. This "awake and fearless" realization, alone, can change anyone's life.

Like I said, I don't agree with everything Milt did or believed. He wasn't unethical… and I know he went out of his way to *never lie*. (This may account for the multiple marriages. I think he tried to be "courteous" to his wife by being discrete with his philandering. He didn't seem particularly bothered, though, with his trail of heartache, either.)

But his overall style left out too much of what I consider important. Like close friends, and making relationships work.

I never saw Milt again. We both resigned around the same time -- he had either found a better gig, or gotten tired of his current circumstances…

… and I finally had mustered the courage to become a freelancer.

I also haven't given him much thought in the passing years. I just Googled him, and there's zero record. That fits -- he guarded his privacy like a spy…

… and I'm sure he had multiple "exit" strategies, also like a spy, that would allow him to change identities and nationality, if necessary.

He just popped into my mind as I considered the concept of *experience*.

He wasn't directly responsible for my life of adventures as a freelancer…

… but he played a role in pushing me off the diving board, so to speak.

I don't have complaints about my life so far -- I actually enjoyed being a slacker, and my awkward climb from cluelessness to expert-level savvy has given me amazing insight into human behavior.

But it has for sure been *more* fun since I woke up, and began actively pursuing goals. Milt was not the first guy to "break things down" -- but until I met him, I'd never encountered the concept.

Now, I see that process as integral to having worthwhile experiences. Most folks experience something, and bounce off that experience like a pinball.

Nothing learned, no clues collected.

This is what separates the true teacher from the wannabe.

To do your job well, you first have to learn.

To *teach* well, you must break down the lessons and understand them, deeply.

I hope I've made my point.

Chapter Fourteen:

The Main Goal Of A Life Well-Lived

*And how to bust into the best party in the universe
and demand a seat at the table…*

I've got two important things to cover in this chapter.

First, a bit of advanced philosophy.

Then, an announcement that may bring tears to a few people's
eyes, as well as the rending of garments.

But philosophy first…

Ahem.

I brought up the concept of "**The Feast**" way back at the very
beginning of my guru-dom, many years ago.

It's a metaphor for the state of self-satisfaction and *arrival* you feel
when you finally "make it" in biz, and in life. (It has to be that one-
two punch.)

The phrase came to me while dwelling on the actress Lillian
Russell's famous quote: "*Life is a banquet… and most poor
suckers are starving to death.*"

That concept both delighted and shocked me…

… and also made me think hard about the process of moving from unsuccessful to successful. (I hate thinking hard as much as you do, but it comes with the job.)

I was delighted because it's just a great piece of concise storytelling.

You very clearly get the image of a banquet going on behind closed doors, where it's warm and fun and everyone is gorging on goodies.

And outside, squinting through the window with bloodshot eyes, are the people who can't quite figure out why they aren't *in* there with the others…

… instead of being frozen out, hungry for more of what life offers, but clueless about getting a taste.

And I was shocked because it so clearly described my *own* feelings of being left out, back before I grabbed a seat.

The word "banquet" didn't ring as true as "feast" for me, though.

By changing the image around to a more robust example of raucous fun and debauchery, I both beefed up the goal ahead and super-charged my desire to earn it.

And truly, you must *earn* your seat at the Feast of Life.

No one will invite you in.

And no one will bring you in as a guest.

The bouncer at the door is a nine-headed hell-born bruiser with sharp teeth and no sense of humor. You are *not* getting in without earning your entry, period.

Just in case you're harboring illusions of somehow sneaking in under the radar.

Now, it would be unfair to refer to those outside in the cold as losers. Really, some of them have simply not yet begun or completed their journey inside. But they *are* outsiders, in the most common sense of the term.

Me? I was a stone cold loser.

I grew up so clueless about life that I was a flesh-and-blood "before" example of a complete outsider.

What made it bearable was a simple plot element: I was *convinced* that everyone else DID have a clue about living life well…

… and they just weren't sharing the secrets.

This belief drove me through a decades-long apprenticeship as a slacker. (The Dude in "The Big Lebowski" was where I was headed.)

Slowly, though -- *very* slowly -- I came to realize that my belief of being the only guy left out of the secret path to total enjoyment of life…

… was totally *wrong*.

The truth brought me to my knees, literally: Everyone else wasn't *hiding* their secrets from me.

They didn't HAVE any secrets to share.

I was living in a world filled with zombie sleep-walkers, stumbling through life just as clueless as I was.

The difference: Most of them seemed to be totally *okay* with that.

And it *wasn't* okay with me.

Living life as a piece of driftwood in a stormy ocean was painful.

I was depressed, broke, and increasingly without hope.

You know what saved me?

Biology, for one thing. I cannot physically stand to have my neck constricted.

Wearing neckties literally made me feel like I was *choking to death*.

That made me a bad fit for the buttoned-up corporate realm of the day. (For the youngsters out there, let me remind you that in the bad old days of your elders, beards were verboten... any non-normal hair style -- including shaven heads, Mohawks, and long 'do's -- was a sin... and any attempt at expressing individuality in dress was cause for being immediately *dismissed*.) (The Man is a brutal, controlling bastard.)

(Of course, I've been fired from nearly every "normal" job I've ever held.)

But there was something else, too, that kept me from being absorbed into the belly of the corporate beast.

It was a nagging feeling -- vague and inchoate -- that settling for a "job" would kill my spirit.

Today, people celebrate that kind of rebelliousness. It's what made the current entrepreneurial world what it is.

People like Steve Jobs (who was fired several times by the very company he brought to life, once the Suits tried to take over) are now patron saints of modern business savvy…

… but they had to breach the walls of "inside the box" corporate thinking and habit *first*… and it was a long, bloody fight.

What saved my ass, back then, was a perfect storm of coincidences.

I lost my job, my girlfriend, and my place to live all within a few weeks time, and I spent the next six months on the road. Homeless, unloved, dismissed.

As lost, lonely and illegitimate as a man can be.

I lived off some meager occasional odd jobs along the way. I slept in the car and on friends' sofas, and cruised the entire length of the U.S. Pacific coast, from Seattle to San Diego (including dips into Canada and Mexico).

This is not an uncommon American story. I am well-read, and I know how this novel often ends up -- settling down in some place, and finally finding something to do to while away the rest of your days.

Blend in and vanish.

But I lucked out. Perusing the newspaper one day (after a fitful night on yet another couch in another strange city), I saw Joe Karbo's famous ad with the headline "The Lazy Man's Way To Riches".

It was the first direct response long-copy ad I'd ever noticed before, and the first I read.

It was also the first one I *responded* to. I ordered the book, and God bless Joe for sending it out so quickly.

As you should know, that short tome was essentially a distillation of "Think And Grow Rich" by Napoleon Hill. I soon found that original book, and all the other classic books on entrepreneurship and grabbing life…

… because I had instantly been shoved into a fever of discovery.

I had never before even considered the *concept* of goals.

You mean (I suddenly thought) a guy can actually WANT something…

… and then PLAN to attain it?

And then go out and GET IT?

Are you *kidding* me?

Why didn't anyone TELL me about this before?

I was in my early thirties. Not a puppy. Not stupid, and not uneducated.

What I'd discovered was a crack in the wall of silence in this culture.

Whether by design or by accident, there is no easy way for anyone to break out of the zombie state assigned to you by The Man.

You gotta find your own way out. And it's a painful and disorienting to shed off your old skin and re-emerge as someone new.

It's painful… ***but it's also exciting.***

And *fun*, once you're into it.

At first, I was giddy with this new toy -- my blossoming ability to actually desire something, and then go get it.

Then, I noticed the **Feast**.

I'd never even suspected it was there before. I knew that other people enjoyed "better" lifestyles…

… but I had some hazy idea that they were a different breed, doing things that I had no business even *daring* to dream about (except for the occasional glimpse in magazines like Playboy).

I came in from the storm, and stood at the window gazing in, metaphorically licking my chops.

And I got kinda pissed off about it. Better late than never, sure…

… but it was high time I busted my way in.

It was a gruesome and sloppy process, because I had no clear plan. And only the faint encouragement of dead men and their books to back me up.

Still, the long haul is what made me the dude I am today.

Imperfect, flawed, and by no means a role model for anyone, of course.

But because I crawled through the obstacle course and not just lived but actually *thrived*…

… I am nevertheless completely qualified to *teach* others how to gain entry to this Feast.

Nearly every lesson I send out has **one main thrust:** To help you get closer to The Feast, on your own terms.

I don't write copy for you… I teach you to write it for yourself.

I don't tell you how to market shit… I teach you how to figure out the solutions and get moving in ways that are meaningful for *you*.

And here's the biggest revelation of all: **The Feast is *inside* of you.**

There's no "real" party going on, anywhere, that you need to attend.

There's no lifestyle delineated anywhere that you need to adhere to.

And there's nowhere you need to be…

… except at that special place that is meaningful and sustaining to YOU.

The Feast is within you.

You get to define it, you get to change the details however you wish…

… and you get to sample everything and alter the menu every single day of your life, if that's what you feel you need to do.

One of the big damn discoveries everyone makes when they first encounter goal-setting and attainment is this: Initially, nearly everything you *believe* you wanted with every fiber of your heart…

… isn't such a great treat when you finally get it.

But that's not failure.

No. *It's just part of the process.*

Until you get good at the "game" of attaining goals, you just have to move through the stages that are inherent in your personal system. Each time you attain something, and then decide it's not really what you wanted, you just learn the lesson and move forward.

And the grandest realization of all is that this kind of movement IS life.

There are no big "master endgame goals" that you attain, and then it's over.

That's not how it works.

The real joy is in the *pursuit* of goals.

There's no finish line.

The Feast has an endless revolving menu of courses, and the lucky ones among us dive into each one with gusto.

That's the biggest insight I have to offer anyone.

The Feast is within you.

Chapter Fifteen:

Disgruntled Leeches

Wrong diagnoses, government porn sites, and waiting around for the clueless to get clued in…

L et's call this "The Disgruntled Chapter."

Now, I'm not particularly mad at anyone, and I'm having a bit of raw fun this summer.

Still… when I sit down to make notes for the blog or a blistering Facebook post, I keep channeling this dark, hidden part of me that is… *disgruntled.*

It started last month, when I went off on the topic of "experience". I half-thought that diatribe (where I blasted many of the self-described "gurus" out there pretending to be wiser than they really are, lacking the perspective and battle scars of veterans who didn't learn their craft from a book but from actual, you know, *experience*) would have cost me some readers…

… but instead, it hit a nerve.

Turns out, there are a lot of fellow disgruntled out there, a little peeved over the way bad (and often just dead *wrong*) info and advice gets tossed around in the entrepreneurial space by meatheads looking for a quick buck.

So… what the hell.

I've got a little pile of notes here that, alone, would likely never make it into stand-alone posts (because they're disconnected from the subjects I usually write about).

And what I've decided to do… is to just plow through these semi-misanthropic mini-rants, and maybe flush all this gnarly gunk out of my system.

Let's see if you agree with me on these issues that only busy entrepreneurs in the modern landscape ever seem to have to deal with.

Here we go:

Disgruntle #1: I get knocked off so much that one of my assistant's first jobs each week is to go online and find the latest blatant offering of copied materials from my catalog of books and courses.

The online auction site eBay is a major offender. She'll find sloppily-copied versions of my stuff for sale there, and has the direct number for the joint taped to her phone.

It doesn't take long for her to get that auction booted.

Cuz it's, like, illegal.

The customer service folks at eBay are getting sick of hearing from us… but it's their own fault for not having ANY plan for dealing with repetitive rip-off artists.

Now, what's funny (in a grim way), is how the rippers sometimes *react*.

They email me, absolutely in a *snit* about getting their sordid auction bumped.

They actually DEMAND that I explain to them, personally and in detail, *why* they can't sell illegal knock-offs of my products for profit.

Knowing they're in this snit is the only satisfaction I get -- I never answer their emails, but it's nice knowing they're riled up.

Look -- using my ads as blueprints for your own stuff is fine. It's a form of flattery, even. All I ask is that you give me credit once in a while, a nice testimonial or a shout-out in a blog. Nothing fancy.

But actively trying to attach yourself to my coattails -- and steal my thunder -- is just sleazy.

It's being a *leech*.

A few years back, Gary Halbert told me about this odd guy who insisted on traveling to Miami to present something "important and exciting".

Like a fool, Gary agreed.

What the "exciting" something turned out to be… was an exact word-for-word rip of Gary's book "Maximum Money In Minimum Time"… with some very *disturbing* alterations.

This bozo had replaced every verb with an idiosyncratic (and mostly unappetizing) imitation. So, where Gary had written "get your greed glands salivating"… this nutcase had substituted "get your greed glands drooling buckets of spit".

I'm serious.

This is what the guy spent *months* at.

Then he replaced Gary's name with his -- which was *creepy*, because this book was filled with personal stories from Gary's life. So this new version was a stone-cold identity theft.

The punch line: This rip-off artist was *astonished* that Gary wasn't pleased at the result.

The guy had actually thought Gary would break a leg offering this new book to his own list.

It was beyond bizarre.

And yet... *this kind of rip-off thinking is not unusual.*

Another example: The newsletter I produced for eight years was called "The Marketing Rebel Rant". Copyrighted the entire time.

And now word reaches me there's some guy online doing a "Rebellious Marketer's Rant" blog-like thing. It's lame, dreadful reading and I feel sorry for this ripper's utter lack of originality.

But I also think: *Screw you.*

Where is your friggin' *self-respect?*

There is room for everyone in this brave new online world. And God knows I've done my part in urging and pushing people to get their own e-biz going.

Just make an *attempt* to plow your *own* row, all right?

Don't start your acting career calling yourself Marlon *Bando* or Johnny *Depth*, for example. (Unless you really have *uber*-chops and can leverage a little honest irony, like Elvis Costello did when he burst onto the music scene. But irony is a slippery thing, and if you have *any* doubts about the quality of your talent, you need to punt. Unless you're in X-rated films, where there's a tradition of amusing name rips.)

I spent over four years nurturing that newsletter. I thought it was overkill to trademark the term "marketing rebel"... but now I'm glad I did. It was my baby. My *brand.*

And I put my name on it. I actively engage in the sin of pride when it comes to the Rant.

Goddammit.

So when some yo-yo comes along and takes advantage of my hard work with a cheap shot like this … well, I just feel so… *used.* (Sniff.)

Okay, I'm kidding. I'll be fine no matter how many losers hack my efforts. I'll let the quality of my work do my talking for me.

But still. (Plus, I sold the name Marketing Rebel to a good friend, who now has that gruesome job of chasing down copycats.)

I have long known that *every* market out there has an underbelly crawling with leeches. This will never change.

But I don't have to *like* it. None of us do.

There are blood-suckers out there who are *proud* of their efforts, too. Like the guy I met at a recent seminar who made a living buying up URLs close in spelling to existing ones… essentially "drafting" the momentum of someone else's efforts.

He considered himself a "pirate" worthy of respect and admiration. And he had the smirk to go with that attitude. *What a clever, clever boy I am.*

Dude, that's not clever marketing. That's *leech* behavior.

And I'm not saying you gotta be a "nice guy" in business.

Capitalism is, at heart, gladiator warfare. It is, in fact, only a slight upgrade from the law of the jungle – only now, instead of the winner eating the loser and wearing his shrunken head as a necklace, the victor just gets to *bank all the money.*

It's a tad more civilized. But it remains cutthroat, and I have no problem with aggressive competition. (Which often requires a little copycat behavior -- but *not* leeching.)

The free market demands a thick skin for every participant.

Still, you will never be *respected* by your peers until you show some honest originality.

(Just to complicate things... in some markets, rip-offs can be harnessed for *good*. Music artists who fight illegal downloads are earning a bad reputation from fans. Smarter groups, like the Grateful Dead, never stood in the way of bootleggers... intuitively understanding that active trading of live show recordings could be *free publicity* and a way to nurture interest in the music.)

(The greed-head suits at the big labels still haven't figured this out. When everything you do is targeted to profit, it's hard to step out of that paradigm and see how allowing rips can *help* things. Thinking hurts suits' brains.)

Hey, I thought it was funny back when www.whitehouse.com was a porn site, for many years in the early aughts. (Most people forgot to use *.gov* instead of *.com* typing in the site's URL.) The domain has since been redirected to the right source -- I'm sure a little visit by the FBI had something to do with it.

But it's NOT funny when the image-leeching happens to me. And it won't be funny when it happens to you, either.

Jeez, I'm in a bad mood.

Disgruntle #2: I think the pendulum is swinging back... but for the last several years, this country has been in an anti-intellectual fever.

At first, I thought the "don't trust science" shrieking was just another media bender -- a little agitation to get more people to read the newspaper.

But then the polls started coming out... revealing that a *majority* of Americans believe scientists are on some kind of liberal/communist agenda to harsh the mellow of "normal" people.

Somewhere along the line, *critical thinking* has gotten a bad rap.

Actually, this country has been suspicious of egg-heads for a very long time. And not without some reason -- I grew up with sci-fi flicks where the bad guy was always a misguided scientist or deliberately-evil smart guy causing trouble.

This was blowback from the atom bomb and the lingering queasiness of nuking Nagasaki and Hiroshima -- not exactly a highlight of scientific progress.

Yet, the "brilliant" evil mastermind figure goes back even further. Lex Luther, Superman's brainy nemesis, was introduced in 1940 (pre-bomb). Moriarty -- the only man able to outwit Sherlock Holmes -- goes back to Victorian days.

And the original Luddites were a group of early 19th-century folks so distraught at the prospect of new technology ruining things that they ran around destroying all the cotton gins they could find. (The term "Luddite" now refers to anyone allergic to technology. I heard it used twice yesterday on CNN.)

Get straight on this: Technology scares the *bejesus* out of most folks.

Our modern Luddites seem to labor under some delusion that what this country needs is a forced march back to the glorious 1950s... where Mom stayed home baking pies and TV networks went off the air early (right after "I Love Lucy").

Hey -- I have my own grievances against all kinds of modern ills. I think the medical establishment is *criminal* in its reliance on pharmaceuticals and surgery, for example.

I also think every new generation shouldn't be allowed to possess cell phones or drive cars until they've been forced to survive in the wilderness for a while first.

Get a little perspective on what *propels* our quest for high tech and the safety/comfort/ease it brings to the daily grind, if you know what I mean.

And learn that feral beasts aren't really as cuddly as Disney makes them out to be.

But the current wave of anti-intellectualism is more than a robust argument over the ethics of stem cells and accuracy of carbon dating.

It also threatens the biggest social equalizing technology in our history -- the Web.

Information is the life-blood of the Internet. And the people who fear losing the status quo (where they're currently on top, politically and financially) are hot on the case to *corral* the free exchange of ideas and info.

The genius "freedom of speech" protections of the First Amendment are all about censorship. If you are all for censoring *anything* now -- whether it's hip hop lyrics, cable late-night raunch, or middle school sex education -- I suggest you think twice before cheering on the lynch mob.

Because you're probably making a whole boardroom full of smug Fat Cats smile.

You're following their game plan.

First, South Park.

Then, the Web.

Short term, it's easy to understand why people in power want to slam the door on "too much" exchange of free info. It hurts profits.

Information is power, and right now vast libraries of it is *free* online.

Doctors are being challenged on diagnoses. (I recently discovered a doctor had prescribed steroidal medication for me that was *contra-indicated* for my condition. Thank God for AMA-busting info via the advanced sharing on the Harvard School of Medicine site. I went to another doc who was horrified at the mistake, and helped me fix it immediately.)

Politicians and journalists are being fact-checked online as they speak and write. (And boy, do they *hate* that.)

Even car salesmen are feeling the heat. (When we leased our Audi, we knew more about the options than the manager on the lot. Took us twenty minutes online, and we killed *all* the bullshit and profit-gouging cold. The salesman was nearly in *tears* by the time we signed the papers.)

People in positions of power don't *like* being challenged, or proven wrong, or one-upped with better info.

It makes them irritable.

They don't like it… but the *rest* of us *should*.

However, until those being challenged and fact-checked catch up to the "instant bullshit detecting" paradigm of the Information

Age… they will squirm and fight like cornered cats to *stem* the free flow of ideas and info.

If this protection of short-term interests prevails, we're *all* in trouble.

Quick story: The big news of the year 1532 was the successful conquest of Peru in South America by the Spanish conquistador Pizarro.

And it would have gone otherwise if the Incas had a *written language.*

But they didn't… even though their Mayan neighbors a short distance north did. (To understand why, read "Guns, Germs and Steel" -- fascinating examination at how info traveled fast in the analog world of east-west spice routes, yet stagnated in north-south situations, due to climate and vegetation "toll booths".)

Pizarro had around 100 exhausted men, and was facing a lethally-proven Incan army of multiple thousands, fresh from slaughtering other enemies and clearly still hungry for more blood.

He should have been a brief, unpleasant memory in Incan history ("*Remember those hairy dudes with pots on their heads we ate?*")… except there *wasn't* any Incan history.

Without writing, info spread only by word of mouth… making your own wobbly memory banks the largest data-storage unit available.

So the Incan ruler made all decisions straight from the hip. Hunches, essentially.

Or, more precisely, *brain farts*. What he knew about conducting war consisted solely of what he'd managed to learn in his brief lifetime. And the fact his large army routinely made mince-meat of opponents reinforced his self-image as a living God. So why bother with strategy?

Not so for the conquistadors. Pizarro had not only studied centuries of warfare from many different cultures... he'd also read Cortez's best-selling book "How I Conquered the Aztecs" a few years earlier. (I forget the actual title.)

Cortez, too, had been seriously outnumbered and over-matched. But he used old-school street smarts to weasel his way *around* the army, and just kidnapped the Aztec ruler. Game over in one classic move.

Pizarro decided to follow the same tactic. None of his superior technology -- gunpowder, steel weapons and armor, naval savvy -- would have helped much, being so outrageously outnumbered.

But the one technological advantage that DID make the difference... was *knowledge*. (Pizarro kidnapped the ruler, just like his mentor Cortez had, the Incan army fled in confusion, and their civilization was *toast*, in a blink.)

Books like Cortez's were the first step in the "information revolution" that has reached a sort of climax with the Web today.

And people in power have always wanted to keep information *away* from their enemies (and, with tyrants, away from their own subjects -- ignorance is good for the tyranny biz).

People who don't study history don't understand this.

In America, kids now routinely graduate from high school without ever having read a single book. Their main use of the Web is for entertainment and hooking up.

And, anyway, it's *fun* to mock smart-asses.

It's *hard* to stay current, gather knowledge and process it, and put it to good use. (I've heard people complain that reading gives them a headache. Hint: If opening a book causes you pain, then you're doing it *wrong*, all right?)

Much easier to embrace ignorance and pretend the lights and air conditioning go on every day because of magic.

The know-nothings have had their day, including a whole lot of political success. But they can't hold onto that success because, eventually, even outnumbered "smarty-pants" types get pissed off and press their very substantial powers.

They're in charge of the freakin' *Grid*, after all.

Ignorance is bliss only when someone with a brain is watching your back.

Disgruntle #3: I know several people who have used the power of affiliate marketing tactics to get a number-one ranking on Amazon and even the New York Times bestseller list.

It's a *trick*, of course… and now there are multiple publishers who have a menu of prices they offer new authors: Pay us this, and we'll get you this high ranking.

Guaranteed.

There's nothing new about such pay-to-play tactics. Political pundits with vendetta-bent money behind them have simply bought their way to the top of the best-selling lists for years. (They order massive piles of their own tripe, at full price, and dole the book out as a freebie to the yowling base. Expensive, but it gives the desired impression of having swept the land with the force of the ideas.)

And if your marketing plans *require* the badge of having been ranked number one, why the hell *not* use this trick?

Makes sense to me.

In fact, I applaud anyone who levels a shot at the head of the major publishing moguls, who don't give a rat's ass about quality anyway.

Still... since I'm still in the middle of a frothing rant... it may be time to point out that many of these best-selling emperors *aren't wearing any clothes.*

I mean... you can trick your way into lots of things. Like walking into a bar and pretending to be someone you're not, talking up your imaginary Hollywood contacts and piles of cash and mansion in the hills.

This may provide you with short-term results... but you'll soon be found out.

If that's something you can live with, then good for you. *Caveat emptor* and all that.

And the prevailing notion, anyway, is that "quality" is in the eye of the beholder. Why should anyone's idea of what's good or bad hold any more weight than anyone else's?

Thus, the winner of American Idol has earned equal status with The Beatles... metaphysical myth stands shoulder-to-shoulder with science... and hastily-filmed YouTube home videos are the new "Citizen Kane".

Or not.

I've recoiled at the idea of easy quality since I was a kid. (Wanna read a great book that nails the mercurial nature of quality best? "Zen And The Art Of Motorcycle Maintenance". My highest recommendation.)

Movies and television have long fed the notion that skill and talent are merely matters of *minimal effort*. While I know from experience that learning to play the guitar requires hours of bleeding fingers and frayed nerves, you wouldn't get that impression from the last thousand screenplays about musicians, for example.

The general culture seems to NEED to believe that Mozart just channeled his tunes from some unearthly source, without much sweat equity. Or, if there *is* any torture to being an artist, the pain comes from cool, if annoying, personality flaws.

I really enjoy hanging out with people who accomplish stuff.

It doesn't even matter what that accomplishment is -- I've listened for hours to guys who are masters at construction equipment, fascinated at the skill required to wrangle earth-moving machinery.

Heck, I even have lawyer friends who weave amazing tales from case files that would never stand a chance of making it to Law And Order.

I love to listen to *anyone* who has mastered something. Skill and accomplishment is a heady brew… and it matters not a whit if you've earned public applause for your efforts yet.

So, while I'm a fan of any marketing tactic that closes the deal (and leaves a trail of happy customers)… I am continually annoyed at the Kato Kaelins of the world. (Kato, you recall, got famous merely by being a friend of OJ Simpson.)

People who essentially *cheat* to earn their spot at the table… and then insist they *belong* there… may be dominating the culture right now, but their empires are built on sand.

The culture will never change -- rewards will continue to be heaped on talent-challenged puppets backed by cynical marketers. Nearly every reality show star out there is a good example.

And "true" artists will continue to languish in the shadows... perhaps buoyed by a small fan base, like Charles Bukowski, or living in cultural exile like Van Gogh, discovered only after an empty career and early death.

Ultimately, I suppose, this is the way things are meant to be.

Wanting things to be different is a result of too much idealism in my childhood.

I remember the first time I realized that there *weren't* any "gentlemanly" rules to surviving in the streets. Quite literally an "in your face" reality check. (I got knocked out by a guy who didn't wait for me to put my fists up.)

In the movies -- at least the movies I devoured as a kid -- there was a sense that fights were settled with quasi-polite fisticuffs... *and the good guy always won.*

This led to a delusional belief that, if I was simply in the "right", I would *automatically* win any confrontation.

I'm just lucky that my first encounter with a dirty fighter was when we were both too young to put any weight or strength behind our punches. Getting sucker-punched hurt, went against all the rules... and shattered my tidy little universe.

Life *wasn't* fair, it turned out.

It's a brutal lesson, best learned early.

A semi-famous shrink once told me an easy way to judge the potential actions of any given person... was to simply find out if they moved through the world as if it were mostly *safe*...

... or mostly *dangerous*.

When I was young -- and stupid, and eagerly doing stupid things with great stupid gusto -- we had a ready insult for anyone afraid to test their limits: We called them a "Safe". It was a barely-more-mature version of calling someone a "scaredy cat".

On the other hand, we kept our distance from those grinning hoodlums who *truly* seemed to have no sensible fear or shame at all. No fear of injury, no fear of jail, no fear of death.

Somewhere in the middle is a place where you can equally enjoy evil fun as well as sedate and contemplative moments. Too far in either direction, and you end up becoming an anarchist or paranoid gun nut. Moderation rocks.

Part of the reason I left the "normal" world of agency advertising was the utter lack of true creative juice. Madison Avenue considers itself "dangerous" and "daring"...

... but, in reality, they're dull and deluded.

And you can't fully enjoy the thrill of entrepreneurism without having cultivated a taste for a little honest risk and fear.

However, most of the world huddles in the safest corner they can find, suppressing dreams, distrusting too much excitement, and actively angry at anyone who dares do things differently.

Almost by definition, real quality is simply too hot for most folks to handle. And that's just the way it is, and always will be.

Hey -- I have long since lost any urge to stare death down. I've had my car wrecks, my drunken brawls, my dangerous liaisons…

… and while I cherish the memories, I now find more satisfaction in pursuing the dangers of intellectual honesty and -- yes -- the pursuit of *quality*.

Quick story that shows why I believe the universe is correct, working its mysterious ways: Several years ago, I was *happy* being the anonymous "secret weapon" copywriter -- the guy who got the job done, but didn't need the heat of center stage to feel fulfilled.

I was well-known enough in the "inside" world of marketing to feel smug about my reputation, and earn a ridiculously-good living.

What more could I possibly want?

Of course, as soon as that question pops into your mind… it will never go away.

No matter how satisfied you are with your life… when even the *smallest* twinge of yearning for "something else" hits your gut… you are at the end of that movie.

And a new reel needs to be loaded up.

Life isn't stagnant. We just aren't prepared for the *way* dramatic change takes over.

Anyway… I went to a seminar in Phoenix that featured a roundtable brainstorm about advanced marketing tactics. I knew many of the participants, but half of them were strangers. So, to begin things, we all introduced ourselves.

Stay with me here -- I'm sharing a seminal moment in my career. One I never saw coming.

The introductions went around the room, almost like an AA meeting: *Hi, I'm so-and-so, and here's a quick rundown of my resume.*

When it came to me, I just stood up and said I was a copywriter. Those who knew who I was nodded, and a few sent notes my way asking for a private meeting during the first break. I was a very minor celebrity to maybe a quarter of the room, and a complete cipher to the rest.

Fine with me. I didn't need to impress anybody with a list of credentials.

I preferred to rest on my laurels.

I sat down. The woman next to me stood up and introduced herself as an author… and around the table, almost everyone nodded in acknowledgement.

They'd heard of her book. It had caused quite a stir, sitting atop the best-seller lists for a time. She'd sold a TON of copies.

Here is where my big revelation came crashing down on my naïve head: For the rest of the seminar, people referred to her as "the best-selling author", and took copious notes whenever she talked about the craft of writing.

Her single book? A tome titled something like "What Men Know About Women"…

… one hundred *blank pages*, bound in a nice cover and sold at bookstores worldwide.

Get it? Blank book. A gimmicky joke.

Author.

I was stunned every time someone referred to her as a best-selling writer. No one -- *no one* -- acknowledged a drop of irony, and she basked in the attentions that only a best-selling author ignites in a room of marketers.

I'm sure she's a very nice person. Heck, she may even be an excellent writer... and someday she'll publish a "real" book that will blow me away. I certainly give her buckets of credit for marketing a concept that hit a nerve with half the population. (I'm not sure how many men have followed her career, but I have yet to meet a woman who hasn't said "*Oh yeah, I remember that book!*")

Meanwhile, as the seminar attendees chattered around me, I was sent into a cold daze. It wasn't jealousy. It was the realization that it was MY fault most people there didn't know who I was (and were not predisposed to defer to whatever wisdom I brought to the table).

Resting on your laurels is fine... *until you start to expect other people to do any footwork learning what those laurels are.*

If life were fair, the many years of hard, brain-sweating work I'd done perfecting my writing chops would precede me wherever I went.

And when I announced at an event that I was a copywriter, that alone would alert everyone to the high level of craft I had achieved.

That afternoon, the last shreds of naiveté fell from my eyes.

I realized I needed to write a book. A real book, one that actually *would* precede me and do my introductions for me.

In a blink, I was no longer satisfied to be the secret weapon, deep in the shadows stage-right.

So I went home, cancelled all other plans, and spent a few exhausting weeks putting "*Kick Ass Copywriting Secrets of a Marketing Rebel*" into polished shape. From scratch -- the book didn't even exist in my mind until that moment of clarity at the seminar.

Thus -- while I still express a disgruntled exasperation at the unfairness of life and the dominance of mediocrity in our culture -- I'm very happy to have *had* that "in my face" reality check.

No matter what the game is -- life, Monopoly, golf, or dealing with vicious competition in business -- you're a *fool* to believe that being good at what you do, alone, will win the day.

You don't need to play dirty (and I encourage you to refuse to compromise your ethics or sense of moral outrage, and always do the right thing).

But you DO need to understand that the world is not fair... *and you DO need to understand the ways other people will cheat.*

You need to acknowledge the perverse *jokes* the culture and the market you're in will play on you, over and over and over.

And for God's sake... stop *ignoring* those nagging questions in your head about what makes you happy.

Your opportunities for radical change will not announce themselves, and may come in the guise of really *annoying* reality checks.

That's why I sign my emails and blogs with "Stay Frosty". It's Michael Beihn's line in "Aliens"... just before the Space Marines make their final stand against the army of overwhelmingly-scary creatures that -- minutes earlier -- they didn't even know *existed*. For Beihn's character, it was a "go crazy or get your shit together" moment, and he shook himself like a dog, accepted reality, and *got on with it.*

I loved that moment in the flick.

Heck, I *identified* with it.

Final Disgruntle: I mentioned that I've lost most of my need to risk life and limb engaging the world in dangerous ways.

And I'm content with that. I actually *anticipated* this period of life, where my metabolism would finally wind down to the point where I could sit and transcribe the stories and novels and books that have swirled around in my head for decades.

I haven't lost my edge, thank God.

I just no longer need to *test* the sharpness of that edge against the rougher surfaces of life.

And yet...

I still get a thrill on Friday afternoons -- a remnant of the pleasant anxiety over the coming weekend. For most of my life, every Friday evening was the opening act of a fresh adventure that would last for at least two unpredictable days.

Drama, tragedy, romance, comedy... the whole Shakespearean bundle.

And don't get me wrong -- I'm not *through* with loving adventure. Not by a long shot.

I'm just more content with having a little *less* raw experience. I'm not jaded -- just ready to dedicate more time to writing for a while. And yet...

That Friday afternoon thrill used to be so intense, I literally could not sit still. Hormones and adrenaline *forced* me out into the bright lights and chaos of weekend culture.

For many of my longtime friends, losing that urge to go out and cause trouble has turned them into couch potatoes.

This annoys me. I've learned there aren't just two opposite poles of excitement -- either vegging out in front of the tube, *or* getting chased by cops, with nothing in between.

That "in between" is what I'm now cultivating. I still welcome those pangs of anticipation on Friday afternoon…

… but I've learned to channel that energy into more creative outlets.

Reliving some of my more outrageous adventures by writing about them is a real treat -- like watching a favorite movie you haven't seen in a long time.

And yet…

Well, I remain that guy who taunted fear and danger for so many years. I *love* the taste of that sharp, edgy energy of anticipation.

I may not carouse on Friday like I used to… but I'm damned glad I understand what that *feeling* all about.

Hey -- stay frosty.

Chapter Sixteen:

Direct Marketing's Well-Deserved Big Black Eye

What goes around, comes around...

L et's talk about salesmanship, shall we?

It is, after all, the missing "X factor" in almost *all* the bad-to-mediocre marketing you see. If there is one common denominator present in most of the people who come to me for advice...

... it would be a *lack of street-level salesmanship savvy.*

The word "salesmanship" carries a tarnished glow in our culture. Most folks think of used car salesmen in a loud sportscoat lying his ass off to pawn an oil-dripping jalopy on some unsuspecting soul...

... or of shrill-voiced telemarketers stalking innocent families during dinnertime from some dank boiler room...

...or of slick con-men sidling up to gullible rich widows.

And, as I said in the first chapter of "Kick-Ass Copywriting Secrets", salesmanship's very public black eye is mostly *well-deserved.*

Because both Madison Avenue and unethical entrepreneurs routinely lie and spin and drop-kick the truth to get the result they want. Advertisers too often use the power of salesmanship to bully or weasel their way into your wallet.

It has ever been thus... since the first caveman real estate agent conveniently neglected to mention the cave he just sold to another caveman was used by angry, carnivorous bears during the winter.

Heck, Coca-Cola started out as a cocaine-laced "tonic" that promised to cure "all nervous afflictions", from neuralgia to hysteria.

And graham crackers -- you know, one of the ingredients for that Girl Scout staple, s'mores -- were originally concocted as a *cure* for lust and masturbation by a vegetarian minister in the 18th century.

Seriously.

The term "snake oil" even refers to barrels of turpentine and red pepper mixed with rotting rattlesnake heads sold as medicine, which was flogged all over the American Wild West back in the day.

And the list goes on.

Every so often, the government cuts into the advertising dance and starts nailing the most outrageous liars.

When I broke into freelance copywriting in the 1980s, there had been a resurgence of phony diet claims, and the feds were sending scofflaws off to the slammer in droves.

A few years later, the entire savings and loan industry imploded, and took people's savings with it. Financial scams peaked just before the Black Monday stock market crash of '87.

The country was starting to look like a scamster free-for-all.

It was like the crooks were in charge, and all the honest admen were hiding somewhere.

Fortunately, I discovered an entire community of honest marketers and writers, which included legendary guys like Gary Halbert and Jay Abraham.

I was drawn to the direct response side of advertising because it involved *real salesmanship and actual skill at writing copy*. An ad was good only if it brought in orders.

So, I used those result-getting tactics, and (like Gary and Jay) made sure my clients were ethical and selling good products.

That made sense to me. That put the universe back in greased grooves, where high-end salesmanship could be used to spread the word on stuff people needed, rather than just trying to grab their money.

The Madison Avenue side -- the big agencies with the fancy offices and huge budgets -- seemed *afraid* of results. They produced silly ads for millions of dollars, and never had a clue whether they sold any product or not.

At best, they would cite focus groups who "liked" the campaigns a lot.

Hard to cash "likes" at the bank (as companies trying to use social media are also discovering).

It seemed criminal to me for an agency to take a client's money, and not be able to *prove* whether the advertising they created worked or not.

I knew that direct response had a rotten reputation over the years, going back to those bad-old days of unfettered and unregulated claims on lousy products…

… and it seemed to be boiling up all over the place in modern business.

It's even been a bit embarrassing, at times, to admit I write long-copy direct mail letters and advertorials and thirty-page-long websites. I can see people's brains spinning in horror.

I've even had close friends ask me if it's *necessary* to lie in direct response to get results.

Big sigh on my part.

For the record: I don't lie (or even make stuff up) when I write killer copy.

I don't *have* to -- every hook I've used is as true as I could determine (even the one-legged golfer). Writers who do their research can find hooks for *anything*.

I may push the envelope through outrageously-exciting storytelling…

… but it's all honest salesmanship.

I just know how to find the attention-getting *heart* of the story.

Only lazy writers resort to lies. I'm not creative enough to make up the hooks I've discovered in my most notorious ads – they're all straight from research and interviewing.

When you know where to look, life supplies its *own* outrageous details.

My job is simply connecting the dots in a persuasive manner that excites, lights a fire under your butt, and closes the deal.

And in most cases, if you're not happy, you get your money back, no questions asked.

I'm proud to say that most of my clients report extremely low refund rates. My copy isn't *tricking* anyone into buying -- it's just cementing the deal for something the prospect *already* is primed to desire.

What most people fail to "get" about good advertising…

… is just how *difficult* it is to convince another human being to give you money, based solely on a persuasive sales pitch.

It's easy to get a prospect to say "Yeah, that seems like an okay deal".

But moving him from that admission, up a step to actually pulling out his cash, *is a whole course in the psychology of salesmanship.*

That's why "Kick-Ass Copywriting Secrets" is nearly 200 pages long. And it's why "The Simple Writing System" offers you a personal coach (with professional copywriting credentials) for eight weeks.

It takes a bit of dedicated time to understand the process of completing a sale in the real world.

Sure, there are still crooks in direct response. The rise of Web-based marketing seems to have brought them out like cockroaches.

And I believe the liars should be hounded out of business. And certainly sent straight to Hell without dessert, after a long stay in the hoosegow.
But the magic of great salesmanship is *neither* inherently good nor evil.

It is just a collection of ways to persuade.

And the manner of advertising you use is just a *vehicle* for your persuasive pitch.

If you're evil, then your message is evil.

If you're honest, then your message is honest.

It's just a coincidence that you may be using the exact same persuasion tactics.

You can be sold a load of bad stocks by a smiling broker from a nationally-known brokerage house. (Merrill Lynch paid a $100-million fine for its boiler room scams early in this century.)

You can be conned by a smooth talking street hustler pulling the "found wallet" switcheroo on you. (Cops in New York report a startling rise in the number of tourists getting taken in age-old confidence games on the street.)

Even stylish Madison Avenue commercials can actually be sugar-coated poison. (Ads happily shilled for the prescription drug Vioxx even as deaths mounted a few years ago. Not to mention the decades of Mad Ave. ads touting the health benefits of smoking cigarettes right up to the 1960s.)

When I looked at mainstream advertising at the beginning of my career, I saw bullshit piled on bullshit. Bad salesmanship, no skill to the copywriting, and no excuse for any of it.

When I looked at direct response, I saw the potential for harm… *but mostly I saw a fabulous way to use salesmanship for good business.*

I made a simple vow to only work with ethical clients (and have turned down more clients over the years than I've accepted in order to do this).

But I *also* continued to study salesmanship at its deepest levels -- regardless of what use the advanced tactics were put toward.

That meant studying con games and scam artists.

As I've said many times, some of the best sales tactics have been perfected by crooks -- because they only get *one shot* at making the sale. Then they have to leave town. They need to score immediately.

My big realization was this: The tactics that persuade people to go along with scams…

… can *also* work for ethical products and services.

Because the salesmanship used is, again, neither good nor evil -- it's just *persuasion tactics*, developed through a deep understanding of how humans make decisions.

I'm not alone in this realization. The legendary direct mailer Richard Viguerie has used hard-core "push the envelope" salesmanship to build the largest and most influential political mailing list in the world.

The Red Cross, AARP, the ACLU and every other successful non-profit also uses similar tactics.

Even Reader's Digest employs vicious take-away tease tricks (a staple in good salesmanship) to get you to subscribe.

And *all* the large information publishers (like Rodale and Agora) employ the same psychological attention-getting tactics of the most outrageous tabloids out there. (Every single top writer studies -- and rips off -- National Enquirer and World Weekly News headlines. The more wacky and bizarre, the better.)

What confuses folks about hard-hitting, long copy direct response advertising is the way it screws with their internal "Bullshit Detectors".

People are just *numb* from all the mainstream advertising they have to wade through each and every day, without mercy.

In order to simply survive, they try to ignore almost all the sales pitches that come their way.

And then a great letter appears in their mail. Or a killer ad jumps off the page of their favorite magazine. Or they stumble across a website that pulls them in, deep.

Most ads use piss-poor salesmanship, and they're easy to skip over.

But *great* direct response ads are designed to hit your passionate sweet spot with just a *glance*.

And the copy won't let you wander away, because that ad quickly becomes the *most exciting thing* you've read in a long time.

The copy inflames your desire. Teases your dreams of a better or different life. Reignites dormant and hidden goals.

Done right, direct response advertising can *wake you up*.

Big promises will be made, and supported with believable proof. Credibility will be established, beyond doubt. You'll be given oodles of reasons why the offer is something you should jump on, immediately.

In fact, this sudden urgency of desire can make readers *upset*. Because you've knocked them out of their drowsy comfort zone, and presented *new* problems in their life… because now they can see other options.

They no longer need to live their lives as they have until this point. They have a new *choice*.

A new choice they often didn't ask for, or go looking for, and kinda resent. It just arrived. **In an ad.**

So people are suspicious of advertising in general, and hostile toward direct response advertising in particular.

This complicates things, but it doesn't mean good salesmanship is bad.

The world would *not* be a better place without advertising.

If all the ads of the last few decades somehow had never existed, you'd be completely in the dark about nearly everything that is wonderful and helpful in your life right now.

Because advertising is a huge part of the dialog of modern life. And it's not always about *buying* stuff. Not by a long shot.

The most obvious kinds of advertising are the magazine ads, online banners, direct mail letters, email, thirty-second television spots, radio commercials and pay-per-click ads that swamp the media in your life.

But *word-of-mouth* is also advertising.

Every time a friend raves about a restaurant she just ate at… or tells you how some new herbal ointment fixed up his rash… or even just casually mentions something about their last vacation that tweaks your own desire to travel… *that's salesmanship at work.*

Even when the word being passed your way is *negative*… it's still salesmanship.

Talking someone *out* of doing something takes the same level of salesmanship chops as talking them *into* doing something.

My late good friend Gary Halbert did the best job of making this connection, in an early issue of The Gary Halbert Letter.

He made the obtuse observation that almost *everything* we do in life involves salesmanship -- from convincing a teacher your excuse for being late with homework is worthy of consideration, to wooing and winning the love of your life.

We sell all the time.

Or *try* to.

One of my standard teaching methods is to advise rookies to "sell" a friend on going to see a movie they *know* that friend would like. It sounds so simple…

… and yet, in practice, it can be astonishingly difficult to pull off. Most people think their own enthusiasm should be enough to convince a friend of the value of attending the show.

After all… it's a friend. Someone who should *trust* you when you insist on something. So the rookie gets smack into their friend's face and *orders* them to go see the movie.

Because they'll *love* it.

There may even be some shouting involved. Enthusiastic shouting, but loud and obnoxious shouting nevertheless.

And the result of this in-your-face tactic often astonishes the rookie.

Seasoned salesmen know what often happens: The automatic "Shield of Defiance" goes up in the friend's brain. And instead of enthusiastically running off to the movie…

… they unconsciously check off that particular flick as one they'll see when hell freezes over.

Maybe.

Humans are basically contrary beasts. We don't like to be told what to do… even by friends.

This doesn't mean you *cannot* convince a friend to go see the movie, however.

No. You just have to employ *better sales tactics.*

The last time I went to see a movie I wouldn't have seen otherwise, it was due to a conversation that went like this: "Hi Don. What'd you do last weekend?"

"Oh, nothing much. Saw a movie."

"Yeah? Did you like it?"

"Man, it blew me away. But then, I really like dark, funny, weird film-noir type flicks. This one got some great reviews by hard-to-please critics, but bombed at the box office. And it's only playing until Thursday."

I went to the movie. I not only caught the last showing before it left town, but I Googled it before going and got caught up on the backstory.

It was *exactly* the kind of dark, funny, weird film-noir that lights up my world.

However, if Don had said "John, you MUST go see this movie! It's *exactly* what you like…" I would have probably put it further down my list of things to do before I die.

But Don lit the fire of desire under my ass by coming in a *side* door.

He didn't order me to go -- in fact, he did a little "take away" by not addressing the fact that I, too, like that type of film. And the casual aside about the movie only playing until Thursday put some honest urgency into his "non-pitch".

He didn't sell consciously. In fact, he had no personal stake in whether I went or not… and that lack of self-interest made his "non-recommendation" all the more enticing.

Yet, he couldn't have done a better job of *selling* me on going if he had done it consciously.

I made up my own mind to go. Not based on his urgings…

… but based on what seemed to me as a careful consideration of facts and opinion, plus my own inflamed desires.

Nevertheless, I done got *sold*.

And I wouldn't have, if Don had done what most people do instinctively, and tried to *forcefully* convince me.

This resistance to frontal attack is unconscious, and automatic. Until, that is, a *certain kind of trust* is established. Not the pure, "I got your back" kind of trust between friends, either.

No. There's another level of trust that borders on the sinister… and yet is a huge part of almost everyone's life.

Let me preface this with a disclaimer: I *love* people. I truly do.

However, long ago I realized that, as loveable as the human race is… most folks are just dead asleep. Zombies stumbling through life, so utterly clueless they aren't even cognizant of their lack of clues.

So this unconscious resistance to being sold -- despite being inconvenient to marketers -- is a *good thing*.

If the defiance wasn't there, the world would be a very different place. You'd buy everything that was offered, every second of the day. Nothing would get done, we'd all be in debt, and the wheels of commerce would quickly grind to a halt.

Still, because it *is* unconscious, this resistance can be navigated by a skilled salesman who is not asleep.

And once the resistance is breached, an opposite phenomenon occurs: You automatically *accept* as truth almost everything the trusted person says.

In its most benign form, this can simply be a shortcut to getting needed information or acquiring good products or services.

I'll use myself as an example again. I have built my entire career around being professional (by meeting deadlines and delivering the highest quality work I'm capable of every time)… and by honoring the concept of karma.

What goes around, comes around.

So I treat people the way I want to be treated. I'm scrupulously honest, quick to admit mistakes, and aim to do the right thing (even if it means I have to sacrifice to do so).

This doesn't guarantee that I'll never have people mad at me, or never suffer the disbelief of folks who doubt my integrity.

But it does mean that, after you've been on my list for a while and learned to trust me a bit… you will be *more* inclined to accept what I say as true and worthwhile.

Your automatic resistance will be lowered.

And when I offer something for sale, you will not dismiss it out of hand… and even possibly allow yourself to eagerly partake.

A sale is not a given, of course.

You'll only buy if what I offer meets your needs. But you won't automatically *resist* in the way you would if a stranger approached you with the same exact offer.

This is a very basic level of trust, but it's more advanced than the trust you share with your friends. Because you trust your friends for different things -- and your connection with them is not built around a business relationship.

(**Side note:** This also explains why so many partnerships between longtime friends go sour.

Just because you like someone and enjoy getting wasted and playing Nintendo together does NOT mean you will necessarily enjoy the rigors of do-or-die business with them.

The faults you commonly overlook in a friendship -- like constantly being late, or avoiding responsibility -- are *not* forgivable in a capitalistic partnership. Big difference.)

On the other end of this advanced level of trust is the *dark* version:

The Cult of Personality.

I don't want to step on toes, but this includes much of organized religion and all political parties. At least in the most passionate sectors.

The obvious examples are the smaller cults that drink suicide Kool-Aid just because the leader says to. (Google "Jim Jones cult" for the most outrageous American example.)

The *less* obvious examples are when a trusted leader says black is now white… and his followers twist themselves into pretzels trying to explain it to unbelievers. (All my life, I've been listening to politicians insist that their ideology trumps scientific fact, and their respective wing-nuts swoon with delight. Orwell was right.)

There are famous marketers who pull this off, too. What, for example, has the latest self-help guru ever *actually accomplished* in life… except to persuade people to buy his watered-down NLP products?

Seriously -- the entire business model of most self-help gurus is self-perpetuating. He's rich from telling other people how to get rich… and the richer he gets, the more people buy his products on getting rich.

I'm sure of these gurus are nice guys. And they've certainly mastered the art of tickling the greed glands of almost every person they meet with the room-dominating force of their personality. That, I suppose, is a real accomplishment.

But most them weren't rich before they started telling people how to get rich.

This is not a secret among most players in the business world.

But what guys like that really learned to do… is to shortcut their way *past* the natural unconscious resistance of large audiences of people... and set up camp in that ancient part of their brains that yearns for an authority figure to *just tell them what to do.*

Not because of the facts.

Because their personality just *oozes* authority and trust.

Hell, I yearn for that kind of authority all the time. I don't want to spend weeks, for example, researching which flat-screen television to buy -- I just want someone I trust to TELL me which one to buy. I openly asked a dozen of my most-trusted friends which TV they bought or recommend... and NONE of them agreed with anyone else.

Turns out, there are over a dozen choices for televisions right now (including the coming changes that aren't available yet -- one of the recommendations was to *wait* for new technology). And there are excellent reasons for choosing every one of those options.

Oh, how I yearn for an authority to trust.

I'm genetically incapable of kow-towing to authority, of course -- I have a long and troubled history of battling with people in positions of power -- but I still *yearn* for it.

Sometimes I envy people who can give up control to another person.
It's so *easy* to be a follower.

And it's so *hard* to stay awake in this culture of opiated media and hypnotic trends... and to slog out on your own path.
Ah, well.

Most of the really good entrepreneurs I know share my aversion to authority. And while it may be harder to think for yourself, it sure is a hell of a lot more satisfying.

I used to believe I was *not* a natural-born salesman. That belief was a good thing for my career -- because it launched me on a lifelong search for mentors in selling.

I hung out in Jay Abraham's offices for several years, piling up advice on selling and persuasion.

Met Gary Halbert there, and worked damn hard for him for another span of years, sucking up every scrap of salesmanship knowledge I could weasel out of him.

Both men were masters who had honed their skills selling door-to-door, before going deep with self-education from every book on the subject.
It was only after years of studying and applying the craft that I realized I'd actually been selling *all my life.* It just wasn't the kind of selling that involves product and money.

Instead, I was the kid who planned out the afternoon's adventures for all the other kids in the neighborhood. Whether it was a street baseball game, using rules I made up on the spot... or assigning one kid to hide in the backyard and be a monster while we hunted him under rules of engagement I also created... I had to *sell* the other kids on participating.

I wasn't an asshole about it -- every suggestion by other kids was incorporated, if it was good. And I'd have eagerly gone along with anyone else's games, too, because my goal was to have a good time, not dominate the other kids.

It just worked out that I was more creative, and quicker to suggest something to do. I never asked for, nor accepted a leadership role. I was more of a "stealth" leader... who *influenced* things purely with better ideas.

Still, I had to *sell* every idea to the gang. If anyone objected, for any reason, the game was scuttled.

Later, I organized secret newspapers in high school. Quickly took over the choice of songs for bands I was in, and sold the other guys on band names. (My best band name: Bad Dog. My worst: Siddhartha. I'd been reading Herzog, and it was a time of pretentious band names… and Steppenwolf was already named after a Herzog tome. I wish my bandmates hadn't let me sell them on that one, though…)

Salesmanship appeals to me, because it combines tight, street-level psychology (not theory, but *useable* stuff) with the *reality* of human behavior.

Salesmen don't give a rat's ass what people *say* they're going to do. Instead, salesmen observe, very closely, what people actually DO. This requires wakefulness. Like cops and combat-experienced soldiers, veteran salesmen are not burdened with silly belief systems about their fellow humans.

It can be a shock when you first start looking clearly at how everyone around you behaves. But it's absolutely necessary if you desire to perfect your ability to craft a truly killer sales pitch.

Like I said, I love people… but I am under no illusions about their motivations or intentions.

You will not sell anyone by appealing to their altruism.

You will not sell through educating people about a strange new opportunity.

And you will not sell prevention.

No. When you're finally ready to start getting the really huge results, you will appeal to your prospect's greed and selfishness.

You will let others do the educating, and focus your own efforts on monetizing the more base desires that *already* exist in your prospect's heart.

And you will never forget that while most people will not spend a nickel to *prevent* something from happening... they will empty their bank accounts trying to *fix* it once it gets broken.

This is important: I did not start disliking people after I woke up and began to see their behavior for what it was (instead of what I *wished* it was, or thought it *should* be).

I'm riddled with faults myself, for one thing. My ego is too humbled by my wakeful self-realizations to get very big or unruly.

A lot of people *fear* waking up, because they don't know how to act around the truth.

They *enjoy* their denial -- their ignorance of what their neighbors do behind closed doors... their happy belief that all people are basically good and selfless... their certainty that their own "values" are *exactly* what God had in mind.

And I'm here to tell you *not* to fear waking up. It's like the difference between guilt and remorse. With guilt, you do something bad, and you're a bad *person* for having done it.

With remorse, you do something bad, you admit your mistake, try to make things right if you can, learn your lesson and promise (seriously) to do better next time.

Then, you *move on*. And actually DO better the next time.

Remorse is like a pit stop on the road of life. You pause, get your bearings back, clean up your mess, and continue on your journey.

Guilt is like setting up camp. You wallow in your sinful errors, and can't progress.

Remorse is being awake. Guilt is all about staying asleep -- it's a cop-out. For too many people, it becomes *okay* to keep screwing up in the same ways, as long as you feel guilty.

Guilt is anti-life.

Awake, and living fully, you realize that all the people around you are moral pieces of Swiss cheese -- full of faults and aggressively dumb about many things.

And yet, you don't despise them for it. Instead, knowing that you *share* the annoying weaknesses of being human, you are finally able to enjoy the true emotional fullness of uncensored love.

Great salesmen know certain psychological truths.

Like, for example, the fact that ALL superiority complexes are the result of self-hating feelings of *inferiority*.

Someone comes at you with a smirk and a put-down, you can bet it's all defense. They're consciously or unconsciously *protecting* themselves, scared to death the world will discover just how unworthy they really are.

Halbert illustrated this once to me with a simple tactic, and I've never forgotten it. He lived in New York City for a while, arriving there from the considerably less-urbane outlands of Ohio.

New Yorkers pride themselves on being "bullshit immune". They tend to talk loud, interrupt and show hostile skepticism to everything. To them, this is proof of their street-wise superiority. They've seen it all.
You can't pull one over on *them*.

Most people either back away from this kind of in-your-face skepticism, or adopt it to survive.

Halbert, however, being a salesman, saw this loud behavior for what it was: Protection.

Door-to-door salesmen know that the people who put up "No Solicitors" signs on their homes... are the most gullible folks on the block.

In the old days, salesmen used to mark the sidewalk in front of houses where they easily made a sale. This is where the term "mark" comes from -- meaning, sucker or easy target.

The new curbside "marks" are "No Solicitors" signs. And, in personal communication, loud and brash behavior.

New Yorkers were some of the *easiest* sales Halbert ever made. He just came in through the side door -- where there wasn't any protection.

He never tried a frontal assault. Instead, he allowed the other person to begin the conversation, and even allowed them to decide when the pitch would start. Any buying that took place was because they *decided* to buy. They would never *admit* to being "sold"... because in their belief system they were immune to that.

The basic rule: Somebody tells you they're immune to anything... well, that's pretty much what they're MOST vulnerable to.

There's an anecdotal story about the days of the Russian Czars, who were among the cruelest rulers on the planet. Because the Czars regularly used torture to control dissent, rebel groups actually formed torture cults. They trained their entire lives to withstand horrific pain and prolonged torment.

And this one Czar, while visiting his dungeon, found one of these torture-immune dudes near death. Clearly ready to die rather than give up any information. So the Czar pushed his henchmen away, unlocked the binding chains… and *hugged* the man. Called him brother, and apologized for all the pain.

Came in through a side door.

The prisoner, who had been willing to gut out every bad thing they threw at him, collapsed in a sobbing heap while being hugged. And ratted out everyone he knew.

This story might be apocryphal, but it makes a point all salesmen understand.

And, as always, the power of this "side door" tactic can be used for good, or evil.

It's simply a tactic that *works*.

Do you know who a car salesman most wants to see come onto his lot?

It's *another* salesman.

Why?

It's because of the *infectious delirium* of a great sales pitch. When you get good at selling, you just naturally appreciate the construction of a well-designed pitch.

It's a work of art. You allow it in, to savor the tickling of your own greed glands and desire. You indulge in the enthusiasm it generates -- and enthusiasm is like *junk* to a great salesman.

You get caught up in the act. And you get *sold*.

One of the best testimonials I've ever received is from one of the smartest and most successful salesmen in the world. And he wrote: "John really *pisses me off*. I read all his ads to get good ideas on how to write my own copy. And I end up *buying* what he's selling!"

By studying the copy in an ad, you allow the sales message to sneak in through an unprotected side door.

And you can get sold. We're all vulnerable.

Ad writers have been breaking down the process of a good sales pitch for a hundred years now, beginning with Kennedy and Hopkins, and moving through Caples and Ogilvy to Halbert and myself.

Often, we disagree on the details -- whether it's the USP or the big promise that does more work… whether testimonials are essential or just backup… when to introduce urgency, where to reveal the actual offer, why a subhead under the headline may be overkill.

And on and on.

Salesmanship is fluid. A certain pitch that persuaded effectively ten years ago may sound cheesy today.

Or, like Caples' "They all laughed when I sat down at the piano" riff, the underlying offer may be so timeless that you almost *have* to use it at some point when writing to your house list.

But the main message is this: People resist being pitched.

For a great salesman, that resistance is just another objection to be countered.

Don't fight with your prospect -- give him room to make up his own mind.

Chapter Seventeen:

How To Hire A Copywriter.

The essential "Quick Start" checklist for any entrepreneur or business owner looking to find (and get the most out of) a hired-gun freelance copywriter...

It's high time for a little "public service message" here, for any marketer wanting to hire a freelance copywriter to write what you need written to make your biz hum.

Cuz it's a jungle out there.

There's a veritable mob of available writers, of all levels of expertise (from world-class down to *"should be hanged"* incompetent fools), charging all kinds of fees and making all kinds of promises.

It can get confusing, abruptly, and you can end up mismatched (or getting roughed up financially) if you don't know what you're doing.

So, here's a **Quick Start** overview of what you – the dude or dudette doing the hiring – should get straight on before heading into the Big Scary Jungle Of Freelance Copywriters to find your perfect scribe.

(This works for hiring ANY consultant, actually, so pay attention.)

Step One: Deconstruct and list *what you want done.*

Do you need a single ad written, or do you need your entire website created or overhauled?

Do you need someone to write the necessary emails, Video Sales Letters and sales pages for a launch?

Do you need a sales funnel created, starting with AdWords and traveling through landing pages, auto-responders, back ends, and sales support?

Or what?

Step Two: *Admit it* if you aren't sure what you want (or need). *Double* admit it to yourself if you're absolutely clueless.

This is a critical step.

You're about to shell out a lot of money…

… and put a lot of your hopes and dreams on the back of a writer…

… so this is no time to be deluded, or to try bullshitting your way through the process.

Whether you find the perfect copywriter (someone you'll end up working with, successfully, for years) or whether you bring on a misfit (who leaves your marketing efforts sputtering)…

… this is gonna be one of the most time-and-money intensive relationships you have in your business.

Copy is the MAIN ELEMENT in your ability to attract prospects and close them as customers. (Yes, the quality of what you offer matters… but never forget that the Marketing Graveyard is *crammed* with superior products that died horrible and fast deaths *because no one figured out how to sell them.*)

So, if you're an experienced marketer who is positive that you know what you need from a hired copywriter… great.

And if (despite your other experience in business) you're *not* sure precisely what you need… because you're maybe new to a certain advertising tactic, or market forces are crushing you (like changed technology, fresh competition, or the sudden obsolescence of your product), or what you've done before just ain't working anymore…

… you're going to need a *different kind* of freelance copywriter.

This is a *process*. It will become clear in a moment.

Step Three: Figure out your budget. For the entire project, which might include hiring professionals, paying for services (like designers or programmers), buying lists or ad space, every conceivable cost you'll encounter.

Experienced marketers will have a "war chest" for any new project (or any other situation that requires hiring outside help). It's the approximate amount of moolah they're *willing to shell out* to get things rolling.

If you're new to using freelancers, you may not know how much to set aside.

There's no exact formula… but you *can* at least figure out what you can *afford* right now.

Entrepreneurs often learn about the cost of outside services as they go. It can be a shock, so you have to understand what the "value" is to your business of every new move. (In other words, get clear on what a winning ad, in a winning campaign, to the right lists, via the right media will mean in terms of buckets of cash cascading into your life...

... versus how a losing ad in a total bomb of a campaign will harsh your mellow.)

At first, you may have to be vague. Which is fine, because – again – this is a process.

Learning about expenses and figuring out budgets applies to everything you do... from going to a high-priced seminar, taking a course or joining a coaching program, hiring a writer or consultant, designing new product, to investing in new infrastructure, and so on.

There's a "cost" to everything, which includes both the dollars involved, AND your time and invested energy...

... all balanced against the odds of success. If you "save" money doing certain things yourself, and the results are abysmal, how much have you really saved?

Or, if you write a check that makes your hand shake to a top copywriter who produces something that opens the wealth spigot on your head, how much did that writer "cost" you?

When it comes to hiring a freelance copywriter, you have decided that either **(a)** your own ability to craft an ad/website/email/etc is not up to the task at hand...

... or **(b)** it makes "sense" to hire a professional writer... because you have the resources to pay for the help you need...

… and the time saved (by having more people involved in the project) **allows you to move more efficiently toward your biz goals.**

Side Note: If your ability to write your own marketing materials is *zero*… and there is no one already on your staff able to write this material at a level needed in your niche to convert prospects to customers… *then your problem is magnified.* I highly recommend that anyone craving success as an entrepreneur learn how to write fundamentally-solid sales copy…

… so **(1)** you can avoid being *dependent* on outside writers when it's not necessary…

… **(2)** you can write decent copy in a pinch during emergencies…

… and **(3)** you will understand precisely *what* you need from freelancers when you do hire them (and *never* be in the dark about whether their copy is "good" or not).

There are a lot of ways to get this fundamental education in copywriting, including books, courses and online coaching programs (I'll share a list with you later on this topic)…

… and because it's the lifeblood of all your marketing plans, you should consider this *as important as anything else you do in your quest for success.*

But whatever you do, get this fundamental understanding of what goes into good sales copy under your belt asap.

Consider it a primary asset in your business toolkit. A *PRIMARY* asset.
So, continuing…

Step Four: If you're unclear about any of this, *admit it.*

No one is born already knowing how to plan for a business project. And even MBA degrees can leave you clueless (amazing, but true) (and common).

So take stock of your resources: Who amongst your staff has the knowledge to do… or the experience to know how to price out… the things you need done?

If you're a one-man-band, this is easy. And, you may have zero skills, and be mostly riding your passion for becoming independently rich into the entrepreneurial world.

Hey, it can work. I know a lot of entrepreneurs who made a gig successful, all on their lonesome, learning everything as they went.

Not the recommended path, but it's an option.

Eventually, however, every biz owner will have to come to terms with the need to invest in getting help where you need it. Because…

… you can never do everything yourself, if you're going to grow.

If you've never hired a freelancer before, use whatever resources you have to help you make a good decision. Ask colleagues for recommendations, shop around (never just hire the first copywriter you realize exists), and understand that learning how to hire the RIGHT copywriter is a *process*, not an end game.

If you're gonna use writers often, you'll learn as you go.

If you're gonna hire someone permanently as a writer, you better know how to judge their ability to do the work first.

There's no magic. Sorry. And it's not quite like hiring a plumber to fix the pipes – a lot *more* is relying on good copy.

Step Five: There are oodles of ways to find writers. Many advertise their services. Others are well-known within marketer networks.

There are many different *kinds* of freelance copywriters, too. **Quick breakdown:**

[] **The non-advertising writer.** This is the guy or gal who knows how to string sentences together, but does *not* know how to sell. They can be great at providing content for your blog, or writing the special reports you offer as bonuses, or fleshing out the other materials you need that your biz is not relying on for sales.

They should come cheap, too – and work by the article, or by the hour, or by the project. But because they are *not* responsible for your bottom line profits, they are more like a vendor. They provide the raw copy you need, but you will have to instruct them very specifically on what to write.

They are essentially "translators" of your sales message, turning what you do into words that can be used in an ad.

[] **The "regular" advertising writer.** They may come from the world of ad agencies, or from publications. They also are NOT usually steeped in the art of selling – they rely instead on cleverness, slogans, and graphic-oriented advertising that *cannot be tested* because it does not produce actual results.

Their fees will be all over the map. They may have a good resume, having written material for recognizable companies.

For most entrepreneurs, I'm gonna go out on a limb and warn you *away* from any copywriter who doesn't understand "direct response" advertising. (The term "direct response" simply means that your advertising "asks for an action, which can be measured". A sale, an opt-in, a phone call, a reply. The "response action" is where profits will be made.)

[] **The direct response copywriter.** This is the dude who understands how to write copy that will ask for an "action"...

... which (it's worth repeating) includes closing a sale, capturing a lead, or moving a prospect to becoming a customer.

Real salesmanship applies. In nearly all "big" entrepreneurial jobs, *this* is the kind of writer you want.

There are 3 approximate "levels" of expertise to any direct response writer you hire:

Level One: *Raw rookie.* A beginner, with little or no track record, and few if any prior clients.

Believe it or not, a rookie can actually be a decent bet, depending on what you need done. IF he's been trained in direct response, or is in training with a good mentor, then he will at least understand the *fundamentals* of good marketing-oriented writing.

However, they are untested, and you must realize that *you will be paying for part of their education.* If you need something that requires real expertise, the rookie will be in over his head.

Expect to pay under five thousand dollars – all the way down to a few hundred bucks – to hire a rookie freelance writer for almost any project. And you will have to manage him closely, and know exactly what you want (and why you've gone with a rookie to get it).

You may be able to bully a rookie into working fast, or constantly change copy as you go... but remember that he is not experienced at meeting tough deadlines, and may not handle stress well. (A writer needs a *buttload* of time in the front trenches of the biz world to develop the thick skin required to deal with most clients, under deadline, with a lot riding on the ads. *It doesn't come naturally.*)

Remember: A rookie is not a "bargain" if you're relying on their copy for anything critical in your biz. It's like hiring a Little Leaguer to pitch opening day for your Major League team.

Level Two: *The veteran direct response freelancer.* This is a writer with references, success stories, and examples of his work he can point you to that already exist online or in other media.

They will have experience in all forms of advertising and marketing, including direct mail, Video Sales Letters, email auto-responders, web sales pages, print ads, and just about every way in which a sales message can be delivered to a prospect.

More important, the high-end freelance veteran will also have **massive marketing experience...**

... because after being involved in many, *many* different projects over the years, he'll have insight into what has worked, what hasn't worked, what is working now, what isn't working any more, and in many cases what is NEEDED to make your project work (that ain't there yet).

The best veteran writers are essentially **marketing consultants**, who provide the copy once the marketing plan has the bugs kicked out of it.

In other words... you can hire them JUST to provide copy, if you know exactly what you need done, and they'll deliver great ads.

Or, you can allow them to look at your current efforts...

… and they may help you discover where the "real" problem is with your sinking sales (hiding behind what you *thought* was the culprit)… where unseen problems are murdering your bottom line… where new problems may develop down the line…

… as well as pointing out what may be *missing* in your product or marketing plan.

Top writers earn their fees in many ways, and you can expect to shell out from ten grand up to thirty grand (and more) just for fundamental advertising (like a Video Sales Letter, or a web sales page, or a sales funnel that includes AdWords, name capture, email auto-responders directing readers to sales pages, and so on).

Plus, you may have to pay *continuing royalties* on the ads they produce (on top of the initial fee). This is a very common way for marketers to "defer" larger payments to the best copywriters, so you're paying out of profits. (Which also means you're only paying when an ad works.)

This is why knowing WHAT you need done… and WHY you need it done… can be so critical. If you don't have a clear idea of how great copy is going to produce a pile of new profit for you, you cannot "fit" a high-end freelancer into your plans…

… without realizing that you're *gambling*.

A lot of entrepreneurs have done just that. Some have thrived, hiring a writer to do their first campaign without really knowing what to expect… while others have gone under, because they didn't earn enough back to justify the expense of a top writer.

When you *know* (or strongly suspect, based on reality) that great (or even just "better") copy will bring in more prospects, and turn those prospects into customers…

… then you're in a perfect position to hire a freelancer.

Expect to compete with other marketers looking to book any good, respected writer… and they'll need *weeks or longer*, minimum, to produce copy for a project.

Warning: I recommend you do NOT do any royalty agreements on the first job, unless you already trust the writer without hesitation.

It may sound great to push off part of the fee to result-oriented royalties paid later…

… but you need to remember that you're *just beginning your relationship* with this writer. A good one will often not even propose royalties on the first job… because he doesn't know or trust you any more than you do him.

What you pay to hire him MUST fit into the results you expect from the project. So you must have all your other ducks lined up – your product must be good and ready to go…

… you must have ways to access your target audience (through your house lists, or affiliates, or paid-for lists, or "push" marketing like AdWords or niche publication banner ads, etc)…

… and you must have the **resources** available (in your budgeted war chest) to pay for putting everything into action.

For example: If you're just selling an existing ebook on Clickbank, you may only need to hire a writer and someone to convert their copy to a Video Sales Letter.

However, if you're launching a full-on new product to a competitive market from scratch, you may need an affiliate manager, a project manager, possibly several copywriters, programmers, designers, and more. Just to get things off the ground.

The level of effort required for your project to succeed and run smoothly is important to understand when you're staffing up for any new adventure.

Side Note: Some copywriters will provide ONLY the copy, in manuscript form, to you. And you must then convert that copy into a Video Sales Letter, website, published advertisement, whatever.

Other copywriters bring more to the table, *including* producing the VSL (though unless you're dealing with a copywriter who is part of a full team, it's rare that he will produce camera-ready art for publications, or direct mail, or the programming necessary for web pages).

Be aware of what you're getting. The services AFTER the copy is written are all less important than the quality of the writer, but they *are* part of the process of getting a campaign going.

The copy must contain essential killer salesmanship first – afterwards, you pretty it up for delivering to your prospects.

Level Three: *"A List" writers.* The best in the world.

You may be able to book one of the handful of the best copywriters in the game, but at a minimum you should expect to pay $30k and up past $50k into six-digits... *including* (not in lieu of) some type of royalty, even on the first job.

The best writers will not take jobs that are not *guaranteed* to deliver the kind of profits that make their outrageous fees worthwhile.

These top writers become, in essence, **a partner in the project**, possibly earning more than *you* will...

... and they'll be worth it.

However, you as a client are under more scrutiny than they are. If you have to ask how to find an "A List" copywriter, you aren't ready to hire one yet. You cannot make "deals" with them. They write for the largest direct response marketing outfits on the planet, and are out of the league of nearly all average entrepreneurs.

And they often require three months and longer to create a package. Advance planning (and booking) is mandatory.

Good to know they exist. Down the road, after you've earned your first couple of fortunes, you may be ready to hire one and reap the rewards.

For now, I recommend you get your plan down as well as you can…

… and hire a veteran copywriting professional to help you put that plan into action.

Listen to what he says, if his experience and skills at dissecting current and potential problems suggest a *change* to your plans.

Test what he writes, but never change it without knowing from a reality-based market test if he's right or not.

Your niece with the degree in English literature is not qualified to judge sales copy. Nor is your lawyer (though a good copywriter will work with even the most nervous attorney on your team to keep you on the side of the angels). Nor are *you*, unless you have a better track record than the writer.

You can *test* a professional's copy against whatever else you think should be better… and you'll learn a lot doing this.

The best copy I've ever written has nearly given my clients heart attacks. If they say "hey, this is great copy", then I suspect I've failed to deliver the best ad possible.

I want them up all night, worried sick about how the ad's gonna do… *because great copy always takes you out of your comfort zone.*

Selling is hard. You have to find your prospects (after figuring out who they really are), reach them, get them into your sales message, and wake them up to the point that they will *take action* (like buying).

The fastest-moving, most successful entrepreneurs all know how to craft good sales messages, and get them into shape to deliver to prospects. And then follow through.

If you're not confident, or not in a position to craft a great sales message… or, if you have the budget that allows you to take advantage of hiring your copywriting out…

… then wading into the freelance world makes a huge amount of sense.
There are many more details to this (including the creation and handling of contracts, setting deadlines with teeth in them, and having escape clauses when things go south)…

… and a good professional freelancer will *help* you with all of this. They want a successful gig as much as you do.

This is just a first-blush attempt to help you understand the process better.
Now, be wise and prudent, and get busy after your goals.

BONUS MATERIAL: To get a reality check on what goes down when you deal with a high-end copywriter, I'm sharing my "should you hire me or not" form that I give to everyone asking about hiring me for anything.

You may get some ideas yourself on how to best approach other copywriters from this, too. Here's the form I use:

"To find out if I'm available, and whether I'm your best choice or not, send an email to my personal assistant, Diane, at diane@john-carlton.com... and clearly state your answers to these simple questions:

1. What general market are you in... how long have you been in business... and what products or services do you offer?

2. What website URLs are you currently hosting for your business... and approximately how much are you grossing now, and how much have you grossed at the highest point in your marketing efforts? (This information is completely confidential... and if you're squeamish about stating specific figures, you can just say whether you're grossing more-than or less-than a certain figure. Whatever makes you feel more confident in sharing.)

3. Have you ever worked with a professional copywriter before?

4. Do you have a budget for hiring a copywriter? If so, what are you budgeting, right now, for hiring one?

5. Finally, what do you feel are your biggest advertising problems at this time?

I have set fees for specific projects I take on for clients. We'll know quickly if I'm your best choice as a writer, and if you're a good fit for the kind of advertising I create. And, we'll figure out *right up front* what the exact fees will be for what you need.

Sometimes, the best route is to start with a consultation, then agree on a plan for your advertising, and only then actually produce the ad (or Video Sales Letter, or broadcast media, or whatever you agree you need).

Consultations are good when the problem you THINK you're having isn't actually the main reason you're having problems with being profitable. I bring 30 years of hard-core, front-line experience in marketing to everything I do, and I can help you see things you're too close to, or haven't yet considered.

Other times, you really do "just need an ad", and I will simply and quickly create one for you.

First, however, we need to have that conversation.

So, again, to move this to the next step...

... email my personal assistant, Diane, at diane@john-carlton.com, and include your best answers to the 5 simple questions above.

Diane alerts me immediately to potential clients, and we'll get back to you as quickly as possible. I know you're anxious to get fresh advertising out there, and I want to help you do exactly that."

Resources

John's blog (with free archives dating back to 2004):
www.john-carlton.com

On this blog, you will find instant links to:

- The Simple Writing System

- Kick-Ass Copywriting Secrets Of A Marketing Rebel

- The Platinum Mastermind Group

- The Entrepreneur's Guide To Getting Your Shit Together, Volume One

- Simple Success Secrets No One Told You About

- The Freelance Manual

- How to reach John personally regarding consulting: John@john-carlton.com

Printed in Poland
by Amazon Fulfillment
Poland Sp. z o.o., Wrocław